Derrida, Deleuze, Psychoanalysis

A Critical Theory Institute Book

CRITICAL THEORY INSTITUTE BOOKS

The Aims of Representation: Subject/Text/History
edited by Murray Krieger

The States of "Theory": History, Art, and Critical Discourse
edited by David Carroll

Politics, Theory, and Contemporary Culture
edited by Mark Poster

"Culture" and the Problem of the Disciplines
edited by John Carlos Rowe

Accelerating Possession: Global Futures of Property and Personhood
edited by Bill Maurer and Gabriele Schwab

DERRIDA, DELEUZE,
PSYCHOANALYSIS

EDITED BY
Gabriele Schwab

with the assistance of Erin Ferris

COLUMBIA UNIVERSITY PRESS
NEW YORK

Columbia University Press
Publishers Since 1893
New York   Chichester, West Sussex
Copyright © 2007 Columbia University Press
All rights reserved
Library of Congress Cataloging-in-Publication Data
Derrida, Deleuze, psychoanalysis / edited by Gabriele Schwab.
p. cm. — (Critical Theory Institute books)
Includes bibliographical references.
ISBN 978-0-231-14308-0 (cloth : alk. paper) — ISBN 978-0-231-14309-7 (pbk. : alk. paper)
1. Derrida, Jacques. 2. Deleuze, Gilles, 1925–1985. 3. Psychoanalysis. I. Schwab, Gabriele.
B2430.D484D45   2008
150.19'5—dc22
2006102662

Columbia University Press books are printed on permanent and durable acid-free paper.
This book was printed on paper with recycled content.
Printed in the United States of America
c 10 9 8 7 6 5 4 3 2 1
p 10 9 8 7 6 5 4 3 2 1
References to Internet Web sites (URLs) were accurate at the time of writing. Neither the author nor Columbia University Press is responsible for URLs that may have expired or changed since the manuscript was prepared.

CONTENTS

Acknowledgments vii

ONE
Introduction:
Derrida, Deleuze, and the Psychoanalysis to Come
Gabriele Schwab 1

TWO
The Transcendental "Stupidity" ("Bêtise") of Man and the
Becoming-Animal According to Deleuze
Jacques Derrida, edited by Erin Ferris 35

THREE
Polymorphism Never Will Pervert Childhood
Catherine Malabou, translated by Robert Rose 61

FOUR
Buccality
Sara Guyer 77

FIVE
Resistance, Terminable and Interminable
Dina Al-Kassim   105

SIX
The Rhythm of Pain: Freud, Deleuze, Derrida
Branka Arsić   142

SEVEN
The Only Other Apparatus of Film
(A Few Fantasies About *Différance*, *Démontage*,
and Revision in Experimental Film and Video)
Akira Mizuta Lippit   171

EIGHT
De/Territorializing Psycho-analysis
Gregg Lambert   192

ACKNOWLEDGMENTS

My first and foremost thanks go to Jacques Derrida, with whom I discussed in detail my initial ideas for this project and who actively participated in the early stages during which it took shape. When I consulted with him about topic and format and proposed to focus the contributions on an engagement with the work of Gilles Deleuze around the issue of psychoanalysis, he said he would gladly take up a challenge he had thought about for a long time. Derrida's excitement about a platform engaging both Deleuze and psychoanalysis energized the contributors to this volume and leaves its traces in their essays.

In 2002, while I served as director of the Critical Theory Institute at the University of California at Irvine, I designed an opening conference titled "Derrida/Deleuze: Psychoanalysis, Territoriality, Politics" to prepare a dialogue about the trajectories, intersections, and lines of flight that connect and divide the work of two of the twentieth century's greatest philosophers, Jacques Derrida and Gilles Deleuze. I acknowledge with gratitude that the major support for this volume and the conference came from the Office of

Research and Graduate Studies at UCI. I am also happy to acknowledge the support of the Humanities Research Institute, the Humanities Center, the Program in Russian, the UC Libraries, and the International Center for Writing and Translation.

Some of the essays in this volume originate from this conference; others are new contributions written for this volume. I want to thank everybody who participated in this project, most of all, Erin Ferris, my invaluable assistant editor, who shared my enthusiasm, edited Derrida's essay and worked closely with him on its final translation, offered critical contributions to our editorial committee, and worked tirelessly on the book production and correspondence with contributors. Her collaboration was truly gratifying and inspiring. Jennifer Crewe, our editor from Columbia University Press, gave us her unfailing support and editorial advice. I also thank Juree Sondker, our associate editor, and the many others at Columbia involved in the book production. Finally, we thank the (anonymous) readers whose suggestions helped us give the book its final shape.

At the time of the conference "Derrida/Deleuze: Psychoanalysis, Territoriality, Politics," the illness that would soon put an end to Jacques's life had not yet been made known. We knew how fortunate and privileged we were to have him as a participant, but none of us would have thought that it would become the last public event in his honor at UCI. His death has cast a shadow of inconsolable grief over the completion of this volume. *Derrida, Deleuze, Psychoanalysis* opens with Jacques Derrida's own essay. The fact that he completed it during his illness and assisted in its translation and final editing is further testimony to his resilient philosophical will. In 1984, under the auspices of the Critical Theory Institute at the University of California at Irvine, Derrida presented his Wellek Library Lectures, *Memoires for Paul de Man*, in which he unfolded his most intimate thoughts on death and the impossible task of mourning.[1] Twenty years later, Jacques, facing his own battle for life, gave his last interview for *Le Monde*, titled "Je suis en guerre contre moi-même" (I am at war with myself), in which he invoked the notion of philosophy as an "anxious anticipation of death."[2] Yet, even in the face of death, Derrida once again asserted what he called his "unconditional affirmation of life." Within the logic of this affirmation, survival is "life beyond life, life more than life" (7). "To learn to live means to learn to die.... I have not learned to accept death," says Jacques in the interview (2). I hope that this volume will carry his unconditional affirmation of life into the future and transport some of the joy, passion, humor, and irony that are the signatures of his work.

BIBLIOGRAPHY

"Derrida/Deleuze: Psychoanalysis, Politics, Territoriality." Conference held at UC Irvine, Irvine, California, April 12–13, 2002.

Derrida, Jacques. "Je suis en guerre contre moi-même" [I am at war with myself]. Interview by Jean Birnbaum. *Le Monde*, August 18, 2004.

———. *Memoires for Paul de Man*. Trans. Cecile Lindsay, Jonathan Culler, Eduardo Cadava, and Peggy Kamuf. New York: Columbia University Press, 1986.

Derrida, Deleuze, Psychoanalysis

I

INTRODUCTION

Derrida, Deleuze, and the Psychoanalysis to Come

Gabriele Schwab

At the end of "Freud and the Scene of Writing," Derrida offers his readers two images drawn from Numbers and Ezekiel: one is "the parched woman drinking the inky dust of the law" and the other is "the son of man who fills his entrails with the scroll of the law which has become sweet as honey in his mouth."[1] Highlighting the prominence of orality and incorporation in relation to ethics, politics, and the law, these two images seem to contain in a nutshell some of Derrida's major engagements and concerns with psychoanalysis. Derrida's psychophilosophical reflections on incorporation reach back to the mouth as an organ and figure that prepares the ground for a gradually acquired division between self and other. The mouth and, more generally, the capacity for literal and figurative incorporation are instrumental in the constitution of good and bad internal objects and the boundary between autoaffection and heteroaffection. Throughout his work, Derrida makes use of the challenge psychoanalysis presents for a rethinking of orality in its philosophical and epistemological implications. He explores the oral aspects of encounters between self and other from cannibalism and incorporation to hospitality and appropriative consumption. Incorporation, digestion, and elimination provide the primordial terms for an ethical imperative in which the psychological and the political are inextricably intertwined.

Most important, considerations of psychoanalytic concepts of orality shape Derrida's deconstruction of conventional notions of voice and writing from its inception in *Speech and Phenomena* and *Of Grammatology* to his latest works on psychoanalysis, autoimmunity, cruelty, war, and human rights. The mouth lends itself to be used both as an instrument of voracious attack in the service of the work of death and as an instrument of sociality, hospitality, and an ethics of friendship in the service of the work of life. Eating together, taking the other in, eating what the other eats, and understanding what it means to eat well are as important as incorporating the other in an act of mourning. The traces of Abraham and Torok's work on mourning and incorporation, which Derrida honors in "Fors," continue to pervade his own work. The mouth, however, is also the site of utterance and the generation of sounds, the voice, and the cry. In *Of Grammatology*, Derrida refers to the inarticulate cry as that which one has always excluded, pushing it into the arena of animality or madness (166). Posing the problem of the cry and of speech (voice) within the history of life is part of Derrida's larger concern in opening language to the trace of the other, the unconscious, or *différance*. In her introduction to *Of Grammatology*, one of the first systematic assessments of Derrida's relationship to psychoanalysis, Gayatri Spivak writes: "For Derrida . . . a text, as we recall, whether 'literary,' 'psychic,' 'anthropological,' or otherwise, is a play of presence and absence, a place of the effaced trace" (lvii). This concern with the effaced trace of the other calls for a concept of writing and speech able to discern what Spivak calls the "trace-structure of expression" (liii). Derrida's concern with the inarticulate cry further calls for a concept of writing that includes animality and madness and, more generally, primordiality, or what Deleuze calls the "presignifying semiotic," which he describes as "much closer to 'natural' codings operating without signs."[2] For Deleuze, this presignifying semiotic is a decolonizing force that "fosters a pluralism or polyvocality of forms of expression that prevents any power takeover by the signifier and preserves expressive forms particular to content; thus forms of corporeality, gesturality, rhythm, dance, and rite coexist heterogeneously with the vocal form" (117). In this positive valuation of an inclusive concept of writing that resists the confining force of the signifying and representational regime, Derrida is closer to Deleuze than he is to the overall critique of psychoanalysis Deleuze develops with Guattari in *A Thousand Plateaus* and *Anti-Oedipus*.

During the conference "Derrida/Deleuze: Psychoanalysis, Politics, Territoriality," Derrida shared this resistance to *Anti-Oedipus* in a self-ironical anecdote that reveals the playful spirit that marked the exchanges between Derrida and Deleuze about psychoanalysis: "I resisted the way he [Deleuze] attacked psychoanalysis because I thought it would help the resistance to psychoanalysis, and I didn't want to help. I remember once, the only moment I discussed this with Deleuze was . . . just after he published the *Anti-Oedipus*. . . . Both of us were on the jury of a thesis at Nanterre. . . . I took Deleuze back to Paris. I was driving. It was brief. I said: 'Do you know *Anti-Oedipus*?' 'No, I don't!' he replied. And that was all. Then we arrived in Paris."[3] This little anecdote is emblematic of an encounter deferred all too long. It is also emblematic of the role of negation and resistance in the production of difference. Derrida's and Deleuze's play between self and other is based on a mutual recognition of resistance fully to engage the differences in their positions, especially toward psychoanalysis. Could we say that in this incident Derrida, in a tacit reaffirmation of psychoanalysis after *Anti-Oedipus*, coaxes Deleuze into a self-deterritorializing gesture? Could we say that, by enacting the encounter with Deleuze in a tension between play and history, Derrida defers the encounter into an anticipated future?

In *Anti-Oedipus*, Deleuze and Guattari attack psychoanalysis on the grounds, among other things, of Freud's construction of the subject with the help of the oedipal triangle and the submission to the law of the father this triangulation requires. While this notion of subject formation contains and undermines desire and establishes a fundamental lack in the subject as constitutive, Deleuze and Guattari proclaim the revolutionary power of desire and its resistance against social and psychic repression.[4] According to Deleuze and Guattari, Freud is not radical enough in his critique of civilization's discontents because he naturalizes the oedipal triangulation inherent in the subject's socialization into the (Victorian) nuclear family. The latter entails, for Deleuze and Guattari, a colonization of psychic life: "Oedipus is always colonization pursued by other means, it is the interior colony, and we shall see that even here at home, where we Europeans are concerned, it is our intimate colonial education" (170).

By contrast, Derrida emphasizes political implications of psychoanalysis that still remain to be developed in their full potential. He further challenges a "psychoanalysis to come" to elaborate its implied political and social theory in order to claim a voice in current debates about war, torture, cruelty, freedom, and human rights. Many of Derrida's reflections on the political challenge of psychoanalysis converge on issues of incorporation. Incorporation is not only a psychological concept related to taking in the other; it is also an economic and political concept deeply related to issues of colonialism and global capitalism. The political economy of incorporation is, in fact, suggestively evoked in Derrida's use of the images referred to earlier of "the parched woman drinking the inky dust of the law" and "the son of man who fills his entrails with the scroll of the law which has become sweet as honey in his mouth." Together, the two images point to a political dimension of incorporation, including differences in gender politics. Women and men alike incorporate the law and assimilate it from within their entrails, so to speak. Yet while the woman in the image becomes parched from the law's dust and thus deprived of the fluid vitality of life, the man turns the scrolls of law to his advantage after making them taste like honey in his mouth. While the woman's act illustrates the draining of life in willful subjection to the law, the man's act bespeaks the sweet taste of the psychic life of power. Two kinds of appropriation are at work here: by "drinking" the law, the woman becomes (like) the law, and this "becoming law" inverts the economy of consumption. In consuming the law, the parched woman lets herself be consumed by it. The "inky dust of law" dries up her life juices and makes her shriveled, withered, sterile, and unproductive. By contrast, the man turns the law into nurture and *jouissance*.

Of course, we must analyze the incorporation of the law psychoanalytically in order to see the discontents it will inevitably cause, even as it tastes sweet like honey. In fact, Derrida's use of the image of the parched woman carries a certain affinity to an image Deleuze and Guattari use to describe women's subjection to molar politics. A woman's attempt to confine herself to trying to win back her own history and subjectivity by making her appearance as a mere subject of enunciation, they warn, "does not function without drying up a spring or stopping a flow." And they continue: "The song of life is often intoned by the driest of women, moved by *ressentiment*, the will to power and cold mothering. Just as a desiccated child makes a much better child, there being no childhood flow emanating from it any longer" (*Plateaus*, 276). Like Derrida, Deleuze and Guattari thus also attribute the desiccation of the molecular flows of desire to a subjection to the law. But here it is the law of molar politics with its segregation of flows into entities and identities, species and subjects. In contrast to feminist positions that argue for the reclamation of a woman's voice within the laws of the symbolic order, for Deleuze and Guattari, such politics always entail a psychic colonization that can only be countered with uncoded flows of desire.[5]

Derrida's notion of incorporation is more ambivalent. Once incorporated, the law can become a good or bad object, depending on the specific role one accords to it in shaping an ethics of relating to the other. The ethics of hospitality that concerns Derrida so deeply forbids the killing or eating of the other, but it also knows the laws of "eating well," of eating with the other, and of eating what the other eats. Derrida himself took great delight in playing with this ethics that Sara Guyer in her essay in this volume calls a "buccal ethics." In 1986 Jack Peltason, then chancellor at the University of California at Irvine, hosted a celebratory dinner with a small group of colleagues in honor of Jacques Derrida's appointment. Waiters appeared with fancy plates of food, decorated with colorful orchids. Confident that not everybody was in on the new craze of edible flowers, Jacques whispered, with nearly childlike pleasure, "Look, if I as guest of honor eat this flower, everybody must do the same in order not to embarrass or offend me." With ceremonious flourish, he lifted the orchid with his fork and announced: "Thank you all for this beautiful California cuisine!" The orchid disappeared into his mouth. A moment of pronounced silence followed before a boisterous colleague broke it: "Well, if Jacques can eat his orchid without fear of being poisoned, so can I!" and down went the orchid. It was not long before most guests had followed Jacques's example. A sequel to this story occurred fourteen years later, in the year 2000, at a reception in honor of Ngugi Wa Thiong'o, who had just been appointed director of UC Irvine's International Center for Writing and Translation. We stood with Jacques when a waiter passed by with a plate of appetizers, this time decorated with clearly nonedible flowers. Suddenly, Jacques handed me one of the flowers: "May I offer you a flower?" he asked before he cautioned with unconcealed pleasure: "Let's not eat this one!" And, with a final twist, he added: "You see, sometimes memory works after all!"

These little episodes enact Derrida's previously mentioned concerns with psychoanalysis that relate to incorporation and the ethics of heteroaffection. We could almost treat them as a footnote on Derrida's discourses on flowers, hospitality, and cannibalism. Trying to shock his hosts by eating a flower, Derrida willfully used a transgression in order to feed this transgression into the law of hospitality that requires hosts to follow the transgression of a guest in order not to embarrass him. More than a decade later, he deconstructs the transgression by shifting the emphasis to the work of memory and thus establishes a playful link to the fact that the question of eating or not eating the other is, in his work, embedded in his manifold reflections on memory and mourning. Incorporation, in these discourses, bears the mark of a betrayal because it interiorizes the other's fixed and idealized image.[6] Against this betrayal, Derrida remains committed to the notion of an "impossible mourning" that refuses incorporation in order to let the other retain his alterity. This impossible mourning is tied, in his words, to "'original grief' which does not wait for the death called 'real.'"[7] It is in this spirit of refused incorporation that, many years after Deleuze's death, Derrida finally approaches Deleuze's use and critique of psychoanalysis. Perhaps, in the time to come, we will find that our mourning for Derrida already has been inscribed in the traces, vestiges, and spectralities that continue to speak his "original grief." It is in this sense also that mourning is impossible mourning. "Memory projects itself toward the future, and it constitutes the presence of the present," writes Jacques Derrida in *Memoires for Paul de Man* (57). Hopefully, this volume on Derrida, Deleuze, and psychoanalysis will count as a work of mourning that carries our memories of Jacques Derrida into the future.

While they have not gone unnoticed, the uncanny closeness and affinity of concerns in the work of Gilles Deleuze and Jacques Derrida have barely begun to be explored. Given the fact that the very same series of major themes—difference and alterity, territoriality and politics, time and space, the mouth and the face, the voice and writing, the animal and the machine—runs through both of their work, this avoidance is so striking that it cannot be dismissed as a mere coincidental omission. At the time I began planning this volume, the first major collection of essays on Derrida and Deleuze, *Between Deleuze and Derrida*, coedited by Paul Patton and John Protevi, was in the works, but it did not appear until 2003. Surprisingly, to this day, there is no volume that focuses on the relationship of Deleuze and Derrida to psychoanalysis. Such a volume will most likely ignite controversies over differences in politics, but this particular volume is designed to facilitate a productive encounter that refrains from merely setting up the two philosophers against each other. This choice reflects the ambivalence that made Derrida and Deleuze remain different and yet in close proximity to each other. Maybe a closeness too close for comfort brought the two philosophers together in a dance of rapprochement and withdrawal performed at a guarded distance? They barely quoted and willfully ignored each other all too long, like twins who pretend that the other is not even there. Derrida titled his eulogy of Gilles Deleuze "Il me faudra errer tout seul," and Leonard Lawlor translated this title as "I'm going to have to wander all alone." Derrida's own word "*errer*," however, also contains the suggestion of an error—the risk of "erring" that Deleuze left as a legacy for Derrida, who then spoke, somewhat mournfully, of the long discussion the two were supposed to have together yet systematically avoided. Both knew, of course, that such discussion would one day inevitably emerge from their work, and Derrida inserted himself, somewhat mischievously preemptive, into Deleuze's "serial singularity" with his laconic statement, "Yes, we will have all loved philosophy, who can deny it?" (*The Work of Mourning,* 193).

Derrida's statement is, in fact, a highly performative understatement. More than a mere love for philosophy, he shared with Deleuze a lasting passion for literature and for the same authors (Artaud, Joyce, Beckett, Melville, and many more). Theoretically, they shared a persistent critical concern and engagement with psychoanalysis and Marxism as well as a philosophical preoccupation with issues of space, territory, and concomitant politics of appropriation and resistance. They also share dislikes, and, as Derrida confesses, they had the same enemies. Together, they changed this century's sense of writing and speech, allies in their scrutiny of what Deleuze and Guattari call the "signifying regime." But even in this alliance what matters is the "difference that makes a difference," as Gregory Bateson put it in "Form, Substance and Difference." One might be tempted to think of a narcissism of minor differences, but, as Derrida says, they had monumental consequences. Think, for example, of the following statement: "Lies and deception may be a fundamental part of the signifying regime, but secrecy is not" (*Plateaus,* 115). What challenge would Derrida's work on the secret present to this statement? In *Limited Inc.,* Derrida, for example, argues that lies and deceptions are coeval with the possibility of proffering speech acts.[8] Or if Derrida asks of Freud "what the imitation, projected and liberated in a machine, of something like psychical writing might mean" ("Freud," 199), what turn would this question take from the perspective of a Deleuzian "writing machine" (*Plateaus,* 117)? And if Derrida concludes: "If there is neither machine nor text without psychical origin, there is no domain of the psychic 'without text' " ("Freud," 199), how does this relate to Deleuze and Guattari's notion of the "presignifying semiotic" (*Plateaus*, 117)? The latter emerges in forms of corporeality as gesturality, rhythm, dance, rite, and perhaps even cry—forms that, as the authors assert, coexist heterogeneously with the vocal form and constitute a bodily semiosis with its own intentionality. And how does this semiosis relate to specific organs or to the face and faciality? Derrida begins *The Ear of the Other* with a quotation from Nietzsche's *Zarathustra*: "for there are human beings who lack everything, except one thing of which they have too much—human beings who are nothing but a big eye or a big mouth" (3). Deleuze and Guattari write: "The face is the Icon proper to the signifying regime, the reterritorialization internal to the system. The signifier reterritorializes on the face. . . . The signifier is always facialized. Faciality reigns materially over that whole constellation of signifiances and interpretations . . . . Conversely, when the face is effaced, when the faciality traits disappear, we can be sure that we have entered another regime, other zones infinitely muter and more imperceptible where subterranean becomings occur, becomings molecular, nocturnal deterritorializations overspilling the limits of the signifying system" (*Plateaus*, 115). How would Derrida assess the idea of such different regimes in his own terms? Questions such as these inevitably push the stakes beyond both surface resemblances and narcissisms of minor difference between the two philosophers. The present volume critically scrutinizes many of the themes and concerns shared by Derrida and Deleuze. Coverage being undesirable if not impossible, we have opted for a specific perspective, namely, the psychological in relation to and inseparable from the political. With this focus, the essays predominately explore psychoanalysis as a social theory.

The three opening essays, by Jacques Derrida, Catherine Malabou, and Sara Guyer, trace this relation in the sociocultural formation of figures such as the animal and the infant. Derrida's essay, "The Transcendental 'Stupidity' ('Bêtise') of Man and the Becoming-Animal According to Deleuze," focuses on the figure of the animal and the "becoming-animal" according to Deleuze, approaching psychoanalysis and the question of the unconscious by challenging the alleged transcendental "stupidity" (*bêtise*) of man. "The animal," asserts Deleuze, "is protected by specific forms which prevent it from being 'stupid' [*bête*]" (*Difference and Repetition*, 150, quoted in Derrida, 36). How does stupidity advance to this position of being exclusively reserved to and thus marking the boundaries of the human? Derrida traces this Deleuzian assertion to the issue of freedom, will, individuation, and the capacity to say "I." "In other words, the animal cannot be bête, stupid, because it is not free, it has no will, and its individuation, which gives it shape or form, doesn't appear on the background of a ground, which is freedom itself" (51). By grounding this "stupidity" that defines the human in terms of freedom, Deleuze in turn links freedom and by extension "stupidity" to sovereignty, cruelty, and thought. "A tyrant institutionalises stupidity, but he is the first servant of his own system and the first to be installed within it" (*Difference and Repetition*, 151, quoted in Derrida, 52).

This classical motif of tyrants as slaves recalls a Hegelian dialectics of master and slave that has been used and revised in psychoanalytic theories of colonization and "isomorphic oppression."[9] The institutionalization of stupidity, tyranny, and oppression operates as a system that affects the agent who installs the system as well as those subjected to its modes of operation. In a similar vein, Deleuze argues that "cowardice, cruelty, baseness, and stupidity ... *are structures of thought as such*" (*Difference and Repetition*, 151, quoted in Derrida, 52; his emphasis). According to Derrida, this places Deleuze's psychological model in the same tradition of philosophy that also informs Lacan's model of "bestiality" as reserved for human agents exclusively. It is a tradition, in other words, that defines the human in distinction from the animal through the exertion of freedom and responsibility for one's actions toward others. "Properly human animality" in this tradition is "supposed to be free and responsible and not reactive, able to discern between good and evil, able to do evil for the sake of evil, and so on" (55).[10]

Derrida challenges this tradition from a psychoanalytic perspective on the question of the unconscious, a question that, as he asserts, Deleuze dismisses too quickly (56). If Derrida finds it hard to share Deleuze's sarcasm with respect to psychoanalysis, it is because the conceptuality he analyzes in Deleuze and Lacan "does not provide any assured criterion" (57) to propose that only man is exposed to stupidity (Deleuze) or bestiality (Lacan). Derrida's tour de force consists in opening the question of free will and responsibility that grounds Deleuze's and Lacan's positions to that of the unconscious as an agency capable of interfering with free will.[11] In this context, Derrida reminds us of Lacan's insistence that the animal has no unconscious. In a related move, Catherine Malabou, in her essay "Polymorphism Never Will Pervert Childhood," to which I will return later, reminds us of Deleuze's insistence that the child has no unconscious, either. Is it the unconscious, then, that marks the boundaries of the human subject? Insisting that Deleuze's "philosophy of bêtise" is inconsistent with reference to the unconscious (58), Derrida links Deleuze and Lacan's position to a philosophical and anthropological tradition of thought that "supposes with Descartes and Kant that the animal cannot constitute itself as an I" (57). Difference here is linked to differentiation and individuation, and the agency of the human subject is conceived as bounded by the egological form. This form is where Derrida locates his critique:

> Without having to credit such or such construction of Freudian metapsychology, one cannot reduce the whole psychological or metapsychological experience to its egological form, and one cannot reduce all life to the ego or every egological structure to the conscious I. In the psychological or phenomenological experience, in the self-relation of the living being, the relation of the living being to itself, there is something one could call nonego, on the one hand, and there is even, as Freud would say, the unconscious ego. So, even if one doesn't want to rely on the authority of Freudian discourse, it is enough to admit that the living being is divisible and constituted by a multiplicity of assemblages, instances, forces, different intensities, and sometimes tensions and even contradictions.
>
> (58)

Derrida resists what he calls the "hegemonic tradition from Descartes to Levinas, including Lacan and Heidegger, and so on," because for him the distinction of "man and the beast" on the basis of a distinction between response/responsibility and reaction, sovereignty and nonsovereignty, freedom and nonfreedom is founded on an untenable anthropocentric bias (58). For Derrida, this distinction becomes obsolete as soon as one admits "that there is no finite living being, human or nonhuman, that wouldn't be structured by" differential forces that allow for antagonisms, resistances, repressions, or simply "'la raison du plus fort,' the reason/right of the strongest" (59). What is at stake in Derrida's challenge to Deleuze and Lacan regarding the figure of the animal and the question of the unconscious is the problem of anthropocentrism in defining the boundaries of the human. This anthropomorphism has profound political consequences. After all, the same epistemological move has often led to other forms of exclusion, colonizing in their nature, such as the exclusion of children and indigenous people from the defined boundaries of the human.

The figure of the child is at the center of Catherine Malabou's "Polymorphism Never Will Pervert Childhood." Malabou comments on the fact that "Deleuze maintains that a child does not have an unconscious, that he or she must *produce* it" (71). Criticizing Freud's assumption of the child's "polymorphous perversity," Deleuze insists that there is no polymorphism but an assemblage of raw materials that have to be invented and played with, an assemblage that resists any deterritorialization or fixation to the sign and to meaning (71). If Deleuze and Guattari identify the child as simultaneously the most deterritorialized and the most deterritorializing figure, it is highly significant that the ideal incorporation of the deterritorialized child is the orphan, that is, the child most prone to escape the territorializing forces of familial oedipalization and the transversal energies of substitution.[12]

In contrast to Deleuze, Malabou reads Freud's polymorphism as itself a deterritorialized state. Moreover, she locates a reinscription of polymorphism in Deleuze's own text. The "internal proliferation," "contamination," and "invasion" that Deleuze names as the forces of deterritorialization, as Malabou points out, correspond precisely to what medical discourses call the polymorphism of viruses, microbes, or pathogenic bacteria (74). Likewise, the polymorphous machine in electronics is a machine that produces assemblages of different voltages and currents. Malabou asks: "Shouldn't we therefore assume there to be, at the origin of any metamorphosis, a polymorphous machine that carries out the transmutation of the polymorphous into what Deleuze and Guattari call the 'polyvocal'?" (74). This assumption, however, is precisely what collapses the difference between the polymorphous and the polyvocal on which Deleuze bases his critique of Freud.

What is at stake in these controversies about the figure of the animal and the figure of the child as they are used to define the boundaries of the human? According to Malabou, the stakes for Derrida lie in "the immense question of a polymorphism of difference" (74). Reading this polymorphism of difference in light of Derrida's rejection of an anthropomorphism that draws the boundaries between the human and the animal along the lines of free will and responsibility, we see that the child has always escaped this anthropocentric definition. Isn't this why Deleuze sees the child as the site of deterritorialization? In this light, "becoming animal" or "becoming child" could be seen as pertaining to a process of deanthropomorphization. If this process is polymorphous, and if some call it perverse, it is because it unfolds beyond the logic of the cogito or the self-constitution as an I. Operating outside the categorical limitations and differentiations of consciousness, this process begs the question of the unconscious and takes into account the divisibility, multiplicity, and difference of forces in a living being. Because of this very shift from anthropomorphism to a polymorphism of difference, it is too hasty, Derrida insists, to conceive of the "becoming animal or child" from within a refutation of psychoanalysis.[13] Perhaps Freud's model, he suggests, can be rethought in a way that makes it less anthropocentric than Deleuze would have it.

The figure of the child is also prominent in Sara Guyer's essay, "Buccality." Guyer looks at the child from a Kleinian perspective of the infant's unconscious fantasies, placing a particular emphasis on critical revisions of the Kleinian model by Deleuze, Derrida, Nancy, and de Man. It may be helpful to recall that, at the end of "Freud and the Scene of Writing," Derrida writes: "Melanie Klein's entire thematic, her analysis of the constitution of good and bad objects, her genealogy of morals could doubtless begin to illuminate, if followed prudently, the entire problem of the archi-trace, not in its essence (it does not have one), but in terms of valuation and devaluation. Writing as sweet nourishment or as excrement, the trace as seed or mortal germ, wealth or weapon, detritus and/or penis, etc." (231). Like Derrida, Guyer sees the emergence of a genealogy of morals or, as she calls it, a "buccal ethics" in the infant's earliest fantasies formed even before the differentiation of self and other. What do infantile fantasies—surging before the psychic differentiation of a body with organs, a body separated from others and the breast that feeds it—tell us about the emergence of self and other, of voice, speech, and poetry? How do infantile fantasies compel us to rethink the rhetoric of figures and the ethics of responsibility toward the other? "What if we began to read according to the mouth," asks Guyer, "the opening, eating, kissing, biting . . . mouth—and its depths?" (79). The mouth eats and "reads" before the constitution of a face and a differentiated subjectivity. Levinas grounds the ethics of responsibility—the *thou shalt not kill thy neighbor*—in the face-to-face encounter. Highlighting the anthropomorphism inherent in this ethics, Derrida asks if there is an ethics of responsibility that precedes the constitution of the face. It would be an ethics tied to "eating well" (*il faut bien manger*) and responsively or responsibly, an ethics that opens up the association of eating the other and hence of eating and guilt. Klein, we recall, grounds her concepts of introjection, projection, and reintrojection in the infant's fantasies of devouring and mutilating the mother's body. Consequently, the infantile world of orality is populated by persecutory "bad" objects that are introjected, spat out again, split off, and placed into others in the form of projections. The move from this "paranoid-schizoid position" to a "depressive position" is, in a sense, an ethical move based on identification and substitution. It is a move from orality to vocality, from incorporation to identification, and from mere objects and part objects to signs. Or, as Guyer describes this transition, to a "melancholic vocality": "the good object (absent-present) becomes the object of a voice (*fort-da*)" (87). According to Guyer, Deleuze's revision of the Kleinian model brings the voracious (paranoid-schizoid) and the vociferous (depressive) mouths to cross. "The voice (the vociferous mouth) 'steals' the 'sonorous *prevocal* system' of orality (the voracious mouth)" (87). This is why Deleuze will come to distinguish between a literature of the face and a literature of the mouth. In a similar vein, Jean-Luc Nancy conceives of a "first philosophy" that issues through the mouth. It is, as Nancy states, a mouth that is neither mind nor body, neither substance nor figure, reminiscent perhaps of the disembodied mouth in Beckett's *Not I*. It is a mouth without a face, prior to signification and prior to the eye as the carrier of a gaze (Guyer, 98).

It is in this mouth, this buccality, that Nancy locates the emergence of the ego: "The Freudian child ... opens [*il s'ouvre*] first of all in a mouth, the open mouth of a cry, but also the mouth closed around a breast to which it is attached by an identification that is older than any identification with a figure; and the half-open mouth, detaching itself from the breast in a first smile, a first mimicry whose future is thought. The mouth is the opening of the *Ego*, *Ego* is the opening of the mouth" (Nancy, *Ego sum*, 162, quoted in Guyer, 91).[14] We are reminded here, of course, that, in *The Ego and the Id*, Freud defined the ego as first and foremost a bodily ego (20). By grounding subjectivity in a primarily bodily relation to the other that precedes language, naming, and the face, Nancy tries to perform a crucial revision of the egological history of subjectivity. Derrida in turn "translates Nancy's analysis as a fundamentally ethical account of the subject that coincides with a nonfigural rhetoric" (91). It is an ethics that is organized around incorporation and the dynamic of eating and being eaten, an ethics established, as Derrida reminds us, in the name of the mother who is "being eaten" and incorporated by the infant (Guyer, 95). Buccality, then, is a relation to the (m)other prior to the self because the mouth precedes the division between autoaffection and heteroaffection, self and other (93).

Finally, de Man links this nonfigural rhetoric to poetry, arguing that a relation to the mother is only possible through poetry and language (Guyer, 96). De Man, in other words, marks the transition from the infant as hungry mouth to the infant as mirrored in its mother's eyes and as responsive to this mirroring. We must be cautious, however, not to perceive this transition from the mouth to the face and the gaze in merely developmental terms as a transition to a different ethics grounded in a gradually emerging distinction between self and other. As Guyer insists in a provocative turn against this developmental narrative, for de Man, the infant becomes a poet only because he "with his soul drinks in the feelings of his Mother's eye" (Wordsworth) and thereby incorporates his mother's feelings. The infant's affection through nursing by the mother's feelings is why in this buccal ethics of otherness the origins of language and poetry become aligned not with facing the other but with "mouthing" (98). Guyer's perspective on "buccality" in Deleuze, Derrida, Nancy, and de Man is consistent with Derrida's challenge to a tradition that defines the boundaries between human and animal along the lines of a division between (irresponsible) reaction and (responsible) response. In the buccality of the mouth, Guyer locates an ethics of responsiveness to the other that precedes the constitution of a subject capable of saying "I." This ethics will not be replaced but rather supplemented by an ethics of the face-to-face that will henceforth remain contemporaneous with it. We must understand the profound political implication of this epistemological move. In consequence, the boundaries of the human will no longer exile the animal or the infant and the child (and by extension indigenous people) according to the colonizing hegemony of a subject who pronounces an "I" without the benefit of a doubt. "I, say I, unbelieving," says Beckett's *unnamable*, a master in polymorphism and polyvocalism. The boundaries of the human have become more tenuous, and the ethics of self and other less exclusive, hegemonic, and anthropocentric. Moreover, as far as human ethics are concerned, the remains of the child inscribe themselves forever as an archaic trace in the adult subject's ethics of otherness.

"These remains of the child never emerge as the personal recollections of the speaking subject. Rather, they can only be spoken as analysis or as a 'construction of analysis,'" writes Dina Al-Kassim in "Resistance, Terminable and Interminable." She reminds us that the figure of the child in psychoanalysis refers not only to infancy and childhood proper but to the traces and remains of the child in adult life: "Freud speaks in place of the departed child whose traces remain as an 'archaic inheritance' in the discourse of the adult patient" (118). Rather than as a reconstruction of lost memories, the analytic process evolves as the co-construction of "a lost fantasy, a desire that could not survive the censorship of repression entire but persists, a resistant element, in a compromised and symptomatic form" (118). The lost fantasy of the "departed child" becomes a site of resistance against the censorship and repression that accompany the forces of socialization and acculturation or the access to the symbolic order. At the same time, however, the fantasy also becomes the site of psychic suffering. Political resistance, argues Al-Kassim, "can never sever itself from the psychic suffering that also goes in the name of resistance" (106). Both Derrida and Deleuze, Al-Kassim points out, have addressed the connection between resistance and human suffering. While Deleuze emphasizes creation and creativity as resistance to death, servitude, shame, and "the present," Derrida highlights that psychoanalysis, itself with its "difficult form of thought," constitutes a practice of resistance against the leveling of difference in a conformist or neoconformist culture (*Resistances of Psychoanalysis*, 45; quoted in Al-Kassim, 110).[15] Moreover, he reminds us that psychoanalysis is the only available body of knowledge that addresses "the paradoxical problem of cruelty to oneself" (Al-Kassim, 115). We recall Derrida's insistence that this psychoanalytic knowledge about the intractable cruelty of humans toward other humans and toward themselves should inform sociopolitical reflections about changing the present. Rather than establishing a unified concept of resistance, psychoanalysis uses transference to work with and through resistance. Transference is a paradoxical site for both the enactment of resistance and its working through and eventual overcoming. It proceeds by mobilizing the lost fantasy of the "departed child" as well as the traces and endlessly repeated patterns of affect it has retained from its history of attachment and loss.

Derrida is interested in the ways in which the psychoanalytic process of transference uses the "suffering in repetition" that underlies the repetition compulsion as a chance for a transformational working-through (Al-Kassim, 120). In the same vein, Al-Kassim argues that "in the field of political resistance there are interventions analogous to the analyst's successful working-through and -with the other's resistance, but . . . such interventions . . . cannot prevent resistance from branching out in other ways and as a source of other sufferings" (121). In her reading of *Uku Hamba 'Ze! (To Walk Naked)*, a documentary about the women's protest in South Africa in 1990 against the police's destruction of their homes in a shantytown, Al-Kassim highlights resistance as a source of new suffering. Even though the women who bare their breasts in protest follow a traditional practice and semiotics of shame, she argues, the paradox of violating the customs of home to protect the home haunts them. When they look back at their act of baring themselves in front of the police and the media, they internalize the shame they were trying to expose.

The traumatic effect of this act of resistance unfolds, I think, within the familiar temporal dynamic of trauma, *Nachträglichkeit*, belatedness. Retroactively, from within the symbolic norms of their home, the women fall back into shame and suffering. "They remain there as the melancholy survivors of a public shame," Al-Kassim states. Their act of resistance against power and authority reverts into an act of cruelty toward themselves. Al-Kassim ends her reflections with a question: How are we to integrate this story of public shame with the epic of anti-apartheid resistance? At the beginning of her essay, she refers to Derrida's affirmation of psychoanalysis as a storehouse of knowledge about cruelty and suffering and the transfiguration of resistances (115). Perhaps it is one of the most crucial sociocultural and political functions of psychoanalysis today to help us conceive of the conflicts and contradictions of both resistance's relationship to trauma and traumatic resistance. In this context, Al-Kassim also quotes Derrida's admonishing psychoanalysis to "take stock of technological transformations in knowledge and social relations" (130). The fact that the South African women saw their nakedness exposed and broadcast through the public media was crucial in creating the delayed traumatic effect. It was as though technology worked retroactively to convert an act of protest into an act of shame by taking it out of context and time. Instead of operating in a Deleuzian sense, as a creative act to resist servitude, shame, and death, the image of exposure broadcast by the mass media helped to invert, if not pervert, the resistance by freezing shame into a timeless aftereffect. Here, too, resistance has—as both Deleuze and Derrida maintain—become inextricable from human suffering. Yet, instead of liberating the resisting subject from suffering, resistance, in Al-Kassim's reading of the documentary, is reconverted into suffering through media co-optation.

While both Derrida and Deleuze maintain the link between resistance and human suffering, they part ways when they assess the status of, and difference between, suffering and pain. In "Freud and the Scene of Writing," Derrida reminds us that Freud privileges pain as the primary source of memory: "In a certain sense, there is no breaching (*Bahnung*) without a beginning of pain, and 'pain leaves behind it particularly rich breaches'" (202). Pain can become unconscious, but it leaves traces, inscriptions, and, more important, it becomes the source of our actions and politics because, unknowingly, it feeds our political unconscious. "But beyond a certain quantity, pain, the threatening origin of the psyche, must be deferred, like death, for it can 'ruin' psychical 'organization'" (202). If pain is too unbearable, it is eclipsed from consciousness and memory. Then we encounter trauma and traumatic amnesia. Hence there is not only pain as the origin of the psyche and memory as its essence (201); there is also the necessity to defer pain, to displace it, mute or deny it, or seek it out and transform it as, for example, in masochism.[16]

Branka Arsić's essay deals with the role of pain and suffering in the work of Freud, Deleuze, and Derrida more generally, claiming that it is the question of pain and suffering that puts both philosophers at a certain distance from psychoanalysis. Deleuze, Arsić claims, resists any Freudian notion of the interiorization or the "becoming metaphor" of pain. For Deleuze, it is rather excitements or intensities and their habitual reproduction that produce pain or pleasure. Pain is not translated or transformed but literal and unrepresentable, emerging from passive syntheses that are subrepresentative (Arsić 151). For Deleuze, Arsić argues, passive syntheses are the constructive force of life itself. Everything in the organism is made of a primary sensibility and passivity that constitutes impersonal life, that is, a life of pure immanence, neutral, beyond good and evil (151–152). Desire emerges from this "plane of immanence" as an endless dissemination of passive syntheses. By contrast, pleasure is bound to an "active synthesis" that forms organs and attempts the unification and integration of distributed larval selves. Arsić maintains that, for Deleuze, masochism is not—as in Freud—subordinated to the pleasure principle but constitutes a "strategy that works against pleasure, against the ego and therefore against the politics of globalization.... For the masochistic contract is, in fact, the very resistance to the law" (155–156). In this sense, Deleuze can maintain that masochism is about neither pain nor pleasure but the suspension of the "I" and the law in an "extension and intension of desire" (157). We find in masochism, then, yet another mode of resistance against the egological construction of the subject. In a Nietzschean transvaluation, Deleuze recasts what is traditionally perceived as a deficient state as the undoing of a bond and hence as liberation and resistance. After all, for Deleuze, the egological construction of the subject is nothing but a "becoming trapped in one's molar form and subject" (*Plateaus*, 275). Similarly, the direction of what René Major calls Derrida's "desistantial psychoanalysis" aims against the egological construction of the subject: "The logic proper to *desistance* leads to the destabilization of the subject, to its disidentification from every position in *estance*, from all determinations of the subject by the ego" ("Derrida and Psychoanalysis," 301).

In certain respects, both Derrida and Deleuze share the interest in a "deterritorialized" subject formed before or beyond the egological construction that requires a subjection to the symbolic order and the law. Moreover, both Deleuze and Derrida insist on the productive energies of the unconscious and share an ethos of permeable boundaries and inclusion rather than exclusion in defining the human. Derrida's notion of pain and suffering is, however, as Arsić remarks, closer to Freud's than to Deleuze's. For Derrida, the most primary form of pain emerges from the subject's formative and continual exposure to a wound created by the abyss of separation. It is the pain of separation that propels the vicissitudes of unconscious psychic life. In relation to the latter, Derrida emphasizes that the psychoanalytic goal to gain access to the unconscious generates an "economy of the secret" (160). By contrast, Deleuze and Guattari assume a state of original plurality marked by a free flow of affects. There is no sense that the process of differentiation between self and other is experienced as a painful separation or an original wound. Hence, for Deleuze and Guattari, the economy of the secret related to the unconscious is entirely different. Rather than being "a simple box containing secrets," they argue, "the Unconscious has been assigned the increasingly difficult task of itself being the infinite form of secrecy" (*Plateaus*, 289). Ultimately, the unconscious becomes a ubiquitous state of continual molecular becoming: "The more the secret is made into a structuring, organizing form, the thinner and more ubiquitous it becomes, the more its content becomes molecular, at the same time as its form dissolves" (289). The operation of the secret and hence the dynamic of the unconscious are, in other words, nonrepresentational. Arsić emphasizes that Derrida, too, understands the secret in nonrepresentational terms. This is crucial since it indicates an epistemological shift from thinking in terms of a psychoanalytic revelation of an unconscious content or dissimulated representation of unconscious material to a more structural unconscious in which the secret is not the effect of repression but constitutive of psychic life. This structural unconscious is, according to Arsić's reading of Derrida, generated by an "abyss of separation whose meaning neither speaks nor hides anything. It is neither reflective nor anamorphic; rather, it is simply in the mode of nonbelonging, a passive 'there is something secret'" (162). For Arsić the difference between the psychoanalytic and the Derridean notion of the secret resides in the fact that, for Derrida, the secret escapes the specular order and representational economy of subjectivity (163). Or, as Spivak pointed out in her introduction to *Of Grammatology*: "In Derrida, via Freud, there would be a difficulty in setting up the opposition between the conscious and the unconscious within the subject as the founding principle of a systematic study. The unconscious is undecidable, either the always already other, out of reach of psychic descriptions, or else it is thoroughly implicated in so-called conscious activity" (lix). In light of this ubiquitous operation of the unconscious, we could then say that the economy of the secret is generative for the very formation of subjectivity. Recent developments in psychoanalysis are, in fact, closer to Derrida's position than the classical Freudian notion he engages. Anton Ehrenzweig, Christopher Bollas, and Alessandra Piotelli, for example, have emphasized a similar structural and nonrepresentational unconscious as a supplement to the unconscious generated by repression.[17] It is an unconscious that can never be "revealed" but structurally divides the self against itself. The economy of the secret is one in which subjectivity always remains partly hidden from the subject's conscious grasp.

For Derrida, this separation cuts like a wound, and the only thing that remains "legible" is the living trace of the wound. "The self exists as this passive, incommunicable exposure to the wound," Arsić says (165). Reading Derrida with Deleuze, she then concludes that, if the suffering from this wound is, for Derrida, "outside the economy of representation," then suffering "would be a dissemination of intensities of passions without the intimate gathering and erection of the subject within itself" (166). We are close, then, to the formation of the self before the egological structure, close indeed to the phase of self-formation described by Guyer in her reflections on the bodily self before the acquisition of language, close also to Deleuze's notion of the "presignifying semiotic." For Arsić this dynamic belongs to "another" psychoanalysis, one in which laughter and tears and other raw emotions override consciousness and make the body speak in spasms and rhythms and waves. While this may or may not unsettle classical representational psychoanalysis, it certainly calls for what Arsić refers to as enduring "the groundlessness of psychoanalysis," because this turn to a nonrepresentational unconscious also means enduring the pulsations, rhythms, and intensities of a mode of being we encounter in the traces left from early infancy (167). This endurance in turn requires a different politics toward psychoanalysis, namely, one less resistant than the one Derrida criticizes in *Resistances of Psychoanalysis* and therefore better suited for doing justice to a reading of Freud.

Here we encounter yet another instance where Derrida and Deleuze part ways. Derrida never shared Deleuze's—and, for that matter, Foucault's—resistance to psychoanalysis. On the contrary, he insists that this resistance is but a symptom of our time that is itself in dire need of analysis. Arsić argues, however, that Derrida comes close to Deleuze when he develops a notion of the self that exists as the privation of selfhood. This notion can be approximated to Deleuze's presignifying semiotic and the passive syntheses of impersonal life (151–152). It also can be approximated to the post-Freudian turn in psychoanalysis to earlier and earlier modes of being before the constitution of the subject and of personhood, a mode of being that unfolds in a transitional space between impersonal and bare life. It is a mode of being that resists the egological definitions and secondary revisions of a subject interpellated to live according to historical time and the order of the law.[18]

How do we gain access to this unconscious mode of being that is not an effect of repression but is constituted by a ubiquitous unconscious process of becomings that shapes subjectivity even after the formation of a self? Drawing on Deleuze, Arsić looks at how one can access this unconscious through pain waves and their production and distribution of intensities. Perhaps we may even access it through affect more generally. Corporeal and sensual experiences that are cathected with intense affect may open pathways to this unconscious flow, perhaps even via detours through the transitional space of music, poetry, literature, film, dreams, and fantasies or—differently and via free association and transference—through psychoanalysis. Deleuze's concept of deterritorialization is based on experiences of pulsations, rhythms, waves, and intensities that, like the early experiences of infancy, make no distinction among the real, dream, fantasy, and hallucination. From a psychoanalytic perspective, these experiences constitute unconscious psychic life, that is, a mode of being beyond the law and the symbolic order with its requirements of censorship and secondary revision and its territorial confinement of the subject into bounded identities. The very destiny of desire rests on finding access to such modes of being, albeit only temporarily.

For psychoanalysis, access to the unconscious is a matter of technique and the use of "technologies" capable of circumventing the imperatives of censorship and its requirements for secondary revisions of dreams, fantasies, and histories—personal and collective. Drawing on film and its intervention in the cultural unconscious by way of a "secondary revision" of history, Akira Mizuta Lippit's essay deals with technological transformations in knowledge and social relations. "The Only Other Apparatus of Film" revisits Freud's *The Interpretation of Dreams*, especially his concept of the dreamwork, in light of its relevance for exploring techniques of revision in experimental film and video. Ordering the chaotic force of the unconscious, the secondary revision of dreamwork can be viewed, Lippit argues, as a form of defensive editing, revising, and censoring of unconscious material. In this sense, it is a political act: "In psychoanalysis, phantasy represents the very possibility of a politics of the unconscious" (177). How does this politics of the unconscious operate in the uses of fantasy in film? Film operates in a transitional space in which the boundaries between perception and imagination or exteriority and interiority are mediated and renegotiated.[19] It is, as Lippit writes, "a world that is at once inside and out, a world in which the distinction between interiority and exteriority has been momentarily halted" (177). Lippit quotes Christian Metz, who argues that film facilitates the "joy of receiving from the external world images that are usually internal" (*The Imaginary Signifier*, 136; quoted in Lippit, 177). Recalling Laplanche and Pontalis's location of fantasy at the intersection of imagination and reality, Lippit asks how the renegotiation of the boundaries between interiority and exteriority affects the status of the real in experimental film and documentary. He identifies an "aesthetics and politics of revision," "a resistance to the orders inscribed on commercial and national media," in experimental videos that work with "found footage" and other recycled cinemas (180). Jay Rosenblatt's found footage film *Human Remains* (1998), for example, uses disembodied voice-overs of Hitler, Mussolini, Stalin, Franco, and Mao in order to revisit and revise history by creating the haunting interiority of voices from beyond the grave. Straddling the boundaries between history and memory, *Human Remains*, according to Lippit, exposes the general vulnerability of historical representation to fantastic revision. If we recall that, throughout his work, Derrida repeatedly acknowledges the unique contribution of psychoanalysis to understanding and dealing with traumatic histories and their impact on human suffering, then Lippit's approach illustrates a specific instance of such use of psychoanalysis in both the medium and the interpretation of certain techniques in film. Lippit deals with films and videos that focus on, intervene in, or—as we could say—perform a tertiary revision of fantasies that accrue to historical trauma. "Facts assume significance once they have been revised in the economy of phantasy," he writes, insisting that fantasies determine any historiography and that "the secondary revision of a history is what makes history possible in the first instance, always too late" (184). In order to distinguish secondary revision from dreamwork, Lippit mobilizes Derrida's reflections about Freud's dreamwork: "The apparent exteriority of political censorship refers to an essential censorship that binds the writer to his own writing" (Derrida, "Freud and the Scene of Writing," 226, quoted in Lippit, 173). Secondary revision engages this essential censorship to create an intervention in political censorship. Here we encounter another instance of the intricate intertwinement of the psychological and the political. Using Deleuze and Guattari's concept of "deterritorialization," Lippit says of the secondary revision that it deterritorializes the dream by inserting another subject from another temporal order, "leaving a trace of its intervention in the form of a *différance*" (171). We may even add that this trace simultaneously deterritorializes both dream and history. It is a transitional trace inscribed in and straddling the boundary between fantasy and memory as it is reworked/revised in the dream. Lippit's essay illustrates how, in this coupling of fantasy and memory in filmic assemblages of historical material, we may detect and read the political unconscious of found memories and histories.

Gregg Lambert's "De/Territorializing Psycho-analysis" shifts the perspective from production and secondary revision to reception and interpretation. The secondary revisions that rework memory and history become a focus of the psychoanalytic process and interpretation. Lambert invokes Deleuze's notion of psychoanalysis as a "'culture of memory,' which is to say, a knowledge that always advances by means of a veritable 'Return to the Source'" (205). Lippit's exploration of the secondary revision in dreamwork and film, however, insists that psychoanalysis is as much a "culture of phantasy" as it is a "culture of memory" since memories are always already traversed, revised or, as he says, "deterritorialized" by fantasy. Moreover, traumatic histories, collective or personal, cannot be accessed or worked through by a "return to the source." As Freud insists, it is not the original event or the source that causes trauma but a retroactive memory that freezes time, congealing the event into a certain structure of fantasy, thus creating a secondary revision of sorts after the fact, belatedly—under the temporal logic of *Nachträglichkeit*. Access to the original event is forever foreclosed, and if memory either eclipses the event or releases it in intrusive flashbacks, it is because it has fallen off the edge of time and history and become timeless or unconscious. As if enclosed in a time capsule floating in outer space, it comes to haunt the victim from elsewhere, and yet its flashback memories assume a terrorizing interiority that erases history and the present. This is the spatiotemporal dynamic of traumatic encapsulation. Could it be that this is why we need, as Lippit suggests, secondary revisions of history in which memory creatively integrates fantasy?

Here again we see the intimate exchange between exteriority and interiority, history and memory, or the real and fantasy. In this sense, Deleuze is right to insist that we cannot accord to the unconscious an ontological determination or that "there is no unconscious that could be said to be already there, since the unconscious must be produced and it must be produced politically, socially, and historically" (Deleuze, *L'île déserte*, 381, quoted in Lambert, 194). Deleuze and Guattari maintain that psychoanalysis produces the unconscious through an analytic machine of interpretation that operates in the psychoanalytic session at the interstice of speech and silence by one simple procedure: "to negate the subject of the statement in favor of the subject of enunciation" (197). According to Lambert, it is this and only this machine of interpretation that Deleuze and Guattari target in their attacks on a certain Freudo-Lacanian practice on the grounds that it threatens to generate an analytic practice of adaptive normalization (195–196).

Lambert organizes his essay around the question whether there is an unconscious outside of psychoanalytic discourse or the analytic session, a question that assumes a cultural and political urgency in light of the fact that, as he says, "the psychoanalytic apparatus of interpretation is plugged into all sorts of things: culture, film, literature, myth, history, and current events" (197). Is Deleuze right when he states that, in a culture in which anything can become an occasion for the production of the unconscious, the psychoanalytic critic creates the event and offers his services afterward? But what could "production of the unconscious" mean in this context other than the establishment of a transference between a cultural "text" (or event) and its recipient? And what could this transference be based on other than the intertwined memories and fantasies taken from earlier cultural texts and events, including memories of trauma that have been eclipsed? The continual production of the unconscious already operates on the plane of a cultural and political unconscious that comes to bear upon, shape, and revise the experience and memory of events and texts. It is in this sense that Lambert argues that "the unconscious is not in the text, properly speaking, but rather occurs between the text and the enunciating dimension that makes of the text something that is sent, meant to be listened to, even obeyed" (200). And it is in this sense that we must understand the statement that "psychoanalysis is not a matter of interpretation" (201).

Freud in his many writings about transference was the first to warn against the reduction of psychoanalysis to interpretation. This is why Lambert takes his distance from Deleuze and Guattari's attacks on psychoanalysis in *Anti-Oedipus*, arguing that they turn the oedipal construction of desire into a boogeyman: "It's as if psychoanalysis suddenly were being accused of wanting to retain a repressive organization of desire rather than providing an *analysis of the dominant organization of desire*" (202; emphasis mine). Since the latter always exists under specific historical and cultural conditions, the organization of desire must be understood within the context of the political and cultural unconscious and its modes of operation. In this sense, of course, Deleuze is therefore right to insist in *Dialogues* that under the forces of late capitalism and globalization "the unconscious is produced across relations of alliance and affiliation that have supplanted the family, alliances that reproduce themselves in the manner of a plague and in such a way that the family itself only functions as a secondary feedback loop for these later formations of unconscious desire" (quoted in Lambert, 207). Lambert concludes that "in order to discover the true position of the unconscious in social formations today, one must deterritorialize the unconscious and, at the same time, defamiliarize the concepts of psychoanalytic knowledge" (208). Yet he wonders whether Deleuze and Guattari are psychoanalytical enough when they simply displace the site of the unconscious from the family to classes, peoples, races, and masses. We may further ask how, if infants are born and nursed by mothers who—as Malabou's and Guyer's essays illustrate—transmit to them the most rudimentary ethics of otherness, do these infants gain access to, and a sense of, classes, peoples, races, and masses? Aren't that access and sense at least initially enfolded in the early culture, aesthetics, and ethics of care? While the collective political unconscious may be most decisive for processes of subjectivation, isn't it always initially mediated through the early culture and politics of infant care?

Ultimately, these questions provide nodal points for the intersecting trajectories of the essays in this volume. All use psychoanalysis as a social and psychological theory that refuses the epistemological separation of the psychic from the political, social, and cultural spheres. By thinking psychic life through the political and vice versa, the essays work at the interface of psychoanalysis, philosophy, and critical theory. Staging an encounter of the works of Derrida and Deleuze through psychoanalysis, this volume highlights both affinities and differences between the two philosophers within a network of shared concerns. Among these, the essays address, as I have noted, a whole variety of topics that figure prominently in both Derrida and Deleuze: the figure of the animal and the child; the limits of representation, signification, and writing; the ethics of encounters with the other; the mouth and face as constitutive of ethical responsibility; the role of presymbolic signification; and the fluidity of psychic life and meaning production. They also trace a common concern with pain, suffering, trauma, and resistance, as well as the role of dream and fantasy in relation to history and the political unconscious.

In terms of organization, the volume has a double focus. The first three essays by Derrida, Malabou, and Guyer develop three different perspectives on liminal figures and figurations of the human. They use the figures of the animal and the child to reach beyond anthropological definitions of the human based on an egological self-constitution of the subject as an "I." The essays highlight that both Deleuze and Derrida challenge the political implications of discourses of the free will from a perspective that refutes the exclusionary policing of the boundaries of the human. The two philosophers share, the essays suggest, an ethics of relationality that embraces what Malabou calls a "polymorphism of difference." Malabou and Guyer trace this ethics of otherness back to its early formation in the infant. The ethical implications of these reflections on animality and infancy thus bear heavily on history and politics. The subsequent essays by Al-Kassim, Arsić, Lippit, and Lambert move the focus more explicitly toward history, politics, the political unconscious, and resistance. Providing a link between the two sections, Al-Kassim explores the fantasy of the "departed child" as a source that provides the psychic energy for political resistance. She uses the connection both Deleuze and Derrida establish between resistance and human suffering to address issues of traumatic history and shame in a global media culture. Arsić, by contrast, explores pain and suffering in relation to masochism and human agency. Masochism, she argues, is less about pain and suffering than about the suspension of the "I" and the law and therefore a secret act of resistance. Lippit analyzes the economy of dreamwork in relation to technologies of film that grant access to the political unconscious of found memories and histories. The political unconscious in turn becomes the explicit topic of Lambert's essay. Lambert raises fundamental questions about the intertwinement between the psychological and the political in the formation of the subject: "How does the constituted individual in a given society accede directly to this political plane except in bypassing—a bit too precipitously—the entire question of this formation altogether, which is to say, by foreclosing the dimension of the imaginary entirely?" (208). "Can we imagine, one day," he concludes, "a psychoanalysis that would be deterritorializing, that would directly accede to the political enunciation of unconscious desires?" (211). We might further ask, what would such a deterritorializing psychoanalysis look like? One manifestation of the "resistance to psychoanalysis" that Derrida highlights and challenges in his work on psychoanalysis is the stubborn separation of the psychological and the political in philosophies, critical theories, and (Western) epistemologies. If there is one body of knowledge that has challenged and continues to be able to challenge this epistemological error—even though it has not done so consistently and forcefully enough—it is psychoanalysis. The essays in this collection contribute to addressing and redressing this epistemological split. Perhaps the further and more refined development of thinking together the psychological and the political might be a proper task to pursue for the "psychoanalysis to come" that Derrida envisions in *Resistances of Psychoanalysis*.

NOTES

1. "Freud and the Scene of Writing" (hereafter "Freud"), 231.
2. Deleuze and Guattari, *A Thousand Plateaus* (hereafter *Plateaus*), 117.
3. Transcribed from "Derrida/Deleuze: Psychoanalysis, Politics, Territoriality" (VHS, Iain Grainger for the Critical Theory Institute, UC Irvine, Irvine Calif., 2002, available at the Critical Theory Institute and the Critical Theory Archive at UC Irvine).
4. See especially *Anti-Oedipus*, 113–122.
5. See also "Psychoanalysis and Ethnology," in ibid., 166–192.

6. Following Abraham and Torok, Derrida takes incorporation in the process of mourning to be a form of idealization reminiscent of the early internalization of the normative rigidity of the image of the father. In this respect, he shares Deleuze's negative valuation of this formative idealization.

7. "Je suis en guerre contre moi-même" (hereafter "I Am at War"), 2.

8. This introduction is not the place to discuss in detail the very different notions of the secret in Derrida and Deleuze. While Deleuze and Guattari contest that secrets are a fundamental part of the signifying regime, they nonetheless assert its social dimension. In "Memories of the Secret," for example, they write, "The secret has a privileged, but quite variable, relation to perception and the imperceptible. . . . The secret was invented by society; it is a sociological or social notion. Every secret is a collective assemblage" (*Plateaus*, 286).

9. For a discussion of "isomorphic oppression," see Nandy, *The Intimate Enemy*.

10. Derrida's reading may surprise since Deleuze and Guattari do not in general align themselves with the human-animal distinction. Especially in their concept of "becoming-animal," they refute the "irreducibility of the human order" as based on a false culturalism and moralism. Especially states of molecular becomings produce a zone of indetermination in which the boundary between the human and the animal becomes uncertain. See *Plateaus*, 273.

11. See, for example, his reflections on the task of a "psychoanalysis to come," especially the sections on free will and human rights in *Without Alibi*.

12. Deleuze and Guattari, *Kafka: Towards a Minor Literature*, 79–80.

13. One may ask here, however, whether Deleuze does not make a sharper distinction than Derrida acknowledges between polymorphism and "becoming." A discussion of this problem would go beyond the frame of this introduction.

14. The image of the mouth detaching itself from the breast in a first smile points in an interesting fashion to the fact that the smiling reflex evolves coevally with the sucking reflex. This raises the question whether orality and faciality are not more dynamically linked from an earlier stage.

15. He thus shares with Deleuze the sense of responsibility in resisting the present. But while Deleuze sees the creation of concepts as a call for a "future form," for Derrida, resistance exceeds any concept of sovereignty. Rather than locating resistance in a concept, he locates it in a "set

of relations that obstruct, limit, refuse, repeat, and rebel" (Al-Kassim, 114).

16. This relationship between trauma and pain is not reflected in Deleuze's notion of pain because he focuses on masochism rather than trauma.

17. See, for example, Bollas, *The Shadow of the Object*; Ehrenzweig, *Hidden Order of Art*; Piotelli, *From Fetus to Child*; and Schwab, "Words and Moods" and "Cultural Texts."

18. Deleuze and Guattari, in fact, draw explicitly on Althusser's notion of interpellation. See *Plateaus*, 130.

19. For a theory of the transitional space of cultural objects, see Schwab, *Subjects* and *The Mirror*.

BIBLIOGRAPHY

Bateson, Gregory. "Form, Substance and Difference." In *Steps to an Ecology of Mind*, 448–465. New York: Ballantine, 1972.
Bollas, Christopher. *Being a Character: Psychoanalysis and Self-Experience*. New York: Hill and Wang; London: Routledge, 1992.
———. *Cracking Up. The Work of the Unconscious Experience*. London: Routledge, 1995.
———. *The Shadow of the Object: Psychoanalysis of the Unthought Unknown*. New York: Columbia University Press, 1987.
Deleuze, Gilles. *Difference and Repetition*. Trans. Paul Patton. New York: Columbia University Press, 1994. Originally published as *Différence et répétition* (Paris: Presses Universitaires de France, 1968).
———. *L'île déserte et autres textes*. Paris: Minuit, 2002.
Deleuze, Gilles and Félix Guattari. *Anti-Oedipus: Capitalism and Schizophrenia*. Trans. Robert Hurley, Mark Seem, and Helen R. Lane. Minneapolis: University of Minnesota Press, 1983.
———. *Kafka: Towards a Minor Literature*. Trans. Dana Polan. Minneapolis: University of Minnesota Press, 1986.
———. *A Thousand Plateaus: Capitalism and Schizophrenia*. Trans. Brian Massumi. Minneapolis: University of Minnesota Press, 1987.
Derrida, Jacques. *The Ear of the Other: Otobiography, Transference, Translation*. Trans. Peggy Kamuf. Ed. Claude Levesque and Christie McDonald. Lincoln: University of Nebraska Press, 1988.

———. "Fors." Trans. Barbara Johnson. *Georgia Review* 31 (Spring 1977): 64–116.

———. "Freud and the Scene of Writing." In *Writing and Difference*, trans. Alan Bass, 196–231. Chicago: University of Chicago Press, 1978.

———. "I'll Have to Wander All Alone" ["Il me faudra errer tout seul"]. Trans. Leonard Lawlor. *Philosophy Today* 42, no. 1 (1998): 3–5. Reprinted in *The Work of Mourning*, trans. Pascale-Anne Brault, ed. Pascale-Anne Brault and Michael Naas, 189–196. Chicago: University of Chicago Press, 2001.

———. "Je suis en guerre contre moi-même" [I am at war with myself]: Interview by Jean Birnbaum. *Le Monde*, August 18, 2004.

———. *Limited Inc*. Trans. Samuel Weber and Jeffrey Mehlman. Ed. Geoffrey Graff. Evanston, Ill.: Northwestern University Press, 1988.

———. *Of Grammatology*. Trans. Gayatri Chakravorty Spivak. Baltimore: Johns Hopkins University Press, 1976.

———. *Memoires for Paul de Man*. Trans. Cecile Lindsay, Jonathan Culler, Eduardo Cadava, and Peggy Kamuf. New York: Columbia University Press, 1986.

———. *Resistances of Psychoanalysis*. Trans. Peggy Kamuf, Pascale-Anne Brault, and Michael Naas. Stanford, Calif.: Stanford University Press, 1998. Originally published as *Résistances de la psychanalyse* (Paris: Galilée, 1996).

———. *Speech and Phenomena and Other Essays on Husserl's Theory of Signs*. Trans. David B. Allison. Chicago: Northwestern University Press, 1973.

———. *Without Alibi*. Trans. Peggy Kamuf. Stanford, Calif.: Stanford University Press, 2002.

———. *The Work of Mourning*. Trans. Pascale-Anne Brault. Ed. Pascale-Anne Brault and Michael Naas. Chicago: University of Chicago Press, 2001.

"Derrida/Deleuze: Psychoanalysis, Politics, Territoriality." Conference held at UC Irvine, Irvine, Calif., April 12–13, 2002.

Ehrenzwieg, Anton. *Hidden Order of Art: A Study in the Psychology of Artistic Imagination*. Berkeley: University of California Press, 1967.

Freud, Sigmund. "The Ego and the Id." In *The Standard Edition of the Complete Psychological Works of Sigmund Freud*, trans. James Strachey, Anna Freud, Alix Strachey, and Alan Tyson, 19:12–68.

London: Hogarth and the Institute of Psycho-Analysis, 1953–1974.
Major, René. "Derrida and Psychoanalysis: Desistantial Psychoanalysis." In *Jacques Derrida and the Humanities: A Critical Reader*, ed. Tom Cohen, 296–315. Cambridge: Cambridge University Press, 2001.
Metz, Christian. *The Imaginary Signifier: Psychoanalysis and the Cinema*. Trans. Celia Britton, Annwyl Williams, Ben Brewster, and Alfred Guzzetti. Bloomington: Indiana University Press, 1976.
Nancy, Jean-Luc. *Ego sum*. Paris: Flammarion, 1979.
Nandy, Ashis. *The Intimate Enemy: Loss and Recovery of Self Under Colonialism*. Delhi: Oxford University Press, 1983.
Patton, Paul and John Protevi, eds. *Between Deleuze and Derrida*. New York: Continuum, 2003.
Piotelli, Alessandra. *From Fetus to Child: An Observational and Psychoanalytic Study*. London: Routledge, 1992.
Schwab, Gabriele. "Cultural Texts and Endopsychic Scripts." *Substance* 30, nos. 1 and 2 (1994–1995): 160–176.
———. *Subjects Without Selves: Transitional Texts in Modern Fiction*. Cambridge: Harvard University Press, 1994.
———. *The Mirror and the Killer-Queen: Otherness in Literary Language*. Bloomington: Indiana University Press, 1996.
———. "Words and Moods: The Transference of Literary Knowledge." *Substance* 26, no. 3 (1997): 107–127.

2

THE TRANSCENDENTAL "STUPIDITY" ("BÊTISE") OF MAN AND THE BECOMING-ANIMAL ACCORDING TO DELEUZE

Jacques Derrida

EDITED BY ERIN FERRIS

Everything I'm going to say will be first of all a tribute to Gilles Deleuze's work, a sign of an old and lasting admiration, respect, and friendship.[1] But I also would like to pay homage to Paul Patton for his scholarly work on Deleuze, and not only in the Anglophone world. Among so many other contributions, I especially would like to remark his translation of *Difference and Repetition*.[2] Why do I refer to the translation of this book here and, more specifically, to a chapter in *Difference and Repetition* entitled "The Image of Thought"? Even more specifically, why do I point to a particular page of this translation, where Paul Patton's vigilance is so remarkable? Because, within the narrow limits I have prudently and modestly decided to contain my lecture, everything will turn around two French words, a French lexicon, that I consider untranslatable: "*bête*," "*bêtise*." For reasons we could unfold for hours, there are no English words—especially not "stupid" or "stupidity" and not even "dumb" or "dumbness"—that adequately translate "bête" or "bêtise." Even within the borders of the French idiom, there is no stable semantic context that could univocally guarantee a safe translation from one pragmatic use of "bête" or "bêtise" in a given context into another one. Being aware of that, Paul Patton twice keeps the words "bêtise" and "bête," in French, in square brackets, when he writes, translating Deleuze, "Stupidity [*bêtise*] is not animality. The animal is protected by specific forms which prevent it from being 'stupid' [*bête*]" (*D&R*, 150). And Deleuze himself put the word "bête" within quotation marks. Of course, having put the word in square brackets, Paul Patton then uses the word "stupidity" without mentioning "bêtise" again; the reader having been warned once and for all that "stupidity" is supposed to translate "bêtise," there will be no further harm. This will be the case, for instance, for the major question Deleuze asked, "comment la bêtise (et non l'erreur) est-elle possible?" ("how is stupidity [not error] possible?"; 151). This will be, then, my point of departure.

I now am going to select some pieces of a seminar I'm giving at UC Irvine on the beast and the sovereign, although I'll have to skip many developments for lack of time.[3] Beyond sexual difference, the article "la/le"—"la bête," "le souverain," the beast, the sovereign—very well indicates that it has to do with common names, common nouns, such that it is does not have to do with adjectives or attributes. The distinction is all the more critical in that it recalls two pieces of evidence, probably linked to the idiomatic use of the French language. One would never say of La Bête that it is bête or bestial. The adjective, the attribute—bête, bestial, stupid, dumb—is never appropriate to the animal or the beast. So bêtise is proper to man or to the sovereign as man. Later on I'll come back to Deleuze's text in *Difference and Repetition* on the subject precisely of bêtise as essential to, or appropriate to, man. Of course, everyone here knows, too, the very rich chapter of *A Thousand Plateaus* entitled, "1730: Becoming-Intense, Becoming-Animal, Becoming-Imperceptible . . ."[4] One finds there not only references to the wolf—the wolf is at the center of the seminar—and the Wolf Man, the man whom the wolves look like, but also references to the werewolf and to the phenomenon of children-wolf/wolf-children and the becoming-whale of Ahab in *Moby-Dick*. One finds there, too, among a thousand plateaus, many other things, including the question of taxonomy, classification, and the question of animal figures. And, in passing, Deleuze notes psychoanalysis. He laughs at psychoanalysis when psychoanalysis speaks about animals. He laughs at it, as he often does—to me, sometimes a little too quickly—but not only does he laugh at it, he also tells us, which is even funnier, that the animals themselves laugh at psychoanalysis when psychoanalysis speaks about them: "We must distinguish three kinds of animals. First, individuated animals, family pets, sentimental, Oedipal animals each with its own petty history, 'my' cat, 'my' dog. These animals invite us to regress, draw us into a narcissistic contemplation, and they are the only kind of animal psychoanalysis understands, the better to discover a daddy, a mommy, a little brother behind them (when psychoanalysis talks about animals, animals learn to laugh)" (*Plateaus*, 240). He then adds, in italics, *"anyone who likes cats or dogs is a fool."* "Fool" is the translation for *"con,"* which is as untranslatable as "bête": "Tous ceux qui aiment les chats et les chiens sont des cons." "And then," he goes on, "there is a second kind: animals with characteristics or attributes; genus, classification, or State animals; animals as they are treated in the great divine myths, in such a way as to extract from them series or structures, archetypes or models (Jung is in any event profounder than Freud)." That's also Deleuze's absolute originality: in France, admiring Jung more than Freud. He goes on:

> Finally, there are more demonic animals, pack or affect animals that form a multiplicity, a becoming, a population, a tale.... Or once again, cannot any animal be treated in all three ways? There is always the possibility that a given animal, a louse, a cheetah or an elephant, will be treated as a pet, my little beast. And at the other extreme, it is also possible for any animal to be treated in the mode of the pack or swarm; that is our way, fellow sorcerers. Even the cat, even the dog. And the shepherd, the animal trainer, the Devil, may have a favorite animal in the pack, although not at all in the way we were just discussing. Yes, any animal is or can be a pack, but to varying degrees of vocation that make it easier or harder to discover the multiplicity, or multiplicity-grade, an animal contains (actually or virtually

according to the case). Schools, bands, herds, populations are not inferior social forms; they are affects and powers, involutions that grip every animal in a becoming just as powerful as that of the human being with the animal.

(*PLATEAUS*, 241)

Of course, the question that explicitly or indirectly traverses the whole seminar to which I refer is what is proper to man, *le propre de l'homme*. On the other hand, whether it's characterized as a perversion or sexual deviation, zoophilia—which compels making love with beasts, or making love to beasts—or whether it's characterized as cruelty, this bestiality, this double bestiality—zoophilic or cruel—also would be the proper of man. That's something I study in detail in another part of this seminar in relation to Lacan. To save time, I'll skip a long series of reflections on the French use of the words "bête" and "bêtise" and the critical reading of Lacan on bestiality as essentially human and related to the law, calling for responsibility and not reaction. Here, I'll simply note that Lacan opposes responsibility and reaction, reaction being essentially animal, response and responsibility being human. So, for this tradition, what is proper to the beast or the animal would be neither bestiality nor bêtise, stupidity, dumbness. Now, then, the question, "How is bestiality possible?" or "How is bêtise possible?"

This question will have been raised, in this form or another, by many people. However, Deleuze gave it a certain form in the text I mentioned a moment ago, in *Difference and Repetition*, which is twelve years older than *A Thousand Plateaus*, older than the chapter from which I just read, namely, "Becoming-Intense, Becoming-Animal, Becoming-Imperceptible." In *A Thousand Plateaus*, which devotes so many analyses to the becoming-animal, Deleuze no longer refers to "la bêtise" the way he does in *Difference and Repetition*. The only occurrence of the word "bêtise," at least that I found, concerns precisely a certain bêtise of psychoanalysis, which you're supposed to know, the stupidity of psychoanalysis, the stupidity or bêtise that psychoanalysis says when it addresses the question of masochism and more generally when it speaks about animals. "We wish," Deleuze says, "to make a simple point about psychoanalysis: from the beginning, it has often encountered the question of the becomings-animal of the human being . . ." I interrupt here to note that for psychoanalysis, and for Deleuze when he objects to psychoanalysis from that point of view, it is always a question of humanity, of man, of the becoming-animal of man, of the history and histories of man, in its or in their becomings-animal. In other words, it's a question of the becoming-anthropomorphically-animal of man and not a question of the animal or the beast, if one may say, themselves: "We wish to make a simple point about psychoanalysis: from the beginning, it has often encountered the question of the becomings-animal of the human being: in children, who continually undergo becomings of this kind; in fetishism and in particular masochism, which continually confront this problem. The least that can be said is that the psychoanalysts, even Jung, did not understand, or did not want to understand" *(Plateaus,* 259). Deleuze insinuates that all these psychoanalysts denied or denigrated understanding. They acted as though they didn't understand, they wanted not to understand, something that, consequently, they understood very well. And they have some interest in not assuming, in not confessing, in not declaring, that they were understanding. So, they were understanding what they were understanding and wanted not to understand, as though they were not understanding, which is a symptom more than a simple nonknowledge. It's a symptomatic misrecognition, so to speak, on the background of an unconscious knowledge. This active miscognition, misrecognition, or symptomatic misrecognition is a mistreatment. It is a cruel and violent mistreatment of the becoming-animal of man and the child. Cruel violence. Deleuze goes on, "They killed," the translation says—in fact it's "they massacred"—"They killed becoming-animal, in the adult as in the child. They saw nothing. They see the animal as a representative of drives, or a representative of the parents. They do not see the reality of a becoming-animal, that it is affect in itself, the drive in the person, and represents nothing. There exist no other drives than the assemblages themselves." This concept of affect—like the concepts of machine or assemblage and of plan(e), *le plan*—is, as you know, the central concept of this analysis and of all the Deleuzian strategy.

After some lines on the becoming-horse of little Hans with Freud and the becoming-cock of Arpad with Ferenczi, Deleuze approaches the interpretation of masochism. It is at this point that the word "bêtise" is imposed on him in order to qualify the discourse of the psychoanalytic type: "Psychoanalysis has no feeling for unnatural participations, nor for the assemblages a child can mount in order to solve a problem from which all exits are barred him." Here, Deleuze is criticizing the idea of a phantasm as a natural representative, an indication of a deeper and natural drive, for which Deleuze wants to substitute the more technical, less natural, more mechanistic figure of the plane (*le plan*). The assemblage and the plane, the flat figure of the plane, are always involved. Deleuze goes on precisely with the word "stupidity," bêtise consisting here in believing in the profundity, in the depth, of the phantasm there where there is only flat plane:

> Psychoanalysis has no feeling for unnatural participations, nor for the assemblages a child can mount in order to solve a problem from which all exits are barred him: a *plan(e)*, not a phantasy. Similarly, fewer stupidities [*moins de bêtises*] would be uttered on the topic of pain, humiliation, and anxiety in masochism if it were understood that it is the becomings-animal that lead to masochism, not the other way around. There are always apparatuses, tools, engines involved, there are always artifices and constraints used in taking Nature to the fullest. That is because it is necessary to annul the organs, to shut them away so that their liberated elements can enter into the new relations from which the becoming-animal, and the circulation of affects within the machinic assemblage, will result.
>
> (*PLATEAUS*, 259–260)

In other words, despite all these machinations of becoming-animal that lead men and children, despite the artifices that remain constraints, they affect the affect. Rather, they calculate it voluntarily. Psychoanalysts would speak fewer bêtises, they wouldn't speak stupidities, about the subject of pain, humiliation, and anxiety, if they assumed their own knowledge on that subject. Deleuze is not saying that psychoanalysts are stupid, bêtes, but that, mechanically, their statements are stupidities. They say stupidities, ils disent des bêtises, on that subject. They define bêtise not only as a character, as a feature, a state, or as the essence of what one is, but also as the affect of what one does or what one says. They are events and even operations, les bêtises, stupidities, and not a phenomenal essence, The Stupidity, La Bêtise. So psychoanalysts are not stupid when they say stupidities because they know and they understand what they try not to understand, what they want not to understand. They have the intelligence of what they want, what they want not to understand, for reasons to be analyzed.

This gesture and this moment, this denunciation of stupidities, despite this unique occurrence of the word "bêtise" in *A Thousand Plateaus*, are all the more significant and strategically decisive in this book in that, not only are they inscribed in the logic of the desiring machine, of the Anti-Oedipus, but also in that their necessity is announced in the very first pages of *A Thousand Plateaus* around the concepts of rhizome and deterritorialization, which are put to the test as examples like the wasp or the orchid—the wasp or the orchid make rhizomes, so to speak, heterogeneous, the wasp itself becoming a piece of the apparatus of reproduction, the reproduction apparatus of the orchid—or the examples of the baboon and the virus, DNA of the baboon and the cat, the crocodile, and so forth.

In the second chapter of *A Thousand Plateaus*, entitled "1914: One or Several Wolves?" Deleuze's sarcasm is unleashed against the treatment of the Wolf Man by Freud. There is a reference to Kafka's story "Jackals and Arabs." I'll delay citing the first sentences and the conclusion, namely, an indictment of Freud, who is charged not with believing in what he was saying, which is also a machine in which he hypocritically pretends to believe. Rather, he is charged with having done everything here, everything he could—and the indictment here is ethical and even political—to make the patient believe in what psychoanalysis was telling him and trying to make him subscribe to it. And to subscribe to it with another name, a name different from his own, a name becoming the name of another, the name of the father, patronym, there where there was not the name of the father, there where the new name, the brand-new name that he had made for himself, that he had stolen, so that it's a question of recognizing a theft and a substitution of someone's proper name by psychoanalysis, a dispossession that motivates, on the side of Deleuze and against psychoanalysis in the name of the Wolf Man, a style and logic of the complaint, of the counterindictment. This is not far from looking suddenly like Artaud's discourse about the theft of his own first name, of his new proper name, and his own body, which is supposed to be organless, without organs, which means that the so-called bêtises of psychoanalysis are not only the sign of a poverty of knowledge, that is, nonknowledge or incomprehension, but also of ethical violences, machines, and war machines for subjecting—for stupefying, so to speak—ways of making the passions more stupid, "more stupefied" than they are in truth.

There is, at the beginning of this chapter, a date, at the beginning of the narrative, a series of events, and Freud's analysis of the Wolf Man at the time, that is, before or during the First World War. This is the sarcastic opening of the chapter, "1914: One or Several Wolves": "That day, the Wolf-Man rose from the couch particularly tired. He knew that Freud had a genius for brushing up against the truth and passing it by, then filling the void with associations. He knew that Freud knew nothing about wolves, or anuses for that matter. The only thing Freud understood was what a dog is, and a dog's tail." This is an allusion not only to the well-known dogs of Freud but also to those of Lacan; each was famous for having a dog. And the name "Lacan" will soon appear in the genealogy of psychoanalysts: "It wasn't enough. It wouldn't be enough. The Wolf-Man knew that Freud would soon declare him cured, but that it was not the case at all and his treatment would continue for all eternity under Brunswick, Lacan, Leclaire"—which is true. "Finally, he knew that he was in the process of acquiring a veritable proper name, the Wolf-Man, a name more properly his than his own, since it attained the highest degree of singularity in the instantaneous apprehension of a generic multiplicity: wolves. He knew that this new and proper name would be disfigured and misspelled, retranscribed as a patronymic"

(*Plateaus*, 26–27). Before returning to *Difference and Repetition*, here is Deleuze's conclusion of the chapter "1914: One or Several Wolves":

> The proper name is the subject of a pure infinitive comprehended as such in a field of intensity. What Proust said about the first name: when I said Gilberte's name, I had the impression I was holding her entire body naked in my mouth. The Wolf-Man, a true proper name, an intimate first name linked to the becomings, infinitives, and intensities of a multiplied and depersonalized individual. What does psychoanalysis know about multiplication? The desert hour when the dromedary becomes a thousand dromedaries snickering in the sky. The evening hour when a thousand holes appear on the surface of the earth. Castration! Castration! cries the psychoanalytic scarecrow, who never saw more than a hole, a father or a dog where wolves are, a domesticated individual where there are wild multiplicities. We are not just criticizing psychoanalysis for having selected Oedipal statements exclusively. For such statements are to a certain extent part of a machinic assemblage, for which they could serve as correctional indexes, as in a calculation of errors. We are criticizing psychoanalysis for having used Oedipal enunciation to make patients believe they would produce individual, personal statements, and would finally speak in their own name. The trap was set from the start: never will the Wolf-Man speak. Talk as he might about wolves, howl as he might like a wolf, Freud does not even listen; he glances at his dog and answers, "It's daddy." For as long as that lasts, Freud calls it neurosis; when it cracks, it's psychosis. The Wolf-Man will receive the psychoanalytic medal of honor for services rendered to the cause, and even disabled veterans' benefits. He could have spoken in his own name only if the machinic assemblage that was producing particular statements in him had been brought to light. But there is no question of that in psychoanalysis: at the very moment the subject is persuaded that he or she will be uttering the most individual of statements, he or she is deprived of all basis for enunciation. Silence people, prevent them from

speaking, and above all, when they do speak, pretend they haven't said a thing: the famous psychoanalytic neutrality. The Wolf-Man keeps howling: Six wolves! Seven wolves! Freud says, How's that? Goats, you say? How interesting. Take away the goats and all you have left is a wolf, so it's your father.... That is why the Wolf-Man feels so fatigued: he's left lying there with all his wolves in his throat, all those little holes on his nose, and all those libidinal values on his body without organs. The war will come, the wolves will become Bolsheviks, and the Wolf-Man will remain suffocated by all he had to say. All we will be told is that he became well behaved, polite, and resigned again, "honest and scrupulous." In short, cured. He gets back by pointing out that psychoanalysis lacks a truly zoological vision: "Nothing can be more valuable for a young person than the love of nature and a comprehension of the natural sciences, in particular zoology."

(*PLATEAUS*, 37–38)

So this was the only occurrence of the word "bêtises"—in the plural, "stupidities"—in *A Thousand Plateaus*. Twelve years before, in 1968, in *Difference and Repetition*, Deleuze opens a long paragraph, more than a page, with the following statement: "La bêtise n'est pas l'animalité. L'animal est garanti par des formes spécifiques qui l'empêchent d'être 'bête' " ("Stupidity [*bêtise*] is not animality. The animal is protected by specific forms which prevent it from being 'stupid' [*bête*]"; *D&R*, 150). The same paragraph is concluded by a question this time. The question is, "how is stupidity (not error) possible?" (151). Or, more precisely, Deleuze says at the end of this paragraph, "Philosophy could have taken up the problem with its own means and with the necessary modesty, by considering the fact that stupidity is never that of others but the object of a properly transcendental question: how is stupidity (not error) possible?" ("Comment la bêtise [et non l'erreur] est-elle possible?")

Now, two remarks at this point on the very form and the first implication of this Deleuzian question. The great interest of this question, its irony, the laughter of this ironic and serious question—

how is stupidity (not error) possible?—has to do first of all with the gap opened up by the parenthesis, "et non l'erreur." It's a gap related to a great tradition of transcendental questions of possibility, great critical questions, and first of all in the form of the Kantian question in which Deleuze reinscribes the question of bêtise. It's the question, "how is it possible?" Under what conditions is it possible? What are the conditions of possibility for what is already a fact, what is already possible? Under what conditions is science possible? And so on. Under what conditions is the synthetic a priori judgment possible? But, following this tradition of the transcendental question of the Kantian type in order to apply it to bêtise, what is, of course, a surprise, a provocation, is that Deleuze pulls it out from—and rightly so—its epistemological economy, from its usual territory, namely, the territory of knowledge, judgment on truth and error, and, I would even say, of objectness, because it's always starting from a determination of being as an object that the transcendental question of possibility is determined, not only with Kant but even with Husserl. It's always a question about the object in general: How is an object in general possible? How is the objectness of the object possible? So Deleuze pulls his question out from this epistemological regime, out from this theory of knowledge, and he does this in a parenthesis when he specifies "la bêtise (et non l'erreur)," "stupidity (not error)," when he excludes the question of error from the question of bêtise, which means that la bêtise is not the relation of a judgment to what is, it's not a modality of knowledge, it's not an error, or an illusion, or a hallucination, or a mistake in knowing in general. One can be true, one can be in the truth, one can know everything, and nevertheless be bête. At the limit, there might be a bêtise in absolute knowledge, and this is probably the example of which all the people who speak about bêtise think; especially in Flaubert's *Bouvard et Pécuchet*, one dreams of this stupid form of absolute knowledge that an encyclopedic knowledge "of the totality of being" might be. So bêtise, whatever it means—and we are far from having done with it—has nothing to do with knowledge or with the adequation of a determining judgment to truth or error. Nevertheless, we'll see, there remains a certain proximity. Deleuze doesn't say this, but, if he's so careful to distinguish bêtise from error and judgment, it's because the proximity is troubling even if it cannot be reduced to identity.

French usage of the word "bêtise" implies not an error, not a bad judgment, but rather an inability to judge, a flaw in judgment, a defect in judgment. It's not a nonrelationship to judgment the way we could say a stone doesn't judge. But it's a blunted, dulled faculty, a nonfaculty, but "non" by some fault, by some secret perversion of a faculty that is not very well oriented, that is debilitated or diverted in judgment. The reference to justice, to *jus*, here, to the juridical, the judiciary, in the sense of *justesse et justice*, is behind all this trial, this indictment, of bêtise. Someone who is called bête lacks judgment there where the faculty of judging, of judgment—according to this critique of the faculty of judgment that the trial of bêtise always is—is altered, but altered in the sense of bêtise as a supposed permanent feature of character, an idiosyncrasy, to be distinguished from idiocy; it affects a certain quality of judgment there where the judgment, as Descartes noted, implies perception and understanding. Judgment implies, at the same time, perception and understanding, that is, intelligence and the intervention of the will, the voluntary decision, so that, according to this Cartesian terminology, la bêtise would be at the crossroads of the finitude of the intellect and the infinity of the will. So, the precipitation to judge, the excess of the will over understanding, intellect, would be proper to man and would lead to bêtises, that is to say, stupidities, out of precipitation, the precipitation of the will, which is disproportionate to the finitude of the understanding. That's why there is an abyssal implication, a vertiginous one, of bêtise, which in this case always touches, or is touched and moved by, a certain infinity of freedom in a Cartesian sense.

Of course, Deleuze doesn't say this. But we'll see later on how what he says finally about the ground, *le fond*, of bêtise, what relates bêtise to a certain abyssal depth of the ground, is perhaps not unrelated to what I just suggested in Descartes about freedom. In any case, this implication of a mistake in judgment, there where the judgment is not only the determining judgment that leads to the true or the nontrue but the judgment of the judge, the judgment from which one expects some right, *justesse*, as well as some justice, suggests that one cannot think stupidity, bêtise, or at least the pragmatic use of this word—and that's what I'm interested in for the moment—without this reference; there is no pragmatic use of the word "bêtise" that wouldn't imply some obscure reference to *jus*, the law, the immense semantic abyss that hollows the word, the lexical semantic family of *jus*, justice, judge, and so on. Another use, another meaning, and another implication of the category of bêtise this time touch not only the event but the action, the way one acts when one makes or does misdeeds, so to speak, a certain way of misdoing or the bêtise that one does, not stupidity as an idiosyncratic feature as a way of being, *exis*, Aristotle would say, *habitus*, but rather as the accident of what one makes/does: "j'ai fait une bêtise," "I've done/made a stupidity." It's not that I am bête in that case, but, on the contrary, although I'm supposed not to be stupid, I was surprised that I made/did something stupid, a bêtise. So there is always nominally or marginally, but ineffaceably, an insistent reference to the comprehension of meaning, if not knowledge of the object, a stubborn reference to a certain opening of meaning, intelligence, that is not simply knowledge or science. That's what accounts for the risk that is always present, always threatening to confuse stupidity, la bêtise, with the error and illusion that it is not, to which it cannot be reduced. That's why there is the parenthesis in Deleuze—"how is stupidity (not error) possible?"

Now, in its French usage—in the pragmatics of the French idiom—which risks resisting the tradition, on what ground, on what groundless ground, does la bêtise open and close? I mean the adjective "bête" and the noun "bêtise," which still point to a truth of the meaning. They count with the truth of the meaning even if this truth, this appearing or this revelation of the meaning, can never be reduced to an objective knowledge of the object. La bêtise is always a certain way of not understanding, not being able to explain oneself or to explain, but a not understanding on the order of the analytic comprehension of the meaning, at least of something we call in France, in colloquial slang, "la comprenure." It doesn't mean intelligence or comprehension, a way of having an access to something, a meaning that should appear, but the deprivation of la comprenure.

The second preliminary remark is this. By saying that stupidity is never the other's (la bêtise n'est jamais celle d'autrui), by calling philosophy to modesty—when Deleuze says "philosophy could have taken up the problem with its own means and with the necessary modesty"—he suggests that stupidity is at the heart of philosophy, which invites philosophy to modesty, and, especially, Deleuze implies that stupidity, the possibility of bêtise, is never that of others because it is always mine or ours, always on our side, on the side of what is close to me, proper to me, or similar to me, the side of my neighbor, *mon semblable*. Now, the word "bêtise" belongs to the language of indictment; it's a category of accusation, a way of categorizing the other. You know that in Greek *kategoria* meant accusation, blame. And, with some distance from Deleuze's text—he doesn't refer to "category"—I would add that bêtise, la bête de la bêtise, is a funny category because it is most often manipulated as an accusation, a denigration, an incrimination, blame that tries to discredit not only a mistake in intelligence or knowledge but also a misdeed, an offense, an ethical misdeed, or quasi-juridical accusation. This category is precisely a category whose signification is never assured. It's a category without category in French—it's untranslatable within French itself. I would add this in parenthesis, with no direct relation to Deleuze's text or intention when he mentions the properly transcendental question of bêtise: Either, if there is a category of bêtise, it's a category whose meaning cannot be determined, in any case, not as a meaning or sense as such, a sense whose conceptual ideality could be translatable and that is distinguished from the idiomatic and pragmatic body of its occurrences. It's a word that, more than any other word, means, each time, something different, according to the pragmatic singularities, conscious or unconscious, that engage it or are engaged or involved in it. So bêtise is not one category among others. Or it is a transcategorial category. One will never be able to isolate a univocal meaning of a concept of bêtise in its irreducible link to the French idiom. Now, if it is a category, then bêtise, as an accusation and as an attribution, an attribute, a predicate, a predication, if this category doesn't belong to the regime of the normal series of categories, if it is an exceptional category, a transcategorial category, then it corresponds to the first literal definition of the transcendental in the Middle Ages. Long before Kant, "transcendental" meant *quid transcendi omni genus*. It's a category that transcends all the categories and doesn't belong to the series or table of categories. So bêtise would be in a position of the transcategorial category, that is, of the transcendental; it's transcendental in that respect, or quasi-transcendental, and we should draw all the consequences that follow from this. If I had time, I would add a development on Heidegger and the categorical here, but I'll have to turn back to Deleuze.

Saying that stupidity is never the other's, Deleuze suggests that stupidity is at the heart of philosophy and invites it to modesty. He declares, I repeat, that the possibility of stupidity is never the other's because it's mine, it's ours, it's on our side, on the side of the human, of the *semblable*. Similitude. It looks like me, and I can assimilate it because it's on my side, which means at least two things. First—and this is a very classical motif—bêtise is always human, always of one of my fellow creatures, of my neighbor. So, bêtise is human and not bestial, not animal, and, mutatis mutandis, with this motif of the semblable, the similar, the fellow creature, of a bêtise that is always proper to man, bêtise, stupidity, would find an analogous problem—I don't say identical—with that of bestiality, which I treat in the seminar with respect to Lacan; Lacan says that bestiality is properly human and not animal. Nevertheless, Deleuze's gesture remains specific, and in order to follow the reasoning that leads him to say that stupidity is proper to man, is never that of the other, one can follow a trajectory that associates bêtise with three motifs: one, the figure of sovereignty that one calls tyranny; two, cruelty; and three, what is indispensable to attribute stupidity to man and to understand its link with philosophy, namely, stupidity as a problem of thinking, or of thought, of the thinking being that man is, which implies that it's not proper to animality, or to the beast. So, bêtise is a thought. Bêtise is thinking. It's a thinking and thought freedom. It is in this link of thought with individuation that Deleuze will identify the spring of bêtise, bêtise always supposing a relation with what Deleuze called "le fond," "the ground" in Schelling's tradition, the Schelling to whom Deleuze refers in a footnote, Schelling, the author of *Philosophical Research on the Essence (or Nature) of Human Liberty.*[5]

I think that one could not understand anything in Deleuze's argumentation on the subject of stupidity—which implies thinking as human freedom in its relation to individuation, as a phenomenon of individuation, *Vereinzelung*, which is determined on the ground, on the background of the ground—one would understand nothing of this argumentation if one could not reconstitute the whole of Schelling's discourse on freedom and human evil and, notably, what Schelling called the ground, the originary ground, *Urgrund*, which is also a nonground, a groundless ground, *Ungrund*. In a moment, I'm going to quote some lines by Schelling that Deleuze doesn't quote but that are visibly the source of his argumentation here, and he refers to Schelling in a footnote, without quoting him. When Deleuze says that stupidity is "possible by virtue of the link between thought and individuation," he distinguishes what is proper to man, stupidity as proper to man. Or, again, when he says:

> Individuation as such, as it operates beneath all forms, is inseparable from a pure ground that it brings to the surface and trails with it. It is difficult to describe this ground, or the terror and attraction it excites. Turning over the ground is the most dangerous occupation, but also the most tempting in the stupefied moments of an obtuse will. For this ground, along with the individual, rises to the surface yet assumes neither form nor figure. It is there, staring at us, but without eyes. The individual distinguishes itself from it, but it does not distinguish itself, continuing rather to cohabit with that which divorces itself from it. It is the indeterminate, but the indeterminate in so far as it continues to embrace determination, as the ground does the shoe.
> (*D&R*, 152)

The animal cannot be bête. That's why Deleuze had written previously, "Stupidity [*bêtise*] is not animality. The animal is protected by specific forms which prevent it from being 'stupid' [*bête*]"

(D&R, 150). In other words, the animal cannot be bête, stupid, because it is not free, it has no will, and its individuation, which gives it shape or form, doesn't appear on the background of a ground, which is freedom itself. Just after the passage on individuation I mentioned a moment ago, Deleuze writes, "Animals are in a sense forewarned against this ground, protected by their explicit forms" *(D&R*, 152). That's why they couldn't be bête. But one cannot deny that the phrasing here is very vague and empirical. The expression "en quelque sorte," "in a sense"—"les animaux sont en quelque sorte prémunis contre ce fond par leurs formes explicites" ("Animals are in a sense forewarned against this ground by their explicit forms")—introduces something vague, out of focus, as to the explicitness of a form. At what moment is a form "in a sense" explicit? And, finally, what are the forms Deleuze has in mind here when he designates, in such a general and indeterminate fashion, "the animals"?

Couldn't we say that man also has explicit forms that forewarn him "in a sense" against the ground, that is, against stupidity? The passage by Schelling concerning the ground that I wanted to quote, and whose principle, it seems to me, supports or sustains the whole Deleuzian discourse here, can be found in his *Philosophical Research on the Essence (or Nature) of Human Liberty.* Schelling is explaining, and trying to justify, his distinction between Being (*Wesen*) as ground (*Grund*) and being as existing (*Existenz*). Discussing this problem, he states that there should necessarily be a Being (*Wesen*) prior to any ground or any existence, being, and thus, in general, prior to any opposition, any duality. He says (I quote), "How could we call this anything other than originary ground (*Urgrund*) or, better, nonground (*Ungrund*)?" or groundless ground; "since it precedes all oppositions, these oppositions cannot be discerned or present in another way in themselves. It cannot be thus characterized as identity but only as absolute indifference as to principle (*die absolute Indifferenz*)."[6] Within this logic, which is Schellingian as well as Deleuzian, man takes shape, is determined in his form, on this background of the ground, by keeping with it a relation, a free relation. That's his freedom, a relation to the groundless ground, which would be denied to animals who are nevertheless "in a sense forewarned," "en quelque sorte *prémunis* contre ce fond par leurs formes explicites." We should read Schelling again, and Heidegger on Schelling, and in particular what Schelling says on this human sickness that stupidity (*Blödsinn*) is. *Blödsinn* is at the center of a remarkable book by Avital Ronell, *Stupidity*. "Stupidity," "bêtise," is it exactly the same thing?

Now, to come back to Deleuze, only this experience of freedom that bêtise is, as human freedom, only this freedom that has a relation to the groundless ground, can account for the fact that not only is bêtise foreign to "animals," but it may be linked to the three motifs I indicated a moment ago, namely, sovereignty, cruelty—and thus evil, disease, or sickness, as Schelling would say—and then thought, thinking.

First, sovereignty, in the figure of the tyrant:

Deleuze notes, in the passage on bêtise, "This is why tyrants have the heads not only of beasts but also of pears, cauliflowers or potatoes. One is neither superior nor external to that from which one benefits: a tyrant institutionalises stupidity, but he is the first servant of his own system and the first to be installed within it. Slaves are always commanded by another slave" (*D&R*, 151). This is a very classical motif, a Platonician one, that tyrants are slaves.

Second, evil or cruelty in their essential link to bêtise:

Here Deleuze is very eloquent and insistent. What he says is consistent with the gesture that makes bêtise the phenomenon of freedom as human freedom. What is remarkable is that the distinction between stupidity and error remains the essential condition for this interpretation and this problematic. Deleuze writes, "how could the concept of error account for this unity of stupidity and cruelty, of the grotesque and the terrifying, which doubles the way of the world? Cowardice, cruelty, baseness and stupidity are not simply corporeal capacities or traits of character or society; *they are structures of thought as such*" (*D&R*, 151; emphasis added). Before coming back to these structures of thought, philosophic and transcendental, I underline, through some quotations, the essential importance that Deleuze attributes to the link between stupidity and cruelty, and thus between stupidity and evil, between stupidity and freedom, between stupidity and responsibility—all traits that are supposed to be human and not animal:

> All determinations become bad and cruel when they are grasped only by a thought which invents and contemplates them, flayed and separated from their living form, adrift upon this barren ground. Everything becomes violence on this passive ground. Everything becomes attack on this digestive ground. Here the Sabbath of stupidity and malevolence takes place. Perhaps this is the origin of that melancholy which weighs upon the most beautiful human faces: the presentiment of a hideousness peculiar to the human face, of a rising tide of stupidity, an evil deformity or a thought governed by madness. For from the point of view of a philosophy of nature, madness arises at the point at which the individual contemplates itself in this *free ground*—and, as a result, stupidity in stupidity and cruelty in cruelty—to the point that it can no longer stand itself. 'A pitiful faculty then emerges in their minds, that of being able to see stupidity and no longer tolerate it.'
>
> (D&R, 152; EMPHASIS ADDED)

It is at this point that Deleuze inserts the footnote that refers to Schelling, which reads: "Flaubert, *Bouvard et Pécuchet*. Schelling wrote some splendid pages on evil (stupidity and malevolence), its source which is like the Ground become autonomous (essentially related to individuation), and on the entire history which follows from this, in 'Recherches philosophiques sur la nature de la liberté humaine'" (*D&R*, 321–322 n. 15). Continuing after the inserted footnote, Deleuze says, "It is true that this most pitiful faculty also becomes the royal faculty when it animates philosophy as a philosophy of mind—in other words, when it leads all the other faculties to that transcendent exercise which renders possible a violent reconciliation between the individual, the ground and thought" (*D&R*, 152).

Third, then, thought:

What is interesting in this structural link that Deleuze sees between bêtise and thought, what he calls the structure of thinking as such, "la structure de la pensée comme telle," is what he denounces as totally unable to think this thought of bêtise. What he charges or indicts here is the weakness or defect of thought. It is a double figure, a guilty figure of the same sin, the same fault, the same crime: bad literature, pseudoliterature, on the one hand, and, on the other hand, philosophy. These are the two faults, the two flaws. Both of them would have missed the essence of bêtise, the essence of stupidity, as a problem of thought. Deleuze explains why. If philosophy and pseudoliterature miss stupidity as a thing of thought, so to speak, the best literature ("la meilleure littérature"— this is Deleuze's phrase), even if it doesn't address thematically or systematically the stupidity of thought, stupidity as the structure of thought, the best literature is "haunted"—again Deleuze's word—by stupidity; it is haunted by "the problem of stupidity." Deleuze thereby introduces the spectral lexicon of haunting that will carry the equivocal charge of the difference between pseudoliterature and philosophy, on the one hand, and the best literature, on the other hand.

How can we recognize this haunting? What are the signs, positive, negative, denigrative, denials, presence of symptoms, absence of symptoms, explicit or implicit thematization, to what degree, and so on? Deleuze writes:

> The transcendental landscape comes to life: places for the tyrant, the slave and the imbecile must be found within it—without the place resembling the figure who occupies it, and without the transcendental ever being traced from the empirical figures which it makes possible. It is always our belief in the postulates of the *Cogitatio* which prevents us from making stupidity a transcendental problem. Stupidity can then be no more than an empirical determination, referring back to psychology or to the anecdotal— or worse, to polemic and insults—and to the especially atrocious pseudo-literary genre of the *sottisier*. But whose fault is this? Does not the fault lie first with philosophy, which has allowed itself to be convinced by the concept of error even though this concept is itself borrowed from facts, relatively insignificant and arbitrary facts? The worst literature produces *sottisiers*, while

the best (Flaubert, Baudelaire, Bloy) was haunted by the problem of stupidity. By giving this problem all its cosmic, encyclopaedic and gnoseological dimensions, such literature was able to carry it as far as the entrance to philosophy itself.

(*D&R*, 151)

Now, on the other hand, to say that stupidity is never stupidity of the other doesn't mean only that it is always reserved for my fellow creatures, my *semblables*, as human beings. It means also that I— the I, as a philosopher, theoretician or not—always risk being compelled to attribute stupidity to myself, the I to which I refer or the stupidity that I think, automatically, in a stupid manner, *bêtement*, that I identify in others. Here, to follow this, to interpret Deleuze's intention, we could follow Flaubert's track, and, of course, Deleuze refers to it also. But let me get to my conclusion.

I'm not saying this in order to discredit discourses that do whatever they can to specify as much as possible the humanity, the properly human character, of bestiality (Lacan) or bêtise (Deleuze). I'm not saying this in order to confuse humans with animals, to say that there is no difference between human animals and nonhuman animals. On the contrary, it's in order to refine the differential concepts that I underline a certain nonpertinence of the concept and of the logic that are put to work here, in order to reserve the privilege of what one thinks one can define as human bestiality and human bêtise, that is, to reserve this to the properly human animality, supposed to be free and responsible and not reactive, able to discern between good and evil, able to do evil for the sake of evil, and so on. I would like to conclude by specifying my reading of the original form that this tradition takes in Deleuze. I think that Deleuze both belongs to this tradition and, on the background of this tradition, remains absolutely originary.

When, in the Schellingian vein I recalled, Deleuze says "la bêtise n'est pas l'animalité" or "the animals are in a sense forewarned against this background by their explicit forms," he implies that man, even where his form, the determination of his individuation, protects itself against the groundless ground, the *Urgrund* as

Ungrund, man remains nevertheless as an undetermined freedom in relation with this groundless ground, and that's where this properly human stability comes from. But what permits saying this in this form? Let's reexamine this statement: "Les animaux sont *en quelque sorte prémunis* contre ce fond par leurs *formes explicites*" (emphasis added). If they are prémunis, forewarned, it means that they are in relation, that they have some relation with this ground, and they are under the threat of this ground. Of course, one is often tempted to see with respect to many animals a relation to the groundless ground, a relation more fascinating and fascinated, anxious and abyssal, as abyssal as with man. Even in what could forewarn or protect them we can feel a proximity, an obsessing, threatening proximity, of this ground against which, but like humans, animals would protect themselves. Moreover, when Deleuze, in such a sharp fashion, wants to separate man from animals as to bêtise by saying, in a determined and decided fashion, "la bêtise n'est pas l'animalité," why does he introduce phrases that are so resistant to sharp opposition, such as "en quelque sorte," "in a sense?" Or "forewarned," "prémunis," a notion that always implies a degree—again the problem of immunity. There's always a degree of more or less, more or less protection against something to which one remains related, a more or less of protection, the way some animals sense the coming of an earthquake that remains imperceptible to man. Above all, what could we do with a phrase like "formes explicites?" What about implicit forms? So this question of the implicit, of the difference implicit/explicit, not only opens on gradations, a differentiality with no opposition, a gradation of more or less, but also opens on the question of the unconscious.

That's why I started with psychoanalysis. Psychoanalysis is a space where, of course, I admire Deleuze and where I also have some resistance to him. The question of the unconscious, which doesn't appear at all in this context, Deleuze quickly will have dismissed, the way Lacan himself does when he says that bestiality is not animal and when he says that the animal has no unconscious.[7] Even the unconscious of man, repression, and resistance are not taken into account in this Deleuzian analysis of bêtise. It is at this point that—however funny and necessary sometimes is Deleuze's ironical vigilance, his sarcasm as to psychoanalysis—it's difficult for me to laugh with him for too long. Why should we not recognize, why should we not say conversely that, to the extent that he also has explicit forms of individuation, man protects himself against the groundless ground? To that extent, at least following Deleuze's logic, man would ignore pure stupidity, as the animal does. Without homogenizing things, without wanting to erase the differences, I believe that the conceptuality just analyzed here does not provide any assured criterion to propose, in such a decisive way, that "la bêtise n'est pas l'animalité" and that only man is exposed to stupidity.

For example, in the following sentences in Deleuze's text, I don't see why the very equivocal figures of *minage*, which relates to the ground or the underground and the work of *minage*, and of *travail* and being worked by, *travailler par*, couldn't apply to animals, unless one supposes with Descartes and Kant that the animal cannot constitute itself as an I. That's a constant prevailing belief with philosophers, that the difference between animal and man, between animality and humanity, is that the animal cannot say "I," but also with anthropology, that the essence of what is proper to man is circumscribed by the possibility of saying "I," even the ability, the power, to say "me/I." This is a question I would have liked to develop but will have to leave aside for now and make do with a sketch of how I'd approach it:

> Animals are in a sense forewarned against this ground, protected by their explicit forms. Not so for the I and the Self, undermined by the fields of individuation which work beneath them, defenceless against a rising of the ground which holds up to them a distorted or distorting mirror in which all presently thought forms dissolve. Stupidity is neither the ground nor the individual, but rather this relation in which individuation brings the ground to the surface without being able to give it form (this ground rises by means of the I, penetrating deeply into the possibility of thought and constituting the unrecognized in every recognition).
>
> (D&R, 152)

This amounts to saying that stupidity is the "I," is the thing of the I, of the ego. It avoids naming something, in the form of a psychic life, that we could call ground or not, that wouldn't have the figure of the I. Without having to credit such or such construction of Freudian metapsychology, one cannot reduce the whole psychological or metapsychological experience to its egological form, and one cannot reduce all life to the ego or every egological structure to the conscious I. In the psychological or phenomenological experience, in the self-relation of the living being, the relation of the living being to itself, there is something one could call nonego, on the one hand, and there is even, as Freud would say, the unconscious ego. So, even if one doesn't want to rely on the authority of Freudian discourse, it is enough to admit that the living being is divisible and constituted by a multiplicity of assemblages, instances, forces, different intensities, and sometimes tensions and even contradictions. I purposely use here, speaking of differential intensities, of forces, a Nietzschean language that would be more acceptable to Deleuze. Everything turns around this egologic of the I and the Self and the ego.

I would have liked to go on with this question of the ego and, of course, with the distinction between response and reaction—which is part of, or which belongs to, the hegemonic tradition from Descartes to Levinas, including Lacan and Heidegger, and so on—between responsible response and irresponsible reaction, and thus between sovereignty and nonsovereignty, freedom and nonfreedom, as the difference between man and the beast. Despite the originality of the way Deleuze asks this question, I think these pages of *Difference and Repetition* belong to this tradition. It may surprise us when this distinction appears in a discourse on the side of Lacan that is produced in the name of psychoanalysis in the return to Freud or in a discourse such as Deleuze's, which speaks of a production of the unconscious. In both cases, at least, they admit the possibility of the unconscious. And I think this philosophy of bêtise is inconsistent with this reference to the unconscious. But at that point one doesn't need the word "unconscious" or any theoretical or metapsychological construction—the I, the id, the superego, the ideal ego, the ideal of the ego, or the real, symbolic, and imaginary of the I as in Lacan. It is enough, a minimal condition, that we take into account the divisibility, multiplicity, or difference of forces in a living being, whatever it may be. It is enough to admit that there is no finite living being, human or nonhuman, that wouldn't be structured by this differential of forces between which a tension, if not a contradiction, cannot not locate or be located in different *instances*, apparatuses, if you will, one resisting others, one repressing or suppressing others, or trying to put forward or make prevail what La Fontaine, in his "The Wolf and the Sheep," called "*la raison du plus fort*," the reason/right of the strongest. In these antagonisms made possible in every finite living being, made possible by differences of forces and intensities, stupidity is always necessarily on both sides, on the side of the who—man, ego—and the side of the what—the side of what happens to the one who poses himself as sovereign, free, etc., or on the side of what the free ego or sovereign denounces or attacks as the stupidity of the other. If I had time, I would move from Deleuze to Flaubert, and to Valéry and Monsieur Teste when he says—again untranslatable—"la bêtise n'est pas mon fort," translated as "I'm not strong on stupidity"—and how stupid one would be to say "la bêtise n'est pas mon fort."

NOTES

1. At Derrida's request, his essay was transcribed from conference recordings and edited by Erin Ferris. With the exception of a few minor revisions he made following transcription, this text reproduces the lecture Derrida delivered at the conference "Derrida/Deleuze: Politics, Psychoanalysis, Territoriality," held at the UC Irvine, April 12–13, 2002.
2. Deleuze, *Difference and Repetition,* hereafter *D&R*. Derrida often translates from the original as he lectures; those translations are reproduced here in addition to any published translations he cites.
3. "The Beast and the Sovereign/La Bête et le Souverain," spring 2002.
4. Deleuze and Guattari, *A Thousand Plateaus,* hereafter *Plateaus.*
5. Schelling, *Philosophische Untersuchungen.*
6. "Wie können wir es anders nennen als den Urgrund oder vielmehr

Ungrund? Da es vor allen Gegensätzen vorhergeht, so können diese in ihm nicht unterscheidbar, noch auf irgend eine Weise vorhanden sein. Es kann daher nicht als die Identität; es kann nur als die absolute *Indifferenz* beider bezeichnet werden" (ibid., 78).

7. See Derrida's analysis of Lacan on the animal in "And Say the Animal Responded?"

BIBLIOGRAPHY

Deleuze, Gilles. *Difference and Repetition*. Trans. Paul Patton. New York: Columbia University Press, 1994. Originally published as *Différence et répétition* (Paris: Presses Universitaires de France, 1968).

Deleuze, Gilles and Félix Guattari. *A Thousand Plateaus: Capitalism and Schizophrenia*. Trans. Brian Massumi. Minneapolis: University of Minnesota Press, 1987. Originally published as *Capitalisme et schizophrénie. Tome 2: Mille plateaux* (Paris: Minuit, 1980).

Derrida, Jacques. "And Say the Animal Responded?" Trans. David Wills. In *Zoontologies: The Question of the Animal*, ed. Cary Wolfe, 121–146. Minneapolis: University of Minnesota Press, 2003.

Ronell, Avital. *Stupidity*. Chicago: University of Illinois Press, 2002.

Schelling, Friedrich Wilhelm Joseph. *Philosophische Untersuchungen über das Wesen der menschlichen Freiheit und die damit zusammenhängenden Gegenstände*. Hamburg: F. Meiner Verlag, 1997.

Valéry, Paul. *Monsieur Teste*. Paris: Gallimard, 1946.

3

POLYMORPHISM NEVER WILL PERVERT CHILDHOOD

Catherine Malabou

TRANSLATED BY ROBERT ROSE

Gilles Deleuze and Jacques Derrida. Their difference does not bear any resemblance. From one difference to another, there exists no immediately visible way of passage, no path, no indications. From differ*a*nce to difference, from the archiwriting to lines of flight, from traces to regimes of signs, from dissemination to immanence, from destinerrancy to strata or blocks of becoming is drawn an immense labyrinth, the struggle through which is perilous, if not hopeless. They themselves never undertook it. Maintaining silence, they always kept at a respectful distance from each other with the exception of a few, virtually insignificant references or mentions made in passing. A lack of awareness, hostility, esteem? The secret of such a differing remains intact.

So then how does one respond to the invitation made to us to bring their thoughts face to face? To take up the question that Deleuze poses at the end of his study of *Bartleby*, are Derrida and Deleuze "false brothers sent by a diabolical father to restore his power over [the] *overly credulous* Americans?" (89). Should I, as an heir, as a daughter, unify these two brothers in one and the same paternal figure, that is, reoedipalize them?

Since the question of filiation is inescapable here, the only thing to do, it seems to me, is to let the child speak. By overturning the terms, first of all, by letting Jacques Derrida and Gilles Deleuze come to me as little children. No longer as fathers, no longer as brothers, no longer perhaps even as sons, but as children. I will therefore ask them, which child are you, who is the child for you, and, to take up a question of Derrida's, "how is a child possible in general?" (*Of Grammatology*, 146).

Why the child? To begin with, because the child has not yet said anything. I think back to the silence that Derrida and Deleuze have mutually observed. To say nothing about the other, is this not to keep him in reserve, to consider him still to be possible, possible, indeed, as other? The liveliest figure of a possible other, in every sense of the term, is without a doubt that of the child. Hence it is appropriate to think that Derrida and Deleuze have been led, one in front of the other, like children, children between whom all is still possible, between whom all remains to be played.

Why the child? Second, because the child is not a common motif for them. Derrida and Deleuze do not share the child, even if so many children show up in both of their texts: themselves, and Alice, Ernst, Heinele, Sophie, Fritz, Jean-Jacques, Hans, the Wolf Man, Deligny's autistic children, Tweedledee, Tweedledum, the slave of Ménon, little Nambikwrara who reveals to Levi-Strauss all the proper names of the tribe, Emile, Norbert, Jean, Pierre, Gregor, Kafka, Marcel; it would be impossible to name them all. These children who show up forbid any attempt to put into perspective their thoughts on childhood. With them, we can only invent a game and play for a moment.

Which game? Each in his own way, irreducibly different, Derrida and Deleuze put again into question the famous Freudian postulate concerning the existence, in the child, of a "polymorphously perverse disposition" (*polymorph perverse Anlage*): "It is an instructive fact that under the influence of seduction children can become polymorphously perverse, and can be led into all possible kinds of sexual irregularities. This shows that an aptitude for them is innately present in their disposition. There is consequently little resistance towards carrying them out, since the mental dams against sexual excesses—shame, disgust and morality—have either not yet been constructed at all or are only in course of construction, according to the age of the child" ("Three Essays," 7:191).

Perversion, as we know, designates deviation with respect to the aim of sexuality. Now, it is not perversion, or perversity (both substantives are possible), that constitutes the object of critical attention for Derrida and Deleuze in their readings of Freud but, to the contrary, polymorphism. That the child is perverse, the cause is understood. On the other hand, that this perversity, or this disposition for perversity, is polymorphous, susceptible of taking various forms, this is what neither Derrida nor Deleuze seems to admit. Polymorphism never will pervert childhood. We should be more precise: polymorphism never will pervert the perversity of childhood. Such are the rules of the game.

Why the child? The third and final reason is that the critique of polymorphism does not constitute, for either philosopher, a motif or a theme that is easy to locate. This critique, whereby the child is inscribed in the text, remains itself a child, the childhood block of writing. It is not finished and neither is it very sure of itself; in thought, it draws the hearth of tenderness and malice where is prepared the eternal return of what is critiqued. What does this mean? The child, perverse but not polymorphous, is the one who, on every page of their books, asks Derrida and Deleuze: is not difference the other name for a polymorphism that is being ignored, that is to say, for a polymorphism without perversity?

Let's pretend that Deleuze and Derrida agree on what a game or play is. Here's the definition of play in Derrida, which I will borrow from *Of Grammatology*: "One could call *play* the absence of the transcendental signified as limitlessness of play [*illimitation du jeu*], that is to say as the destruction [*ébranlement*] of ontotheology and the metaphysics of presence" (50). Here's the definition of play in Deleuze, which I'll borrow from *The Logic of Sense*: play is the distribution of sense: "sense . . . as surface effect and position effect, and produced by the circulation of the empty square in the structural series (the place of the dummy, the place of the king, the blind spot, the floating signifier, the value degree zero, the off-stage or absent cause, etc.)" (71). So let's pretend that these two definitions say the same thing: the sign does not refer to a presence, and neither is it its messenger. It is sent from nothing. Its destination is that of pure difference. The absence of the transcendental signified is the empty square, the degree zero that, in fact, allows for sense to circulate, that is to say, to play. Now, to play is to transform, *passer*, from one square to another, from one series to another. Derrida would say "substitution"; Deleuze would say "transmutation."[1]

Now, these transformations, these transferential upheavals—substitutions, supplements, and transmutations—have absolutely nothing to do with the deployments or the displacements of a polymorphous energy as conceived of by Freud. The famous observation of his grandson Ernst playing with his wooden spool in *Beyond the Pleasure Principle* is proof: for Freud, childhood is never anything other than a certain relationship to the sign and therefore to sense. The polymorphous sexual disposition itself only indicates a certain way of relating to the sign's structure of referral, the "to be worth" (*valoir-pour*): toy, fetish, body part, image, and so on. Polymorphous perversity should therefore be understood as a yet-untamed and hence free possibility of associating signifiers and signifieds, signs and referents, signs and pleasures, starting from the blank square of an infinitely transformable energy.

We can certainly consider polymorphous perversity as the first name given to the absence of the transcendental signified, to the psychic and somatic inscription of difference—with *e* and with *a*—in the history of thought. Freud is the first to call childhood—that is to say, the origin, the law of sense—the law of unlimited exchange. To be perverse, etymologically, is to be able to turn, to turn away, invert, overturn, indeed, to pervert, in short, to give oneself up to twisting and turning. Now, sense, like sexuality, is necessarily perverse, twisted, bent; it is born from all the contortions to which, from childhood, the absence of the master signified destines the floating signifier.

At the same time, in Freud, it is precisely this recognition of the perversity of sense that is covered up by the concept of polymorphism. Polymorphism, in a way, occults perversity. The manner in which Freud thinks of the energy of transformation, the capacity to be transformed in general, is, indeed, a problem. As Deleuze declares in "Coldness and Cruelty," the Freudian conception of transformation remains *transformist*: Freud conceives of transformation as a movement that is necessarily genetic, evolving, teleologically oriented—a conception that supports another, one that is very traditional, of childhood as a process of development and of maturation in phases and stages. In this evolution, the same energy—form and matter at once—unfolds and folds back on itself, lossless, always new, always childlike. Thus, for example, for Freud, masochism is only ever a loop in, an about-face of, or a *twist* on, sadism. They would "deriv[e] masochism from sadism," maintains Deleuze ("Coldness," 108–109). Freud, he continues, intends "to treat sadomasochism as a particular entity within which transitions (*le passage*) occur from one component to the other" (103). It's in this sense that there is, according to Deleuze, a Freudian "transformism."[2] Freud takes for granted, he continues, "the possibility of any manner of transformation" (109). The Freudian concept of transformation—for which the words "*Umgestaltung*" and "*Wandlung*" are the two principal mouthpieces—assumes therefore an originary entity, at once force-matter-form, that can deal with every sort of turn without aging or weakening. Polymorphism ends up being confused with the transcendental signified at the same time that it is supposed to inscribe the trace of its absence.

"With regard to the Death Instinct," says Deleuze, "sadism and masochism are differentiated in every possible way: they have intrinsically different structures and are not functionally related; they cannot be transformed into each other. In short, the true nature of sadism and of masochism is revealed not in any supposed genetic derivation but in the structural ego-superego split, which occurs differently in each of them" ("Coldness," 129). Contrary to what one might believe, Deleuze does not play difference against transformation here, since difference is not thinkable without a certain economy of metamorphosis, but he recalls that the condition of this economy, tied to originary scission, obeys rules, a *regime*, rules that are not those of polymorphism. Polymorphism, in fact, implies the movement of an infinite modification of an agency that, paradoxically, remains identical to itself. Polymorphism characterizes, in biology, the property that certain organisms have to take on different forms without changing their nature. So, in reality, talking about polymorphism comes down to presupposing invariability and unity, what Deleuze calls "infrastructure." He asserts, in *Dialogues*: "We do not believe in general that sexuality has the role of an infrastructure in the assemblages of desire, nor that it constitutes an energy capable of transformation. . . . Sexuality can only be thought of as one [flow] amongst others." (Deleuze and Parnet, *Dialogues*, 101). Polymorphism respects neither the clinical point of view nor the critical point of view, and thus is witness to a blindness "to the very tissue of the 'symptom,'" to take up an expression of Derrida's from *Of Grammatology* (159).

As for Derrida, he gives this transformism a name that might seem surprising, "archive fever." "Archive fever" designates a certain suffering of the substrate, a certain discontent in psychoanalytic "*Kultur*" with regard to the writing surface, or the "subjectile." This suffering, this discontent, is manifested in an ambivalent, if not contradictory, attitude vis-à-vis the archive and the impression that it conserves. Freud is the first thinker of a psychic writing that does not transcribe the psyche but produces it as such, a writing that forms that on which it writes insofar as it writes. Derrida declares: "On the one hand, Freud made possible the idea of an archive properly speaking . . . , of the substrate or the subjectile," by conceiving of the psychic apparatus from a topical point of view as a "spacing" (*Archive Fever*, 91–92). "But *on the other hand*," he continues, recalling the conclusions from "Freud and the Scene of Writing," "this does not stop Freud, as classical metaphysician, from holding the technical prosthesis to be a secondary and accessory exteriority. . . . From which we have the archaeological outbidding by which psychoanalysis, in its archive fever, always attempts to return to the live origin of that which the archive loses while keeping it in a multiplicity of places" (92). What this signifies is that Freud obliterates in a way his own discovery by remaining tributary to an idea of the independent sense of his substrata, to a signifying energy susceptible of taking any form and of leaving its vehicles in order better to regroup.

Neither does Derrida oppose difference and transformation. Difference, he writes, is at once both "the being-imprinted of the imprint" and "the formation of the form" (*Fever*, 63). The two do not oppose each other because each is the condition of possibility of the other. But, in that case, if the imprint, while imprinting, forms the surface, that on which it is inscribed, if in return the formation of the imprint depends on the state of the substrate, then no power of originary formation or impression conditions writing. There is no archipolymorphism.

The rules having been laid, how does one play? There is a big temptation, to which I already succumbed, to turn childhood into a polymorphous function that would authorize bringing together Derrida's and Deleuze's thought. "We must be attentive," says Deleuze, "to the sliding which reveals a profound difference underlying these crude similarities." "A little girl may sing 'Pimpanicaille'; an artist may write 'frumious'; and a schizophrenic may utter 'perspendicace.' But we have no reason to believe that the problem is the same in all of these cases and the results roughly analogous. One could not seriously confuse Babar's song with Artaud's howls-breaths (*cris-souffles*)" (*Logic*, 83). So, neither is it any more serious to confuse the logic of sense with the supplementary condition. What does one do in order not to slide?[3]

I suggest simply that we look at the perversity of the children at play in Deleuze and Derrida. In which becoming is perversity involved?

For Derrida, the child's perversity is attached to the manner in which the child precipitates, in a single stroke, from the cradle, the first part of my paper, that is, the long explanation of the rules of the game, the long explanation of the ambivalence of Freud, of his thought at once both traditionally metaphysical and deconstructive of the play of sense. A child is perverse insofar as he or she endlessly substitutes deconstruction for metaphysics and metaphysics for deconstruction. The child endlessly transforms one into the other, alternately showing their cards, their changing faces, casting doubt on the very origin of the deconstruction of the origin. A child is perverse in his or her very manner of posing the question of the origin. And if deconstruction were only ever the child of metaphysics? An effect of its unconscious polymorphism?

For Deleuze, the perversity of the child is attached to the fact that a child can refuse to be born, that is to say, to play. He or she can remain in the depths, not rise to the surface. There are always two children in the child: the one who lends existence to the depths and thus justifies the very ground of psychoanalysis; the other who sweeps the very concept of the unconscious off of the surface of life. There are always two children in the child, who do not meet, like Artaud and Carroll. "Artaud thrusts *the child [enfonce l'enfant]*," "Carroll, on the contrary, awaits *the child* . . . : he waits at the point and at the moment in which the child has left the depths of the maternal body and has yet to discover the depth of her own body. This is the brief surface moment in which the little girl skirts the surface of the water, like Alice in the pool of her own tears" (*Logic*, 93). The two have nothing to do with each other, maintains Deleuze, which is true. But, despite everything, the perversity of the child consists in putting on display (*mettant en scène*), in the face of and against everything, both of them: surface and depths.

This is what takes place in Kafka's "The Metamorphosis," in regard to which Deleuze concludes, a bit too hastily for my taste, that it is a failure (Deleuze and Guattari, *Kafka*). Metamorphosis is a monstrous coexistence, in the child, of the depths and the surface, of transformism and mutation, of the incestuous triangle and the oedipal triangle. Metamorphosis is the story of the coexistence of two transformations. It's the story of the coexistence of Freud and Deleuze. And the child, child Gregor, already grown-up, asks Freud and Deleuze in his whimpering voice: Where does the energy for metamorphosis come from? Polymorphism or lines of flight? A child slides so easily! He or she turns the critique of polymorphism back on itself so easily!

We only have to take a look at Emile and Ernst playing together. In *Of Grammatology*, Derrida analyzes the passage from *Emile* in which Rousseau wonders how to teach generosity to children. "To teach the child true generosity," notes Derrida, "is to make sure that he is not content only to imitate it. What does it mean to imitate generosity? It is to give signs in the place of things, words in the place of sentiments, money in the place of real goods" (204). The child is not spontaneously generous. He or she only gives away things that do not matter, old pieces of metal, devalued signifiers. "A child," writes Rousseau, "would rather give a hundred coins than one cake." But if the child is not generous, if he would be more willing to give away signs or substitutes than things themselves, it's not because he or she is perverse, but rather, according to Rousseau, it's because he does not have an immediate, natural relationship to the sign. Derrida notes: "The child desires naturally to keep what he desires. It is normal and natural. Here vice or perversity would consist of not attaching oneself to things that are naturally desirable but to their substitutive signifiers. If a child loved money for money's sake, he would be perverse; he would no longer be a child. *For Rousseau the concept of the child is always related to the sign. More precisely, childhood is the non-relation to the sign as such*" (204). Emile is therefore present before the thing, he is unaware of the sign, and for that reason he gets rid of it and allows it to circulate. "According to Rousseau, the child," says Derrida once more, "is the name of that which should not relate in any way to a separated signifier, loved in some way for itself, like a fetish." Now, Freud says exactly the opposite. Have a look at Ernst. He transforms his toys and that to which he is attached the most, his very mother, into tools, that is to say, into signs. Describing the game with the wooden spool, Freud declares: "I eventually realized that it was a game and that the only use he made of his toys (*Spielsachen*) was to play 'gone' (*fortsein*) with them" (quoted in Derrida, *The Post Card*, 310). Derrida notes: the child is perverse because he or she does not play with his toys. "[Freud] calls a game the operation which consists in not playing with one's toys: he did not employ them, he did not use (*benütze*) his toys, he says, he did not make them useful, *utensiles*, except by playing at their being gone. The 'game' thus consists in not playing with one's toys, but in making them useful for another function, to wit, being-gone" (311). So the perversity really does consist in a turning away. The child, contrary to what Rousseau says, is susceptible to transforming everything into signs, to turning presence away toward its substitute, to playing at distancing that which is most cherished. And it is not a separated signifier that the child fetishizes thus but really the play of language in its entirety, the game itself. The child is perverse in his or her infinite possibility of turning away. For him or her, "the objects can substitute for each other to the point of laying bare the substitutive structure itself" (321). It's as if the substitutive structure—the game or play itself, the absence of the transcendental signified—entered into presence by the grace of the child (cf. child Nambikwara [*Of Grammatology*, 107–108]). It's as if the perversity of the child went so far as to turn away the turning-away itself, to the point of gathering the substitutive structure back onto itself, no longer substituting anything for it.

Before coming to the example of the wooden spool, Freud explains that his grandson likes to toss his toys away from him, forcing his parents to gather them back up. But with the wooden spool, the child appears capable of both dispersing them and gathering them back up again all by himself. "In this exemplary example the child throws away and brings back to himself, disperses and reassembles, gives and takes back by himself: he reassembles the reassembling and the dispersion, the multiplicity of agents, work and play into a single agent, apparently, and into a single object" (*Post Card*, 309).

The child gathers back up the dispersion. A perverse gesture, eminently duplicitous. Indeed, with this gesture, says Derrida, "What is going on no longer concerns a distancing rendering this or that into presence; what is going on concerns rather the distancing of the distant and the nearness of the near, the absence of the absent or the presence of the present. But the distancing is not distant, nor the nearness near, nor the absence absent or the presence present. The *fortsein* of which Freud is speaking is not any more *fort* than *Dasein* is *da*" (*Post Card*, 321). The duplicity of the child's play is attached to the fact that it is allied at once with both metaphysics and its destruction, with Plato and Rousseau, as well as with Heidegger, and that a choice or a decision between the two cannot be made—between presence and proximity, between parousia and being-there, between absence and *Entfernung*, between not being-there and the distancing of the distant. But what's more, this duplicity inevitably raises a question: where does this perversity come from, this capacity to turn, simultaneously, metaphysics and deconstruction, into each other? Shouldn't we allow for a certain conceptual and/or psychic metabolism that would oversee the phoronomic destiny of differance? That being the case, couldn't one say that phoronomy requires polymorphism as a structural invariant?

No, there's no polymorphism here, responds Deleuze, but an *assemblage (agencement)*. Difference assembles or sets up its exchange with metaphysics or with philosophy by constituting planes. The same goes for the child; he or she lays out different surfaces, that's all. It is psychoanalysis that turns the assemblage into a sort of syncretic tendency: "As soon as desire assembles [*agence*] something—in connection with an Outside, in connection with a becoming—the assemblage is broken up," says Deleuze in *Dialogues*. "There are always too many [desires] for psychoanalysis: 'polymorphously perverse'" (*Dialogues*, 78–77).

Against this reductionistic vision, Deleuze maintains that a child does not have an unconscious, that he or she must *produce* it: "You have to produce the unconscious . . . as a raw material to experiment with," says Deleuze once more (*Dialogues*, 78). Here, we are far away from polymorphism to the extent that this raw material has to be invented. This invention presupposes as well a certain perversity. The book consecrated to Kafka explores this perversity in every one of its turns. Concerning the "Letter to the Father," in particular, Deleuze and Guattari write: "To augment and expand Oedipus by adding to it and making a paranoid and perverse use of it is already to escape from submission, to lift one's head up, and see passing above the shoulders of the father what had really been the question all along: an entire micropolitics of desire, of impasses and escapes, of submissions and rectifications" (*Kafka*, 10). To make a perverse usage of Oedipus is to deterritorialize it, "deterritorializing Oedipus into the world instead of reterritorializing everything in Oedipus and the family. But to do this,

Oedipus had to be enlarged to the point of absurdity, comedy, . . . the 'Letter to the Father' had to be written." Sexuality is linked to the production of surfaces and zones; what matters is an urbanism, a kind of habitat, a theory of places that does not fit a transformist schema. Behind the oedipal triangle are an infinity of other, non-preformed triangles. In Kafka, the question of triangulation is further confused with the possibility of substitution itself. "All these lines," maintain Deleuze and Guattari,

> are very complicated in Kafka. Sometimes, with the familial triangle as a given, as in "The Metamorphosis," a term of another sort will come to be added or substituted: the chief clerk arrives behind Gregor's door and insinuates himself into the family. But sometimes, too, it is a trio of bureaucrats as a block that move in and take over the terms of the family . . . . Sometimes, as in the beginning of *The Trial*, there isn't even a preexisting familial triangle (the father is dead, the mother is faraway), but there is still the intrusion of first one term and then another that function like policing doubles, and then their triangulations by a third term, the Inspector. We can observe the metamorphoses of this nonfamilial triangle that in turn will become the bureaucratic triangle of the bank employees, the apartment triangle of the voyeuristic neighbors, and the erotic triangle of Fraulein Burstner and her friends in a photo.
>
> (*KAFKA*, 54)

The proliferation of triangles is not the deployment of the diverse manifestations of a form. This is not a matter of an evolution in which the species—here, the species of triangle—would be transformed by filiation. Triangles are not genetic variables. In a word, differences are not engendered but repeat in a serial manner:

> The childhood block . . . shifts . . . in order to reactivate desire and make its connections proliferate. . . . Incest with the sister and homosexual activity with the artist are examples of such childhood blocks. . . . To be sure, children don't live as our adult memories would have us believe, nor as their own memories,

which are almost simultaneous with their actions, would have them believe. Memory yells "Father! Mother!" but the childhood block is elsewhere, in the highest intensities that the child constructs with his sisters, his pal[s], his projects and his toys, and all the nonparental figures through which he deterritorializes his parents every chance he gets. Ah, childhood sexuality—it's certainly not Freud who gives us the best sense of what that is. But in his activity, as in his passions, [the child] is simultaneously the most deterritorialized and the most deterritorializing figure—the Orphan.

(*KAFKA*, 79–80)

Hence the child is perverse because he or she substitutes one structure for another, one triangle for another, exposing there again a "formal structure." In *Proust and Signs*, Deleuze calls the "formal structure" the structure of the work of art, or the structure of "transversality." Transversality is the energy of substitution that secures the communication of differences, the passage from one to the other that guarantees "the unity *of* these parts without unifying them" (169).

Nevertheless, perversity, there again, turns back, completes a twist onto itself. Insofar as the child discovers the substitutive structure and the play of its surfaces, he or she fails at substituting. At least this is the case with Gregor in "The Metamorphosis": There is always the danger of the return of Oedipal force. The amplifying perverse usage of Oedipus is not sufficient to guard against every new closure, every new reconstitution of the familial triangle. . . . In this sense, 'The Metamorphosis' is the exemplary story of a re-Oedipalization" (*Kafka*, 14). One could maintain that this failure only concerns "The Metamorphosis." Deleuze admits that deterritorialization is successful in other texts. But, of course, the perversity of the child's perversity does not concern only Gregor. It goes so far as to reinscribe polymorphism in Deleuze's text itself. Certainly, Deleuze critiques transformism, but does he not reintroduce it surreptitiously at the very moment he denounces it? Triangles, says Deleuze, are in "a perpetual transformation from one triangle to another" (*Kafka*, 12). This transformation is well interpreted as an "internal proliferation," a "contamination," an "invasion"; nonetheless, it's a matter of a perpetual transformation and that, in medicine, one talks about the polymorphism of viruses, of microbes, of certain pathogenic bacteria. Likewise, in the field of electronics, a "polymorphous machine" is a machine that can simultaneously produce different voltages and different currents, that is to say, precisely, assemblages. Shouldn't we therefore assume there to be, at the origin of any metamorphosis, a polymorphous machine that carries out the transmutation of the polymorphous into what Deleuze and Guattari call the "polyvocal"? For Freud, the child is polymorphous. For Deleuze, it is polyvocal, susceptible of completing a "maximum of connections" (*Kafka*, 67). The child asks, between polymorphous and polyvocal, what basically is the difference?

"To the devil the child, the only thing we ever will have discussed, the child, the child, the child. The impossible message between us. A child is what one should not be able to 'send' oneself," declares Derrida in *The Post Card* (25), a book that he himself qualifies as "polymorphously perverse."[4] One should not, and yet a child starts consuming as soon as he or she is touched. Beginning with the first time he or she cries, the child *writes presence*. He or she confronts philosophy with the immense question of a polymorphism of difference. He or she plays at pretending all at once that difference is the daughter of transformation and, on the other hand, that no transformation is possible outside of play, the supplementary condition or the degree zero of the origin. The child of difference forces the text or texts of difference to interrogate their morphological condition, their inherited position as their engendering power at the very moment they attack the values of filiation and derivation. Metaphysics, psychoanalysis, deconstruction, logic of sense: all these are perhaps only a matter of deviation with respect to the aim. And furthermore the child also could ask Heidegger whether the withdrawal of being, the forgetting of the forgetting, could not be interpreted in a way that has yet to be invented, in terms of perversity. And whether the passage from metaphysics to the other thought does not assume some polymorphous agency. Is difference the becoming-minority of metaphysics? Such is the question posed by the minor, the minimal, the small.

Becoming-child. Nietzsche, too, called that a metamorphosis (*Verwandlung*). The "last one." "I name you three metamorphoses of the spirit: how the spirit shall become a camel, and the camel a lion, and the lion at last a child" (*Thus Spoke Zarathustra*, 54). What Nietzsche does not say, and what no one has ever asked, is, from where does this metamorphic power of the spirit come?

Polymorphism never will pervert childhood. A false promise, or something a child would say?

NOTES

1. Concerning "to transmute," "transmutation," and the relationships of the child and metamorphosis, see Deleuze, *Nietzsche and Philosophy*.
2. For the two principal occurrences of this term, see "Coldness," 103 and 109.
3. "The problem is a clinical problem, that is, a problem of sliding from one organization to another, or a problem of the formation of a progressive and creative disorganization. It is also a problem of criticism, that is, of the determination of differential levels at which nonsense takes shape, the portmanteau word undergoes a change of nature, and the entire language changes dimension" (Deleuze, *Logic*, 83).
4. "This book would be of a polymorphous perversity.... Not a word that would not be dictated upside down, programmed on the back (*au dos*), in the back of the post card. Everything will consist in describing Socrates with Plato making him a child in his back, and I will retain only the lexicon required for every line (*trait*) in the drawing. In a word there will only be back (*du dos*), and even the word 'dos,' if you are willing to pay attention to it and keep the memory" (*Post Card*, 187).

BIBLIOGRAPHY

Deleuze, Gilles. "Bartleby; or, The Formula." In *Essays Critical and Clinical*, trans. Daniel W. Smith and Michael A. Greco, 68–90. Minneapolis: University of Minnesota Press, 1997.

———. "Coldness and Cruelty." In *Masochism*, trans. Jean McNeil, 15–138. London: Faber and Faber, 1971. Reprint, New York: Zone, 1989. Originally published as "Le froid et le cruel," in *Présentation de Sacher-Masoch* (Paris: Minuit, 1967).

———. *The Logic of Sense*. Trans. Mark Lester with Charles Stivale. Ed. Constantin V. Boundas. New York: Columbia University Press, 1990. Originally published as *Logique du sens* (Paris: Minuit, 1982).

———. *Nietzsche and Philosophy*. Trans. Hugh Tomlinson. New York: Columbia University Press, 1985.

———. *Proust and Signs*. Trans. Richard Howard. Minneapolis: University of Minnesota Press, 2000.

Deleuze, Gilles and Félix Guattari. *Kafka: Towards a Minor Literature*. Trans. Dana Polan. Minneapolis: University of Minnesota Press, 1986.

Deleuze, Gilles and Claire Parnet. *Dialogues*. Trans. Hugh Tomlinson and Barbara Habberjam. New York: Columbia University Press, 1987.

Derrida, Jacques. *Archive Fever*. Trans. Eric Prenowitz. Chicago: University of Chicago Press, 1996.

———. "Freud and the Scene of Writing." In *Writing and Difference*, trans. Alan Bass, 196–231. Chicago: University of Chicago Press, 1978.

———. *Of Grammatology*. Trans. Gayatri Chakravorty Spivak. Rev. ed. Baltimore: Johns Hopkins University Press, 1997.

———. *The Post Card*. Trans. Alan Bass. Chicago: University of Chicago Press, 1987.

Freud, Sigmund. "Beyond the Pleasure Principle." In *The Standard Edition of the Complete Psychological Works of Sigmund Freud*, trans. James Strachey, Anna Freud, Alix Strachey, and Alan Tyson, 18:7–64. London: Hogarth and the Institute of Psycho-Analysis, 1953–1974.

———. "Three Essays on Sexuality." In *The Standard Edition of the Complete Psychological Works of Sigmund Freud*, trans. James Strachey, Anna Freud, Alix Strachey, and Alan Tyson, 7:125–245. London: Hogarth and the Institute of Psycho-Analysis, 1953–1974.

Nietzsche, Friedrich. *Thus Spoke Zarathustra*. Trans. R. J. Hollingdale. London: Penguin, 1969.

BUCCALITY

Sara Guyer

FOR SADIE CHAPIN STRAUS

> How, for example on the stage of history, can writing as excrement separated from the *living* flesh and the *sacred* body of the hieroglyph [Artaud], be put into communication with what is said in *Numbers* about the parched woman drinking the inky dust of the law; or what is said in Ezekiel about the son of man who fills his entrails with the scroll of the law which has become sweet as honey in his mouth?
> —JACQUES DERRIDA,
> "FREUD AND THE SCENE OF WRITING"

ORAL LAW (DERRIDA)

> Love your neighbor as yourself. But if you bite and devour one another, take care that you are not consumed by one another.
> —GALATIANS 5:13–15

In "'Eating Well,' or the Calculation of the Subject"—an interview with Jean-Luc Nancy—Jacques Derrida undertakes to recast the tragic theaters of thinking and, in particular, those apparently radical discourses of ethics and politics in which there remains "a place left open . . . for a noncriminal putting to death."[1] This opening signals the enduring humanism at work in adamantly antihumanist (or antivirilist) discourses including those of Martin Heidegger and Emmanuel Levinas, discourses that, Derrida goes so far as to say, "remain profound humanisms *to the extent that they do not sacrifice sacrifice*" (113). Whereas Heidegger, in positing *Dasein*, and Levinas, in formulating a structure of hostage, figure a subjectivity apparently foreign to virility, Derrida is concerned with isolating the insistent carnivorousness that accompanies these discourses and recognizing them as profound (if antithetical) humanisms.[2] Yet rather than suggest, simply, that supporting animal rights or consenting to a vegetarian diet could save us from this constitutively sacrificial structure, the interview derives its force and its import from recasting the ethical frontier, that is, from articulating an ethical law ordered by the mouth rather than the face, a mouth that does not simply function as a face. Derrida does this by proposing "il faut bien manger"—the interview's title, at once "one must eat well/one must eat the good/it is good to eat"—as an originary imperative.

In itself, Derrida's analysis stands as a major—if apparently outrageous—contribution to our understanding of a responsibility that would precede or preclude the subject. Moreover, as an attempt to radicalize the ethical command by demonstrating that so long as ethics remains ordered by the face (which also is to say, so long as it is ordered by the injunction "Thou shalt not kill"), the priority of the subject that the ethical critique of humanism would seem to dismantle is instead reasserted, Derrida's interview also provides a preliminary clue for a rethinking of the rhetoric of figures, that other discourse in which a radically antihumanist claim is effected through a consideration of the face, the figure as face, and the face as figure, the figure as what gives and takes faces.

Derrida's examination of responsibility in " 'Eating Well' " and his reorientation of the ethical frontier opens up, by example, a long overdue rethinking of the rhetoric of figures. Yet to undertake this rethinking is not to relaunch the critique of the so-called antihumanism of rhetorical readers like Paul de Man, or J. Hillis Miller, or Cathy Caruth, or, for that matter, Jacques Derrida himself but, rather, to ask what would happen if we were to displace prosopopoeia as the figure of figure, the figure that orders rhetorical reading. What would happen if we began to think about language and literature not in terms of the giving and taking of faces (or figures), the giving and taking of voice and visibility? What if we began to read according to the mouth—the opening, eating, kissing, biting... mouth—and its depths? How might this reorientation of rhetorical reading, a turn from *figural* reading to *buccal* reading, allow for a rethinking of the crucial and contested relationship between literature and ethics?

In order to initiate this reorientation, I begin with Derrida's reading of Levinas and the opening that it effects. As early as *Existence and Existents* (1947), Levinas articulates a responsibility that precedes subjectivity and describes the passivity that attends this undeniable obligation. For Levinas, it is the face that "signifies" this responsibility: "the face is what forbids us to kill" (*Ethics and Infinity*, 86). The face is absolute exposure and fragility (it— and the eye especially—remains unclothed even when one is clothed), and it is this fragility itself, this apparent index of my power to kill, that also forbids me from killing, leaving me more passive still than the fragility before me.[3] This passive responsibility precedes any identification or any sharing (of a language, for example) between myself and another. Yet, as Derrida points out, Levinas's preoccupation with the face (*vis-à-vis*) as the "locus" of an at once excessive and originary (and hence preoriginary) ethical obligation actually limits the responsibility that it solicits.

While Levinas's account of responsibility apparently resists the heroism or virility that Derrida associates with the subject, it also recovers the subjectivity that it seems to withhold. Because "Thou shalt not kill" is what Levinas calls "the first word of the face" (*Ethics*, 89), and because this commandment never has been understood as a prohibition against "killing in general," the injunction, as Derrida shows, means only the more limited "Thou shalt not kill *thy neighbor*." It is an imperative that "is addressed to the other and presupposes him. It is destined to the very thing that it institutes, the other as man" ("'Eating,'" 112). In other words, although Levinas's account bears witness to an anoriginal structure of subjectivity and the passivity (or the trauma) that attends responsibility, it nevertheless assumes as an already existent addressee the subject "who" this obligation is understood to precede.

Levinas offers a twofold discourse. In the first place, it supports a rigid and knowable division between persons and animals (or human and inhuman animals), the very division that his preoccupation with an ethics that precedes subjectivity would seem to contest; and, in the second place, it assumes the subject or man prior to the face of the other in order to articulate the responsibility that is said to precede it.[4]

Responsibility—disarticulated from a sacrificial structure—would coincide with a recasting of the "ethical frontier," with a refiguring or disfiguring, a defacing of ethics ordered by faces. Derrida elaborates this defacement of ethics with the following proposition (in the mode of hypothesis, in the conditional):

> If the limit between the living and the non-living now seems to be as unsure, at least as an oppositional limit, as that between "man" and "animal," and if, in the (symbolic or real) experience of the "eat-speak-interiorize," the ethical frontier no longer rigorously passes between the "Thou shalt not kill" (man, thy neighbor) and the "Thou shalt not put to death the living in general," but rather between several infinitely different modes of the conception-appropriation-assimilation of the other, then, as concerns the "Good" of every morality, the question will come back to determining the best, most respectful, most grateful, and also most giving way of relating to the other and of relating the other to the self. For *everything* that happens at the edge of the orifices (of orality, but also of the ear, the eye—and all the "senses" in general) the metonymy of 'eating well' (*bien manger*) would always be the rule.
>
> ("'EATING,'" 114–115)

Here, two presuppositions condition the deconstruction of ethics. First, Derrida hypothesizes an analogy, a calculation of instability between two limits—the limit between the living and the nonliving and the limit between "man" and "animal." Second, Derrida hypothesizes that the experience of "eating-speaking-interiorizing," a constellation of indissociable actions, "no longer" supports the division between the prohibition against killing man (one's neighbor) and the prohibition against killing in general that serves as the foundation of an ethics. Because one may eat when speaking, speak with a full mouth or eat with an empty one, or eat-speak-interiorize all at once and indistinguishably, the difference between these two imperatives cannot be upheld, and the opposition "Speak or Kill" no longer maintains. The limits between animal and human, living and nonliving proliferate and come undone, as does the limit that would distinguish murder from killing. This means that the ethical is not and "no longer can be" ordered by the difference between "do not eat" or "do not kill," "do not eat man or animal" or between the human and inhuman others; rather, ethics comes into question at every instance that something (some word or some substance) passes the frontier of the mouth—or the eye or the ear, as metonymies of the mouth (rather than parts of a face). Ethics thus is ordered by one rule alone: *il faut bien manger.*

When Derrida offers "eating well" as the rule of the senses, eye (*oeil*) and ear (*oreille*) are made mouths. "All the 'senses' in general" become orifices (114). This orification of face, eye, and ear both translates Levinas's account of the face as a word or a saying (the saying of "Thou shalt not kill") and radicalizes it by acknowledging that, insofar as the face speaks, it participates in the constellation of "eat-speak-interiorize"—a constellation that precludes the distinction between an injunction against killing the neighbor and an injunction against killing in general.

Furthermore, if the ethical dilemma had been understood through the formula "speak or kill," once speaking is understood as orification ("eat-speak-interiorize"), the opposition "speak or kill" becomes indeterminate. In fact, Derrida's reading suggests that, as soon as the ethical frontier was determined by the face as word ("Thou shalt not kill"), the face already will have been a mouth and the ethical frontier already will have become "the edge of the orifices (of orality)." By recognizing the limitation of Levinasian ethics to be its reliance on the face as speaking face, by opening the Levinasian face and considering the face as an opening—an orifice—Derrida indicates a more radical disruption of humanism.

EATING—SPEAKING—NONSENSE (DELEUZE)

When Derrida dismantles "speak or kill" as the foundation of ethicality, he replaces it with the obligation to "eat well," an imperative that acknowledges the inextinguishable violence that remains a part of nourishment and hospitality both. Ethics understood in this manner involves both a refusal to sanction violence and the recognition that its demand is a violent one. Thus, if responsibility emerges in the constellation "eat-speak-interiorize," we are left with the inevitable possibility that eating and speaking will be irresponsible.

Gilles Deleuze explores this possibility of eating badly or of not eating in *The Logic of Sense*.[5] Turning first to Lewis Carroll and then to Melanie Klein and Antonin Artaud, Deleuze identifies two modes of nonsense (or literature) and distinguishes between a literature of the face and a literature of the mouth. On the one hand, he describes a nonsense of face and figure, of the surface, which he associates with Carroll's punning and play; on the other hand, he demarcates a nonsense of depths and orifices, which he associates with Artaud's snapping, grinding, gasping, and swallowing. While both modes are linked to questions of responsibility, to the question of whether it is good to eat and whether one can eat the good, for Deleuze, the opposition between the face and the mouth (surface and depth) remains apparently untroubled.[6] Nevertheless, Deleuze's effort at describing a schizoid literature, or a literature of the mouth, is also an account of ethics and rhetoric.

For Deleuze, Carroll's *Alice in Wonderland* and *Through the Looking Glass* negotiate a singular opposition, at once logical, ethical, and nonsensical: "you either eat what is presented to you, *or* you are presented to what you eat" (*Logic of Sense*, 23). At stake in Carroll's work might be life and death, the life and death of one who needs nourishment as well as the life and death of the food (whether animal or vegetable) one eats or refuses. This opposition, however, is far from simple. It is a matter of presences and presentation, a sovereign subject's acceptance of a gift, and the risk that, as soon as one becomes a sovereign (among others), one will become the subject of another, that is, one will become the subject of the very gift presented. In the case of Alice's coronation dinner, which appears in *Through the Looking Glass,* as soon as the meal—whether a leg of mutton or a plate of pudding—is brought to table, the chain of presentations already has begun. Eating—as the illustrations make abundantly clear—is a face-to-face operation. Indeed, it is the face, the play of faces in which Alice must "face" a cut of meat a bit too large for her to handle or cut into the pudding that addresses her, that leaves her speaking to her food rather than eating it. To eat is then to eat badly, guiltily, and, in Alice's case, against the orders of the other queens, whose power comes into question. And yet to speak, to respect the other insofar as the other has a face, is to remain hungry and powerless, both. But the alternative to this opposition, far from providing nourishment, far from dissociating eating and guilt, far from freeing speech from violence, instead turns words into things that get stuck in the throat or caught in one's teeth.

It is this second mode that Deleuze associates with orality. Deleuze locates orality in the language and the nonsense of the schizophrenic-paranoid position, which is to say, in Artaud's performances and in Melanie Klein's accounts of infancy. Deleuze begins the section of *The Logic of Sense* devoted to orality with the "unforgettable picture Melanie Klein painted" of the nursing infant's "theater of terror" (187), and he goes on to describe the system of "introjection-projection-reintrojection" that makes up this theater (whether of cruelty or infancy) in which bodies, the mother's body above all, are divided into bite-size pieces and in which the question of eating the good emerges. The drama that Deleuze describes involves not only violence against the mother but violence against all that one has ingested, or might have ingested, of her. As he explains:

> Orality, the mouth and the breast, are initially bottomless depths [*profondeurs sans fonds*]. Not only are the breast and the entire body of the mother split apart into a good and a bad object, but they are aggressively emptied, slashed to pieces, broken into crumbs and alimentary morsels. The introjection of these partial objects into the body of the infant is accompanied by a projection of aggressiveness onto these internal objects,

and by a re-introjection of these objects into the maternal body. Thus, introjected morsels are like poisonous, persecuting, explosive, and toxic substances threatening the child's body from within and being endlessly reconstituted inside the mother's body. The necessity of a perpetual re-introjection is the result of this. The entire system of introjection and projection is a communication of bodies in, and through, depth [*en profondeur, par profondeur*].

(187/218; translation modified)

In this system, introjection is made possible by an aggressive attack on the mother's body, one that breaks this body apart into "alimentary morsels." Yet, once these morsels are introjected, the infant that bears them becomes the object of its own destructive aggression, the object of the very aggression that initially it had directed at the mother.[7] Because the body and the breast of the mother can be "scooped out" (to use Klein's idiom) or torn apart, because even what appears "good" may be only a deceptive surface, the possibility of the good, and more specifically the possibility of introjecting the good object, is left in question.

Thus, two forms of mouthwork emerge within Kleinian psychoanalysis: the *orality* of the schizoid-paranoid position, its acts of introjection in which everything is torn apart, torn down, and sent into the hollow abyss, and the *vocality* of the depressive position that substitutes identification for the system of introjection-projection and responds to and suffers from the inaccessibility, the inedibility, of the good object.[8] Deleuze aims both to trace the emergence of the depressive position within the paranoid-schizophrenic position and to distinguish paranoid-schizophrenic orality from melancholic vocality. He aims to understand the schizophrenic not merely as one who has lost his voice but as one who resists and destroys the voice, one for whom "everything is communication of bodies in depth" (192). Yet at stake in Deleuze's account of these positions—and of the relation between orifice and voice, noise and language—is whether the good can be eaten.

Indeed, the question that orients Deleuze's examination of the relation between schizoid-paranoid and depressive positions is whether "the 'good object' (the good breast) can be considered as introjected in the same way as the bad object is" (188). As I suggested earlier, the initial division of the body/breast into good and bad opens onto a paranoia that the good may not be good. Thus the infant or schizophrenic "tears apart" the good object for fear that it is deception and that, beneath its apparent goodness (beneath the surface), evil and destruction lurk. In Klein's analysis, this means that every introjection is an introjection of the bad object; the good cannot be introjected. This is because, as Deleuze explains,

> Melanie Klein herself showed that the splitting of the object into good and bad in the case of introjection is duplicated through a fragmentation [*se double d'un morcellement*] which the good object is unable to resist, since one can never be sure that the good object does not conceal a bad piece. Furthermore, every piece is bad in principle (that is, persecuting and persecutor); only the wholesome [*l'intègre*], the complete, is good; but introjection, to be precise, does not allow what is wholesome to subsist. This is why the equilibrium proper to the schizoid position and its relation to the subsequent depressive position do not seem capable of coming about from the introjection of a good object as such, and they must be revised.
>
> (188/219; translation modified)

In demonstrating that the good is never introjected, Deleuze promises a revisionary history of the depths. Whereas Klein claims that "from the beginning the ego introjects objects 'good' and 'bad'" (116), Deleuze is concerned with recognizing that the schizoid position does not oppose the introjection of good and bad objects, because there is no introjection of good objects, because introjection necessarily involves an object that always is a *bad* part object (even when it appears to be a good one). This impossible introjection of the good leads to the schizoid position that opposes the introjection of "bad partial objects—introjected and projected, toxic and excremental, oral and anal"—to nonintrojection, that is, becoming "an organism without parts, a body without organs, with neither mouth nor anus, having given up all introjection or projection and being complete, at this price" (*Logic*, 188). In lieu of the risky introjection of objects, there remains instead the wholesome and the complete, the body without organs or orifices that allows no entry and resists every division.[9] The body without organs—the sealing-off of the body in order to protect the good—puts into relief the risk and radicality of Derrida's notion of responsibility as eating well, which is to say, an introjection that displaces subjection.

Responsibility is not the abandonment of introjection. It allows for neither the beautiful soul nor the body without organs. Rather, it assumes that "the Good can also be eaten. And it must be eaten well" ("'Eating,'" 115). Responsibility entails eating the inedible as inedible, which is to say, eating the good. We are left with the question of how this responsibility (as orality) differs from the schizophrenic modes of not eating or eating badly that Deleuze describes.

In *The Logic of Sense*, the quasi-opposition—between introjection and the body without organs (rather than introjection of bad *and* good objects)—leads to two distinct figurations of depth, two styles of schizophrenic language, and "two nonsenses of pure noise" between which, Deleuze claims, "everything takes place" (189/220): "The nonsense of the body and of the splintered word, and the nonsense of the block of bodies or of inarticulate words . . . the same duality of complementary poles is found again in schizophrenia between reiterations and perseverations, between jaw-grinding and catatonia, for example. The first bears witness to internal objects and to the bodies they break into pieces—the same bodies which break them to pieces; the second *manifests* the body without organs" (189/220–221). Orality names these oppositional languages of schizophrenia, a language that breaks objects and is broken by bodies (rather than expressing or denoting them) and a language that "manifests the body without organs" (as a mode of performativity).[10] In this sense, orality—and the depths on which it opens—does not describe the good or an approach to the good (for the good cannot be eaten); neither does it describe the depressive position (as it does in Klein and Freud).[11] Instead, the good object—the "complete object" and in this sense a synthesis of the two schizophrenic poles (introjection/projection and body without organs, id and ego)—belongs to a placeless place: it belongs not in the depths but on high; it is the *super*ego, the *surmoi*.

Just as the schizoid-paranoid position yields a split (figured as the acceptance or refusal of introjection/projection), so, too, is the manic-depressive position also split; in it, one identifies with the devoured and devouring objects (the good as lost, introjected, and unintrojectable, one version of which Alice's "gasp" in response to the pudding's speech might represent) *and* with the complete, inaccessible object, at once unharmed and wounded, present and absent, and, as a principle of nondivision, both indestructible and always already lost.[12] The good object (absent-present) becomes the object of a voice (*fort-da*).

Here the voracious (schizoid-paranoid) and the vociferous (depressive) mouths cross. The sounds of voracious orality (and anality)—"clappings, crackings, gnashings, cracklings, explosions, the shattered sounds of internal objects, and also the inarticulate howls-breaths (*cris-souffles*) of the body without organs which respond to them" (*Logic of Sense*, 193/225)—become the material and the model for a language (denotation, signification, manifestation) that, like the good object, is always already there and yet remains inaccessible or ungraspable. In this respect, the voice is equivocal and, to the extent that it equivocates, also is unequivocal: "to the extent that it denotes the lost object, one does not know what the voice denotes; one does not know what it signifies since it signifies the order of preexisting entities; one does not know what it manifests since it manifests withdrawal into its principle or silence. It is at once the object, the law of the loss, and the loss itself . . . . It is no longer a noise, but not yet a language" (194/225).[13] Deleuze's revision of Kleinian psychoanalysis accounts for the simultaneity and difference of voraciousness and vociferousness in relation to the good. The voice (the vociferous mouth) "steals" the "sonorous, *prevocal* system" of orality (the voracious mouth [194/225]). The good object as lost object is not what one eats but what never can be eaten, what introjection destroys. The good object—at once absent and present (like a language), always already and never to be reached (like death)—remains inedible (even when one eats it or offers it to be eaten). It is the voice.

MOUTH WITHOUT FACE (NANCY)

There is—there once was—a mouth that opens and says: I write, I mask myself, I fabulate, I am my body, I am a man—always inextricably uttering: I take refuge in myself or I distinguish myself.

Ego says, or say, neither the presence nor the absence neither the structure, nor the feign of the subject—but the utterly singular experience of the mouth that opens and closes [itself] at once. A tongue moves there.[14]

—JEAN-LUC NANCY, *EGO SUM*

Deleuze reminds us that, for Artaud, "being, which is nonsense, has teeth," and we can say that, in " 'Eating Well,' " Derrida demonstrates that ethics has teeth. The interview raises the question of whether ethics, like Being, is nonsense—a plunge into the orificial depths. The primary orality—or primary orificiality (in which the mouth opens and disarticulates the face)—that Derrida offers as the disruption of ontology and ethics recalls Jean-Luc Nancy's analysis of the radically open and linguistic character of subjectivity. Indeed, in *Ego sum*, Nancy demonstrates that the mouth is the occasion of a constitutive disruption of subjectivity, that is, the emergence of the so-called subject in and as this disruption.

While it is the force of *Ego sum* to articulate the performative status of the cogito, in the book's final section, entitled "Unum Quid," Nancy recasts Cartesian subjectivity according to a convulsive chasm—which is also a chiasm: the opening of the mouth and the saying of the ego (*ego, ego sum, ego existo*) are mutually constitutive.

In his explication of Descartes's second and sixth mediations, Nancy suggests that mind and body are inextricably and inexplicably articulated in the opening of a mouth that belongs to no one.[15] Thus if, for Levinas, first philosophy is ethics ordered by the face of the other that always takes precedence over the I—and leaves the "I" a "me" who responds, for Descartes, in Nancy's reading, first philosophy precedes the "I" as well as the "me." To the extent that there is a first philosophy, it issues through the mouth: "*Unum quid*, a something neither-mind-nor-body opens the mouth [*ouvre la bouche*] and says or conceives: *ego sum*. But this is still to say too much. *Unum quid* does not have a mouth that it can manipulate and open, no more than it has an intelligence that it can exert to reflect on itself. But something—*unum quid*—opens itself (it has therefore the appearance or the form of a mouth), and this opening articulates itself (it has therefore the look of a discourse and so of thought), and this articulated opening, in an extreme contraction, forms: *I*" (157). In attempting to represent this anoriginal emergence, Nancy is concerned with differentiating between a consideration of the mouth that would preexist this articulation, a mouth that therefore would belong to (and serve as the metonymy of) a face *and* a mouth that would be an initial opening, one that would mark the opening or incompletion of the "I." It is this second mouth, the mouth without a face, that Nancy associates with the emergence (and constitutive interruption) of the Cartesian subject. After Paul Valéry, he calls this mouth—which is "neither a substance nor a figure"—"buccal":

> *Bucca* is not *os*, but a later and more trivial term. *Os, oris*, mouth of orality [*bouche d'oralité*] is the face [*visage*] itself, understood as the metonymy of the mouth that it surrounds, bears, and renders visible, the passageway of all sorts of substances, above all the ethereal substance of discourse. But *bucca* is puffed-up cheeks; it is the movement, the contraction and/or distension of breathing, of eating, of spitting, or of speaking. Buccality is more primitive than orality. Nothing has taken place yet; nothing has been spoken there yet. But an opening—unstable and mobile—forms at the instant of speaking. For the instant, one discerns nothing: *ego* does not mean anything, *ego* only opens this cavity. Every mouth is a shadow mouth, and the true mouth also opens onto this darkness, and as this darkness, so as to form its inner hold [*for*].[16]
>
> (162)

In distinguishing between buccality and orality, *bucca* and *os*, Nancy distinguishes between figure and nonfigure and hence links figure and face (*visage*). For Nancy, the difference between buccality and orality is not accounted for by the history of the Latin language (*bucca* came into use later than *os*) but rather by the difference between a mouth that is a figure, for which all activities (including eating, crying, spitting, etc.) are metonymies of speaking, and the mouth that is an opening; the difference between the face as metonymy of the mouth—a mouth that belongs to someone, to a subject who speaks—and the mouth that belongs to no one, the mouth that becomes a mouth in the opening of a one who—opened, disfigured—has no face.

Bucca is the more primitive term in two senses. It signifies an underdeveloped or faceless cavity in which eating-speaking-breathing-spitting, incorporation and introjection, contraction and distension, are undifferentiated; and it is more originary, indicating a mouth before the ego, a mouth that does not communicate but is formed by the word "ego," a mouth prior to the articulated subject (always already the speaking subject) and through which the articulation occurs, a mouth prior to signification, prior to the face, prior to the eye, except insofar as the eye is a mouth.[17] The buccal mouth withholds the face in its movement (breathing, eating, yawning, speaking). Devouring (indeed, engulfing) the sur-face, buccality is the opening that orders Derrida's *il faut bien manger*, as it indicates a linguistic predicament irreducible to figure.

To the extent that Nancy's account of buccality requires that narratives of origin be revised, it also recalls Melanie Klein's displacement of psychoanalytic schema ordered by stages with an account of positions figured in relation to the maternal breast (paranoid-schizoid, depressive) and Deleuze's account of dynamic genesis. Nancy's reading of Descartes indicates a movement (and an implicitly erotic movement) that precedes the oral stage. If readers of Freud have interpreted this movement—the passage between the infant cry to the encircling of a nourishing breast, the opening of the mouth that detaches itself from the breast, the smile and swollen cheeks of satisfaction—as the oral stage, Nancy reads Descartes to show what these readers forget: there is no oral stage. As Nancy writes: "The Freudian child (I do not say the subject) does not start off [*s'initie*] in an 'oral stage.' It opens [*il s'ouvre*] first of all in a mouth, the open mouth of a cry but also the mouth closed around a breast to which it is attached by an identification older than any identification with a figure, and the half-open mouth, detaching itself from the breast in a first smile, a first mimicry whose future is thought. The mouth is the opening of the *Ego*, *Ego* is the opening of the mouth" (162). It is not simply that Nancy here shows that buccality precedes orality, as Freud conceived of it, but also that he turns to Freud's account of autoeroticism in *Three Essays on Sexuality* to show, as Laplanche and Pontalis also show, that Freud "no more speaks here of an oral *stage* or organization than he does of an anal one" (Laplanche and Pontalis, 287).[18] In returning to and recasting Freud's essay, Nancy revises the history of subjectivity, a revision that involves the figuration and refiguration of origins, the possibility and impossibility of an autobiography of the mouth. He also signals a relation to the other that precedes language, precedes naming, precedes the face, and precedes even passive responsibility.

Nancy's fable of the opening of the mouth indicates the existence of a rhetoric of the mouth as a rhetoric before or beyond figure. Moreover, as a mouth prior to language, a mouth that opens and closes around a breast—"attached by an identification prior to any figure"—it also indicates an ethics prior to any face. Responsibility ordered by the injunction *il faut bien manger* emerges as buccality, but what, therefore, can we say of rhetoric, a rhetoric that is no longer beholden to face or to figure but to the mouth?

In *Le toucher: Jean-Luc Nancy*, Derrida makes explicit the extent to which *Ego sum* is a theory of rhetoric. He understands Nancy's analysis of Descartes as a response to the question: "How do two incommensurabilities, of psychic thought and of the body, unite [*s'unissent-elles*] in an expanse [*étendue*] that is itself incommensurable?" (41). In other words, he asks how something that has neither figure nor measure can unite and unite in its enduring dispersion. The answer is "the mouth . . . the originary spacing of a mouth that opens *itself* [*s'ouvre*] between the lips, at the breast of the other, within the other [*aux seins de l'autre*]" (41).[19] Thus Derrida translates Nancy's analysis as a fundamentally ethical account of the subject that coincides with a nonfigural rhetoric.

Derrida is particularly interested in the gesture by which Nancy acknowledges that this mouth is not initially my own and opens (as) the mouth of the other in its first birth cry. The mouth opens—in surrounding the breast [*seins*] of the other—within [*aux seins*] the other. By "scooping out" the breast in the doubling of *sein* as "breast" and *aux seins* as "within" (as womb or entrails) and by recalling that "*sein*" means both "breast" "and womb," Derrida undertakes to return the mother—who remains unnamed in Nancy's account of origins and primary buccality—to this discussion, yet he does so by hollowing her out.

In unveiling a metonymic relation between the part object (breast) and the whole (mother), in remembering her as an opening, and in insisting that the mouth without a face (as her sex) should return a name (the name of the mother), Derrida undertakes to re-member the other whom one eats, to remember that one eats the mother and participates in a relation that, at this "stage," "is marked by the meanings of *eating* and *being eaten*" (Laplanche and Pontalis, 287).[20] These acts of re-membrance issue in the name of responsibility, and Derrida's recollection of the unnamed mother in Nancy's essay responds to the imperative *il faut bien manger* ("one must begin to *identify* with the other who is to be assimilated, interiorized, understood ideally" [*Le toucher*, 115]). Thus he elaborates:

> The mouth . . . stands [*se tient*] between the nonspeaking mouth (*bucca*, without the orality of the *os*) and a mouth that, half-open, begins to detach itself from the breast [*se détacher du sein*] even before the "oral stage." From one to the other, the opening of the mouth responds to a movement of lips—the lips of the other, those of the mother in birth, then my own (if I can say this [?])—but always as close as possible to the birth of the world and to a mother whose name Nancy never pronounces . . . . Despite the obvious and explicit reference to the mother (at the moment of birth and of nursing), despite the reference to the edges of the orifice, to the lips that open the passage to the newborn—the lips between the legs of the mother as the lips of the child who emits its first cry—despite the reference to the breasts that open the infant mouth, the word "mother" does not appear.
>
> (41)

Whereas Nancy's only account of the mouth attached and detached from the breast coincides with a thorough displacement of the oral stage—a reminder that there is no oral stage in Freud and that the infantile sexuality that has been categorized as a stage instead indicates an opening (and what he will call a "spacing")—Derrida understands Nancy merely as claiming a more originary sexual stage in which the child forces the mother open from within, in which the child is this opening, as the mouth opened by a cry. Twice, Derrida points out that the "word" or the "name" (are these the same?) "mother" [*mère*] does not appear in *Ego sum*, even as her body—and the metonymies of her body—remain an important reference (Nancy: "It opens first of all in a mouth, the open mouth of a cry but also the mouth closed around a breast"). Derrida describes buccality as an encounter of more than one mouth and the mouth as more than one; buccality is a relation to the other prior to the self that is ordered by the mouth and not the face.

The question that Derrida addresses to *Ego sum* concerns the recurring reflexive verbs—"*s'ouvre*," "*se distend*," "*s'espace*." If there is no self or referent prior to the opening or spacing of the mouth, the reflexivity of the opening describes an event of initial relation to an other. As Derrida explains, "The nonplace of this place is also opened by the other. *At once* autoaffected and heteroaffected, uniting the two formations *like* two lips, it lets it[self] open [*il se laisse ouvrir*]" (42; emphasis added). The mouth precedes the division between autoaffection and heteroaffection, self and other, yet it also is the figure of their singular-plural relation. Their unity is like the unity of the two lips that make up the mouth. Thus if the mouth (two lips) is the figure of the mouth (the unity of auto- and heteroformation, the unity of "this sex which is not one"), it is this mouth that "renders the figure of the mouth prior to every figure as face (orality) and prior to every identification as a (maternal) figure" (43). The mouth is a figure and a figure of figure prior to figure. But what does this mean? What would it mean to approach figure according to the mouth—not in order to abandon or free ourselves from the failures and destructions that figural reading exposes but rather in order to initiate an exorbitant response, in order to unhinge an antihumanist, deconstructive rhetoric from its enduring attachment to the giving and taking of faces?

Buccality—or the rhetoric of the buccal mouth—at once translates the ethical order "il faut bien manger" and displaces the still "human, all too human" figure of even the most radically nonhumanist accounts of rhetoric, that is, Paul de Man's rhetoric of facing and defacement. Before turning, in conclusion, to give one example of how figural reading might be recast according to the opening mouth, I want briefly to show how Nancy makes this turn possible, even as he seems to demonstrate its impossibility.

At the very moment that Nancy undertakes to figure a mouth without a face, he appears to return the face—as figure—that the fable of the mouth seemed to have displaced: "Imagine a mouth without face (that is to say, once again, the structure of the mask: the opening of holes and the mouth that opens in the middle of the eye; the place of vision, of theory traversed—open and closed simultaneously, separated by an uttering)—a mouth without face then contracts (itself) in a ring around the sound: I. 'You' [*Tu*] have this experience all the time, each time that you utter 'ego' or conceive it in your mind, each time—it happens to you all the time—that you form the *o* of the first person (*first*, before which there is no one): ego cogito existo. An O forms the immediate buckle of your experience" (157).[21] The passage opens in an apostrophe, an address to the reader ("Imagine a mouth without a face"). If Nancy endeavors to give figure to what has no proper figure—if he issues a call to imagine this opening, to imagine a mask in lieu of a face—what we have here is the recovery of a signifying chain that only can lead us back to a drama of faces and defacement, of prosopopoeia as the figure of figure. This passage reintroduces the rhetoric of figures (and face) at the instant when this rhetoric would seem to have been recast.

Yet this passage, which opens in an apostrophe, also ends in a strange dismantling of the figure on which it seems to rely. The "o" is not merely an act of facing or defacement; rather, it is the contraction of a mouth without a face. The "o of the first person" is the "o" of *ego cogito existo,* the "o" of the mouth in its utterance and opening, the "o" of the zero (rather than the two, the you) that precedes the first person. It is also the mark of an apostrophe and hence the mark of a turn away, a turn away from one discourse in order to address someone else, in this case, the "you" ("it happens to you all the time") who is the "I" or the "o," the "you" who says "o": the mouth without a face.[22]

BUCCAL READING (DE MAN)

> Buccal space. One of the most curious inventions of the living thing. House of the tongue. Kingdom of reflexes and of different durations. Discontinuous gustatory regions. Compound machines. There are fountains and furniture.
> —PAUL VALÉRY, "BOUCHE"

If, in "Eating Well," Derrida can be understood to "de-face" ethics, the reading that he performs in the interview would seem to have as its model or its match those rhetorical accounts of language and literature that understand prosopopoeia as a master trope—whether of lyric (de Man), autobiography (de Man), narrative (Miller), or witnessing. In each of these theories, facing is tied inextricably to defacement. Literature or language is understood as the donation of face or sense to the inanimate, dead, or faceless, the donation of figure to what has no figure (sense or shape), thus indicating not the priority of the human and the conceit of infinite appropriation and self-discovery (everywhere!) but rather the deflating acknowledgment that our understanding or sense is conditioned by acts of facing, which is to say, that we are deprived of sense, a privation that figures sometimes help us to forget. Yet I wonder whether this description of language in terms of facing and defacement, that is, in terms of figures, itself masks other accounts of literary negativity. In other words, does the rhetoric of figures—the discourse that has perhaps gone the greatest lengths to separate literature and language from powers of restoration or humanization and that (along with psychoanalysis) has demonstrated the unmaintainability of distinctions between the human and the inhuman, the living and the nonliving—cover over (by facing) a defacement that does not pass by way of the face? An absence of the face that the articulation of face and figure in de Man's work seems to mask?

In "Wordsworth and the Victorians," one of the essays in which he most clearly explains this donation of faces, de Man sets out to read the Blessed Babe passage in *The Prelude* as an allegory of autoformation and specifically to explain how an infant nursing in its mother's arms can become a passionate poet. In some sense, the answer to this question is "poetry" itself, or figure. Just as Nancy describes the opening of the subject as the opening of the mouth that belongs to no one, and just as Derrida sets out to demonstrate the belatedness, the secondariness of the opening—this opening that opens in an opening—de Man considers the possibility of a relation to the mother, a relation that is "possible" only through poetry and language.

The infant is able to emerge as a loved subject, as someone who can appear in his mother's eyes, rather than as the hungering thing at her breast through what Rei Terada has called a "fictive transfer of properties." Two models of relation—between the infant nursing and its mother's breast and the face-to-face or eye-to-eye of recognition—cross in the memorable displacement in the poem of the breast by the eye.

> Blessed the infant babe—
> For with my best conjectures I would trace
> The progress of our being—blest the babe
> Nursed in his mother's arms, the babe who sleeps
> Upon his mother's breast, who, when his soul
> Claims manifest kindred with an earthly soul,
> Doth gather passion from his mother's eye.
> (PRELUDE, 2:237–243)

De Man reads this displacement—as the inscription of an eye in the place of the breast, the cutting off of one source of sustenance/dependence and the substitution of another—to introduce (and to represent) a totalizing system of figure. Yet it strikes me that these lines—which never mention a face—might instead render another, less symmetrical, perhaps even less apparently restorative scene in which the child draws and drinks not only from the mother's breast but from her eye. It is this relation—the mouthing of the eye, a relation that takes place (to recall Derrida's interview) at the orifices—that does not simply designate a face but indicates the confusion of speaking and sucking, claiming and crying, indicates the opening of the system. In other words, I would like to suggest that the figures that de Man understands to indicate both a totalizing understanding and no understanding at all may actually initiate another logic and another rhetoric. Rather than reading this passage as the establishment—through a displacement or figure—of a scene of recognition, one can consider it as witness to a fundamentally distorted and distorting relation ordered not by the eye but by the mouth, not by seeing but by, in this case, eating—or drinking.

The possibility of this reading becomes even more explicit in the apparently less interesting (and thus much less read) 1850 version of the poem, in which the infant's "active verbal deed" ("Claims manifest kindred") of 1805 is displaced by (or remembered as) an ingestion.

> Blest the infant Babe
> (For with my best conjecture I would trace
> Our Being's earthly progress), blest the Babe,
> Nursed in his Mother's arms, who sinks to sleep
> Rocked on his Mother's breast; who with his soul
> Drinks in the feelings of his Mother's eye!
> (2:233–238)

Here, "drinks" takes the place of "claims"—the verb that allows de Man to affirm the performative aspect of figure and the linguistic condition (which is also a displacement) of self-consciousness. If the substitution renders more explicit the crossing of souls and bodies through which the infant incorporates the "feelings" (at once touch and passion) of his mother, through which the infant comes to feel and in feeling (more than other men) becomes a poet, this consolidated narrative relies on the mouth—or the eye as a mouth, the eating eye—in order to account for poetic origins.

Wordsworth's revision might allow us to consider the "conjecture" through which poetry effects autobiography in its relation to other "-jections"—and the constellation of "introjection-projection-reintrojection" through which Melanie Klein, for example, has described the infant's relation to its mother. Here, the child (like a boat) is rocked—moved back and forth or side to side—in order that he may fall—indeed sink, drown—into sleep. But beyond the horizontal and vertical movements through which an infant might enter into self-consciousness—into a rhythm of consciousness and unconsciousness—these lines describe an active nourishment: the infant's active appropriation—through the mouth—of its mother's feelings, as if they were a fluid that could be drunk. This drinking assumes the materialization of passion (more a seventeenth-century than a nineteenth-century notion), and it consolidates "claiming" and "gathering," which are displaced in the strange and surreal scene of drinking the eye (as if tears were a nourishment) and of a drinking eye (as one drinks in a scene). If this passage can be read to describe the liquification of the mother through figure, it also accounts for her liquidation—and thus becomes another way of characterizing her status. As several critics (above all Andrzej Warminski and Cathy Caruth) have shown, Wordsworth's mother is as a surface onto which the infant projects a face and through which the child obtains a face. Read as an account of mouthing, rather than facing, however, this passage may no longer serve as an exemplary occasion in which the substitution of eye and breast assumes a face and the totalizing system of figure (as de Man suggests). Rather, it might indicate a becoming mouth—an opening or a contraction—in which kissing, drinking, and crying may become confused but do not emerge as metonymies of speaking or of the face. This constitutive defacement, this opening (*béance*) of the face and the question of eating well that it seems to evoke, aligns the origins of language and poetic language not with a facing but with a mouthing. If Wordsworth shows that poetry (and autobiography) begins with the buccal mouth (rather than the face), it is Samuel Beckett who demonstrates what this means, what it means to produce a work without figure and without face, a mouthwork.

Beckett's "Not I" is a dramatic monologue—with two actors:

the one a mouth, the other, a silent, shrouded body. Between the opening of the mouth and the deformation of the body, there is a work without face and without figure, a work of testimony and violence, an autobiography of buccality:

MOUTH:
... out ... into this world ... this world ... tiny little thing ... before its time ... in a godfor- ... what? ... girl? ... yes ... tiny little girl ... into this ... out into this ... before her time ... godforsaken hole called ... called ... no matter ... parents unknown ... unheard of ... he having vanished ... this air ... no sooner having buttoned up his breeches ... she similarly ... eight months later ... almost to the tick ... so no love ... spared that ... no love such as normally vented on the ... speechless infant ... in the home ...
(216)

NOTES

Thanks to Steven Miller for encouraging me to take up this line of thinking.

1. " 'Eating Well' " is Derrida's response to the question "Who comes after the subject" that Jean-Luc Nancy posed to nineteen French philosophers; the interview is reprinted in *Points ... Interviews, 1974–1994*. All English references are to *Who Comes After the Subject?*; all French references are to *Points de suspension*. In the passage that I cite, the trope of degrees (e.g., "to the extent that ...") makes manifest the ways in which a certain calculation endures here also.

2. Derrida aligns "virility" with "generosity" (as a mode of "fraternity") in *Le toucher*—a work to which I will return: "Pour le dire trop vite, ce qui dans la mot 'générosité' me gêne, comme dans le mot 'fraternité,' c'est au fond la même chose. Dans les deux cas, on salue quelque généalogie, quelque filiation, un principe de 'naissance,' qu'elle soit ou non, comme on le croit d'ailleurs souvent, 'naturelle.' Et surtout on privilégie une 'virilité' " (35–36).

3. On the naked eye, see Levinas, *Difficult Freedom*, 8. See also Derrida's discussion of "Thou shalt not kill" in "The Animal That Therefore I Am": "What does this bottomless gaze [of the animal] offer to my

sight? What does it 'say' to me, demonstrating quite simply the naked truth of every gaze, given that the truth *allows me to see and be seen* through the eyes of the other, in the *seeing* and not just *seen* eyes of the other?" (381).

4. Derrida explains his use of "animals" (as a multiplicity of species) rather than the monolithic "the animal" to designate every nonhuman being in "The Animal That Therefore I am." For another account of these sacrificial structures, one that has more in common with Derrida's than regularly is acknowledged, see Giorgio Agamben's discussion of "bare life" in *Homo Sacer.*

5. Where in-text citations of this text include two sets of page numbers, the first refers to the translation, the second to the French original, *Logique du sens.*

6. This is not exactly the case in *A Thousand Plateaus.* In that book, Deleuze, together with Félix Guattari, treats "faciality" in a rather different sense, whereby the face is made up of holes or openings; it is the orifices that make up—that open up and to a certain extent destroy—the face they figure. In this essay, I will focus exclusively on Deleuze's early study *The Logic of Sense* (1969). As a result, a more detailed discussion of faciality will have to await another occasion.

7. On the double, see Klein, "Mourning." This "double" is what Deleuze calls the "simulacrum" (*Logic of Sense,* 187).

8. The tearing apart and internalization of the parent—initially the mother, eventually both parents—in Klein apparently translates the paternal feast as Freud describes it in *Totem and Taboo.* If what is at stake in all these texts is a history of depths, it is also the case that they all rely on an originary fiction: the image of a theater (in Klein) or the anthropological-anthropophagic fiction of *Totem and Taboo.*

9. This is not a simple opposition between two processes but the body as introjection-projection machine and the body without organs. Deleuze—with Guattari—approaches psychoanalysis's failure to recognize the body without organs (BwO) from a slightly different perspective in *Plateaus*: "The error of psychoanalysis was to understand BwO phenomena as regressions, projections, phantasies, in terms of an image of the body. As a result, it only grasps the flipside of the BwO and immediately substitutes family photos, childhood memories, and part-objects for a worldwide intensity map. It understands nothing about the egg nor about indefinite articles nor about the contemporaneousness of a continually self-constructing milieu" (165).

10. Here, we must acknowledge Abraham and Torok's work on the

crypt even if a more sustained examination of their analyses of melancholia and of the Wolf Man, as well as Derrida's many analyses of their work, will have to be postponed. I provide some preliminary suggestions for the direction such an inquiry could take in my "Albeit Eating."

11. "It is always a mouth which speaks; but the sound is no longer the noise of a body which eats—a pure orality—in order to become the manifestation of a subject expressing itself" (*Logic of Sense*, 181).

12. One would want to compare this with what Blanchot calls "disaster," particularly with regard to its topography.

13. Again, compare Blanchot on "the fleeting silence of the countless cry" (*The Unavowable Community*, 47).

14. "Il est, il était une fois une bouche qui s'ouvre et qui dit: j'écris, je me masque, je fabule, je suis mon corps, je suis un homme, et toujours cet énoncé inextricable: *je me retranche,* ou: *je me distingue. Ego* ne dit, ou ne dis ni la présence, ni l'absence, ni la structure, ni la feinte du sujet—mais la très singulière épreuve de la bouche qui s'ouvre et se ferme à la fois. Une langue y bouge." All translations of Nancy's *Ego sum* are my own.

15. In the Second Meditation, Descartes writes: "So after considering everything very thoroughly, I must finally conclude that this proposition, *I am, I exist,* is necessarily true whenever it is put forward by me or conceived by my mind" (*Meditations,* 17). In the Sixth Meditation, in accounting for the relation between mind and body, he explains: "I am not merely present in my body as a sailor is present in a ship, but that I am very closely joined and, as it were, intermingled with it, so that I and the body form a unit [*unum quid*]" (56).

16. *For* also can be translated as "heart of hearts," which we would want to analyze in light of all that Nancy has written about and experienced, in particular in a reading of his *L'intrus.* Moreover, *Fors* names Derrida's introduction to Abraham and Torok's *The Wolfman's Magic Word*, a study of melancholic language as encryption that would, on another occasion, have to be read alongside Deleuze's analyses of schizophrenic language.

17. See Derrida, for example, on kissing eyes in the opening pages of *Le toucher.*

18. Laplanche and Pontalis, however, define the oral stage/phase as follows: "The first stage of libidinal development: sexual pleasure at this period is bound predominantly to that excitation of the oral cavity and lips which accompanies feeding. The activity of nutrition is the source of the particular meanings through which the object-relationship is expressed and organised; the love-relationship to the mother, for example, is marked by the meanings of *eating* and *being eaten*" (287).

19. Derrida's question draws its idiom from both *Ego sum* ("The immeasurable expanse [*étendue*] of thought is the opening of the mouth" [161]) and "Psyche," a fragment that Nancy devoted to Freud's posthumous and intentionally (even if not actually, given Nancy's readings) anti-Cartesian note: "*Psyche ist ausgedehnt, weiss nicht davon*" (The psyche is outstretched [*étendue*], without knowing it).

20. This is to suggest that Derrida is talking about the oral stage, except that what has been recognized as the oral stage (in Freud) may be recast as "buccal."

21. "Imagine une bouche sans visage (c'est-à-dire à nouveau la structure du *masque*: l'ouverture des trous, et la bouche qui s'ouvre au milieu de l'oeil; le lieu de la vision, de la théorie traversé ouvert et clos simultanément, diaphragmé d'une profération)—une bouche sans visage, donc, faisant l'anneau [ring] de sa contracture autour du bruit: *je*. 'Tu' fais cette expérience tous les jours, chaque fois que tu prononces ou que tu conçois dans ton esprit *ego*, chaque fois—cela t'arrive tous les jours—que tu formes l'*o* de la première (*première*, avant elle il n'y a rien) personne: ego cogito existo. Un O forme la boucle immédiate de ton expérience." Derrida responds to this passage in *Le toucher*: "Peut-on imaginer une étendue qui ne se touche pas? *Imaginer*, ce n'est pas penser. *Imaginer*, ce n'est pas connaître, certes, mais ce n'est en rien un rien de pensée ou de connaissance. Peut-on, si vous préférez, se *figurer* une étendue intouchable?—une étendue intelligible et sans corps" (237).

22. In response to Derrida's concern with the absence of the mother in Nancy's account of subjectivity and his alignment of this absence with the absence of the figure, the apostrophe makes evident that any account of the mouth without a face, any account of origins, returns the figure and the other (the you here addressed) but does so by remembering the other as a mouth without a face.

BIBLIOGRAPHY

Agamben, Giorgio. *Homo Sacer: Sovereign Power and Bare Life*. Stanford, Calif.: Stanford University Press, 1998.
Beckett, Samuel. "Not I." In *Collected Shorter Plays*, 213–233. New York: Grove, 1984.
Blanchot, Maurice. *The Unavowable Community*. Trans. Pierre Joris. New York: Station Hill, 1988.
Caruth, Cathy. "Past Recognition: Narrative Origins in Wordsworth

and Freud." In *Romanticism*, ed. Cynthia Chase, 98–112. London: Longman Publishing Group, 1993.

Deleuze, Gilles. *The Logic of Sense*. Trans. Mark Lester with Charles Stivale. Ed. Constantin V. Boundas. New York: Columbia University Press, 1990. Originally published as *Logique du sens* (Paris: Minuit, 1982).

Deleuze, Gilles and Félix Guattari. *A Thousand Plateaus: Capitalism and Schizophrenia*. Trans. Brian Massumi. Minneapolis: Minnesota University Press, 1987. Originally published as *Capitalisme et schizophrénie. Tome 2: Mille plateaux* (Paris: Minuit, 1980).

de Man, Paul. "Wordsworth and the Victorians." Chap. 5 in *The Rhetoric of Romanticism*. New York: Columbia University Press, 1984.

Derrida, Jacques. " 'Eating Well,' or the Calculation of the Subject: An Interview with Jacques Derrida." Trans. Peter Connor and Avital Ronell. In *Who Comes After the Subject?* 96–119. London: Routledge, 1991. Reprinted in *Points . . . Interviews, 1974–1994*, trans. Peggy Kamuf and others, ed. Elisabeth Weber, 255–287 (Stanford, Calif.: Stanford University Press, 1995).

———. "The Animal That Therefore I Am (More to Follow)." Trans. David Wills. *Critical Inquiry* 28, no. 2 (Winter 2001): 369–418. Originally published as "L'animal que donc je suis," in *L'animal autobiographique: Autour de Jacques Derrida*, 251–301 (Paris: Galilée, 1999).

———. "Freud and the Scene of Writing." In *Writing and Difference*, trans. Alan Bass, 196–231. Chicago: University of Chicago Press, 1978.

———. *Points de suspension*. Paris: Galilée, 1992.

———. *The Politics of Friendship*. Trans. George Collins. London: Verso, 1997.

———. *Le toucher: Jean-Luc Nancy*. Paris: Galilée, 1998.

Descartes, René. *Meditations on First Philosophy*. Trans. and ed. John Cottingham. Rev. ed. New York: Cambridge University Press, 1996.

Freud, Sigmund. *Three Essays on the Theory of Sexuality*. Trans. and ed. James Strachey. New York: Basic Books, 2000.

Guyer, Sara. "Albeit Eating: Toward an Ethics of Cannibalism." *Angelaki* 2, no. 1 (1995): 63–80.

Klein, Melanie. "Mourning and Its Relation to Manic Depressive States." Chap. 7 in *The Selected Melanie Klein*. Ed. Juliet Mitchell. England: Penguin, 1986.

Lacan, Jacques. *Écrits 1*. Trans. Bruce Fink. New York: Norton, 2002.

Laplanche, Jean and J.-B. Pontalis. "Oral Stage (or Phase)." In *The Language of Psychoanalysis*, trans. Donald Nicholson-Smith. New York: Norton, 1973.

Levinas, Emmanuel. *Difficult Freedom*. Trans. Sean Hand. Baltimore: Johns Hopkins University Press, 1997.

———. *Ethics and Infinity*. Trans. Richard A. Cohen. Pittsburgh: Duquesne University Press, 1985.

———. *Existence and Existents*. Trans. Alphonso Lingus. The Hague: Nijhoff, 1978.

———. *Time and the Other*. Trans. Richard A. Cohen. Pittsburgh: Duquesne University Press, 1987.

Nancy, Jean-Luc. *Ego sum*. Paris: Flammarion, 1979.

Nancy, Jean-Luc and Philippe Lacoue-Labarthe. *The Literary Absolute*. Trans. Philip Barnard and Cheryl Lester. Albany: SUNY Press, 1988.

———. "Psyche." In *The Birth to Presence*, trans. Brian Holmes and others, 393–394. Stanford, Calif.: Stanford University Press, 1993.

Terada, Rei. *Feeling in Theory: Emotion After the "Death of the Subject."* Cambridge: Harvard University Press, 2003.

Valéry, Paul. "Bouche." In *Oeuvres I*. Paris: Gallimard, 1957.

Warminski, Andrzej. "Facing Language: First Poetic Spirits." In *Romantic Revolutions*, ed. Kenneth R. Johnston, Gilbert Chaitin, Karen Hanson, and Herbert Marks, 26–49. Bloomington: Indiana University Press, 1990.

Wordsworth, William. *The Prelude (1799, 1805, 1850)*. Ed. Jonathan Wordsworth, M. H. Abrams, and Stephen Gill. New York: Norton, 1979.

5

RESISTANCE, TERMINABLE AND INTERMINABLE

Dina Al-Kassim

Giorgio Agamben's *Homo Sacer* comes to a provocative conclusion with the claim that "the 'body' is always already a biopolitical body and bare life, and nothing in it or the economy of its pleasure seems to allow us to find solid ground on which to oppose the demands of sovereign power" (187). Critics have countered this provocation by emphasizing the Foucaultian "practices of freedom" that proliferate in resistance movements and emergent alternative practices of the body as evidence that deathly zones of exception are not the *nomos* of our times.[1] Bodily practices of freedom or the indistinction of the biopolitical body: what is missing in this critical encounter is a sense of the body as subject not only to "economies of pleasure" but also to the intermittence of pain and suffering that, while unable to offer a "solid ground" or sovereign position from which to battle a sovereign power, binds the docile subject body to a social network that destines it to resistance as much as it promises a share in power.

It is this quarter of resistance, resistance to power, that calls for analysis. Avowing its desire for freedom, what is often called political resistance and takes the form of protest can never sever itself from the psychic suffering that also goes by the name of resistance. The word "resistance" thus conjures differing yet related scenes of resistances that our philosophies of discourse, counterdiscourse, and power have expressed in the plural rather than in a single or unified concept of pure resistance.[2] Here Michel Foucault: "Where there is power, there is resistance, and yet, or rather consequently, this resistance is never in a position of exteriority in relation to power; . . . the strictly relational character of power relationships . . . depends upon a multiplicity of points of resistance: these play the role of adversary, target, support or handle in power relations" (*The History of Sexuality*, 95).[3] Never exterior to power, never alone, always within the domesticity of its relations with power: this understanding of the coexistence of resistance with power goes astray in so many readings that hope to leave suffering out in the cold, beyond resistance, at once celebrated and coveted, to the point of leveling the difficulties and normalizing the costs of that tie or knot of obligation, resistance to power. Certainly, the call to resistance in the final pages of the best-selling *Empire*, where, we are promised, "militancy makes resistance into counterpower and makes rebellion into a project of love," takes its inspiration from Foucault's formulation of resistance as immanent to power (Hardt and Negri, 413). Yet this celebration of the militant, who need only creatively reconfigure his subjective style to assume his "new world," overlooks not only the ambivalence of any affect, especially love, but also the enigmatic inscription of resistance as performative repetition, a performance with consequences every time. The double suggestion—that resistance may have become indistinguishable from power or unintelligible to the present—complicates our understanding of the biopolitical body in a way that threatens to translate that docility into a form of political agency.

In his attempt to wrest the discourse of rights from absolutist notions of freedom and sovereign power, Jacques Rancière criticizes Agamben for his "radical suspension of politics in the exception of bare life" because it effectively eliminates the process of political subjectivation from the social field. Neither a deed performed once and for all nor an eternal and continuous condition, such a process, in its intermittence and interruptions, recasts the "political subject" as a particular mode of subjectivity defined by its "capacity to stage scenes of dissensus" (304).[4] The political subject is not a property of a given political system, for instance, democracy, but a power to bring to crisis the very framing of the given. And this "division put into the 'common sense' " or dissensus materializes when the difference between the sovereign law and the "rights of man," understood as the general rights accorded a generic "man," becomes an "opening of an interval for political subjectivization." For Rancière, rather than a particularity identifiable as majority or minority, the political subject is a name, a surplus category that performs or has the capacity to perform the disruption of political consensus through a distinctive kind of claim. This claim measures the present dispensation against the abstract or general right; it is only in the enactment of this measure that the political subject appears and, for this reason, that the temporality of the political subject takes the form of a perpetual intermittence.

These qualifications of Agamben's assertion of a progressive indistinction of bare life and law must be complicated in turn by the question, *what conditions the subject who assumes the capacity to make a scene?* Is there not a subjection and subjectivation before *and* after the process of political subjectivization has taken hold? How might we articulate the political subject with its others once we concede that "we no longer know anything of the classical distinction between *zoē* and *bios*, between private life and political existence, between man as a simple living being at home in the house and man's political existence in the city?" (187).

In what follows, I propose to examine intersections of resistance, in its psychic and political manifestations, by way of philosophical sketches of the notion and a singular instance of political dissensus arising from bare life where political subjectivization cannot guarantee a being beyond bare life. Resistance in this instance will call for a different set of critical terms. To excavate this psychic burden of the social text, I turn first to Gilles Deleuze and Jacques Derrida, two philosophers for whom the notion of resistance has been endlessly provocative and whose attention to suffering and to the unprecedented event reveal their common investment in thinking the crisis of the present. Deleuze and Derrida indirectly address political protest or resistance when they take resistance as their central concern; this, too, they share as they carefully distinguish the task of knowledge from the activity of social resistance in its many forms. But each philosopher also lays claim to a resistant act located as a gesture within philosophical writings. For Derrida, this act takes the form of a critical avowal of psychoanalysis as a source for thinking through and shifting sovereignty, power, and pain. In a challenging address to the international psychoanalytic community, Derrida argues that, though psychoanalysis cannot determine an ethics or law of human rights, it has much to contribute indirectly through its analytic engagement with cruelty and suffering. Deleuze also takes up the theme of knowledge production before human suffering when he persistently asserts that philosophy must estrange itself to perform its most essential function, the creation of new concepts. Yet this fundamental estrangement arises only through the intercession of a mediating affect, shame, that draws on suffering but motivates a tropism toward creativity. Like avowal and admonishment, shame intrudes itself into the text of philosophy and addresses others in an act of resistance. In the context of the philosophical concern with knowledge, analysis, and inheritance that emerges in Deleuze and Derrida, I turn to another resistance more familiarly locatable as social protest, an act or event of resistance by a group of South African women and shantytown dwellers that raises questions about the relation of intelligibility to resistance where power itself legislates the border of the socially intelligible.

R IS FOR RESISTANCE

On separate occasions in 1991, Gilles Deleuze and Jacques Derrida produced two very different texts that treat, at least in part, the same theme, resistance or resistances: Derrida's lecture, "The

Notion of Analysis," which became the title chapter of *Resistances*, and Deleuze's *What Is Philosophy?* Responding to the title's question, Deleuze replied from somewhere within the couple Deleuze-Guattari that philosophy is creation, the creation of concepts that "in itself calls for a future form, for a new earth and people that do not yet exist" (107). One finds this development before *What Is Philosophy?* in the interviews with Claire Parnet that became *L'abécédaire* where we learn that "R" stands for Resistance. When invited to speak on resistance and on the letter "R," Deleuze says, among other things, "to create is to resist" (108). Stubbornly, and with a formality that signals the performance of a philosophical gesture rather than the pursuit of an elaborated argument, Deleuze insists on linking creation, creativity, and resistance.

Deleuze offers us a context for understanding his unexpected formulation by sketching the political contradictions of the democratic state, which harbors a discourse on human rights compatible with, "coexistent" with, other imperatives that disavow human rights, "notably those concerning the security of property, which are unaware of or suspend [human rights], even more than they contradict them." He asks us, "who but the police and armed forces that coexist with democracies can control and manage poverty and the deterritorialization-reterritorialization of shanty towns?" This coexistence of rights and wrongs inspires, in his paraphrase of Primo Levi's formulation, "the shame of being a man" experienced "before the meanness and vulgarity of existence that haunts democracies." The feeling of shame, which he claims as a powerful motif for philosophy and for the arts alike and which constitutes the motive of their shared resistance, is compounded by a lack: "We lack creation. We lack resistance to the present." And hence the call to resistance is also a call to gather the strength of this feeling, the shame of being a man, for, as he says, "books of philosophy and works of art also contain their sum of unimaginable sufferings that forewarn of the advent of a people. They"—we may take this to mean both the books/artworks and the people—"have resistance in common—their resistance to death, to servitude, to the intolerable, to shame and to the present" (108).

In a different mood, Derrida also lays claim to resistance, to an act of resistance, this time against the leveling of difference in a culture that seems to have forgotten or to have disavowed the complexity of analysis—here specifically psychoanalysis but perhaps not limited to it: "I consider it an act of cultural resistance to pay homage publicly to a difficult form of thought, discourse or writing, one which does not submit easily to normalization by the media, by academics, or by publishers, one which rebels against the restoration currently underway, against the philosophical or theoretical neo-conformism in general (let us not even mention literature) that flattens and levels everything around us" (45).

Echoing the resistant dimension of philosophy identified by Deleuze in his evocation of creativity, this gesture opens Derrida's argument that psychoanalysis cannot submit to norming without losing itself. If, for Deleuze, philosophy "is by nature creative or even revolutionary" (45), this is so only to the extent that its creativity defies the shame of political injustices and creates the possibility of another affirmation, an alternative set of perceptions. One might say that the philosophical gesture shared by both philosophers itself resists argument in the sense that no argument could replace or substitute for the gesture. To attest or bear witness to an act of cultural resistance is not to supply the argument of that witnessing. Using Derrida's terms, we might say that the gesture of resistance, even when it comes in the form of respect or homage, supplements the argument under way. While it is clearly within the purview of knowledge or the concept to assert the importance of a difficult thought and to specify the complexity of psychoanalysis, which always traffics in the partial and insubstantial traces of social relation, the moment Derrida professes this respect, he cannot fail to bring into view the institutional context of his speaking, the cultural scene of an attack or repudiation of psychoanalytic thinking, and a host of other ostensible outsides. Thus the gesture that exceeds argument becomes the signature of philosophy when it professes its own resistance to all that "flattens and levels everything around us." Derrida's homage multiplies affirmation as a way of contesting "philosophical or theoretical neo-conformism in general." This understanding of resistance as affirmation links the two philosophers, who profess the urgency and responsibility to resist the present by responding to an affective element that spurs thinking without being a part of it; they both link resistance and responsibility to suffering.[5]

But it is precisely here that they diverge most sharply from that common place. Resistance is not enough to keep them, though it will continue to preoccupy their writing. Deleuze repeats the motif of creativity as resistance in several of his late texts, most importantly in *What Is Philosophy?* his final collaboration with Félix Guattari, where they begin by elaborating the conceit of the aged philosopher who reflects on the fundamental task of defining philosophy as a conceptual creation. Stating firmly that "the following definition of philosophy can be taken as decisive: knowledge through pure concepts" (7), the text insists on the constructivist and creative character of that knowledge, which demands of its creations the consistency of a concept (19) on a "plane that gives it an autonomous existence" (7). Internal consistency arises out of the collaboration of overlapping but distinct components of the concept, which then emerges as autonomous and new. Likening this distinctive autonomy of the concept to a style of "becoming stranger to oneself," in "Geophilosophy," Deleuze situates perhaps his most well-known concepts, deterritorialization and reterritorialization, in their relation to world political systems and the theme of human suffering to argue that philosophy resists the ignoble when it creates its concepts (110). Key to the resistant potential of conceptual creation, thinking must lose itself before it can be renewed in the unprecedented concept. Deterritorialization comes first, to be followed by reterritorialization on new grounds such that "philosophy is reterritorialized on the concept" (108). Where philosophy has "not been sufficiently concerned with the nature of the concept as philosophical reality," Deleuze identifies the constitutive relation of philosophy with its other, nonphilosophy, as a "becoming" (11). In passages devoted to the explanation of "becoming," we are introduced to the idea that philosophy renews itself through its resistant creation of the concept only when the philosopher writes "before" the victims of power rather than on their behalf or in their stead. When philosophy is creatively resistant, that is, when it is really philosophy, it is already becoming something other; when philosophy is philosophy it is, perhaps, becoming not philosophy. "The philosopher must become nonphilosopher so that nonphilosophy becomes the earth and people of philosophy" (109). A constitutive outside to philosophy, which Deleuze names suffering, meets thinking in a "zone of exchange" where suffering infects thinking to inspire resistance as their common ground and to create the concept anew.

"The creation of concepts in itself calls for a future form, for a new earth and people that do not yet exist." Deleuze and Guattari's cryptic phrases demand a reading that itself may require the error of wandering far from their texts. The gesture's doggedness retains its enigmatic quality as it refuses to explain itself, thereby resisting its own power to justify the equation of creation and resistance in the absence of the future form that creation would seem to call into being. *What Is Philosophy?* performs this resistance despite having made its excuses elsewhere as when, for instance, in *Negotiations,* Deleuze announces: "Philosophy is always a matter of inventing concepts. I've never been worried about going beyond metaphysics or any death of philosophy. The function of philosophy, still thoroughly relevant, is to create concepts. Nobody else can take over that function . . . . Philosophy's no more communicative than it's contemplative or reflective: it is by nature creative or even revolutionary, because it's always creating new concepts" (136). "By nature" creative, philosophy, like the arts, is nonetheless determined by a supplement that situates it within a particular set of historical and political relations through the added demand that, in being by nature creative, philosophy also must be—and by what power we might ask—resistant. We lack resistance, and, in so lacking, we lack creativity, philosophy, art. Before 1990 Deleuze had already twice theorized what he persists in calling the concept of resistance, notably in two acts of reading other writers, Foucault and Sacher-Masoch, and, through the latter, Freud.[6] In the chapter of *Negotiations* entitled "Life as a Work of Art," Deleuze once again turns to Foucault to address the problem of resistance and, echoing the chapter "Strategies or the Non-stratified: the Thought of the Outside (Power)" in *Foucault,* he offers us an aestheticist theory of subjectivation to account for the difficult relation of power to resistance:

> And it was all very well to invoke points of resistance as "counterparts" of foci of power, but where was such resistance to come from? ... It's a question of "doubling" the play of forces, of a self-relation that allows us to resist, to elude power, to turn life or death against power. ... It's no longer a matter of determinate forms, as with knowledge, or of constraining rules, as with power: it's a matter of *optional rules* that make existence a work of art, rules at once ethical and aesthetic that constitute ways of existing or styles of life (including even suicide). It's what Nietzsche discovered as the will to power operating artistically, inventing new "possibilities of life." One should for all sorts of reasons, avoid all talk of a return to the subject, because these processes of subjectification vary enormously from one period to another and operate through very disparate rules.
>
> (98)

Subjectivation, irreducible to a single subject, styles life as resistance to power but also as resistance to a self whose survival in the play of forces depends on a doubling-back or self-estrangement. Such a self-relation resists itself in order to resist power, and it does so by inventing "optional rules" or willing ways of existence. "No longer a matter of determinate forms," this invention turns against the self to pursue itself not freely but according to a rule-governed style that has some bearing over life. But what determines the rule? How does the rule gain its consistency or secure its footing in life? "Life becomes resistance to power when power takes life as its object. ... When power becomes bio-power resistance becomes the power of life, a vital power that cannot be confined within species, environment or the paths of a particular diagram. Is not the force that comes from outside a certain idea of Life, a certain vitalism, in which Foucault's thought culminates?" (*Foucault*, 92). What we lack is resistance, and therefore we also lack the creative stylization of existence that lends itself to resistance by folding upon or against itself. If we are lacking in creative resistance, by this logic also, we are lacking in life where "living being" has become the determination of that "set of forces that resist" (93).

In another context and another conversation, the same year as *L'abécédaire* but this time with Toni Negri, Deleuze offers another version of this refrain: "What we most lack is a belief in the world, we've quite lost the world, it's been taken from us. If you believe in the world you precipitate events, however inconspicuous, that elude control, you engender new space-times, however small their surface or volume.... Our ability to resist control, or our submission to it, has to be assessed at the level of our every move. We need both creativity and a people" (*Negotiations*, 176). Lacking resistance to the present would seem to be conditioned by this want of belief in the world, which, if only we could believe, would engender the unexpected and unmasterable event productive of a people. Accordingly, a creativity that can style a new subjectivation in a set of new concepts beyond the sovereignty of life, this force of the outside, would stand a chance of resisting the control of power. It would seem that Deleuze's notion of resistance requires a constant flow of newly conceived possibilities of survival well beyond the limitations of a life that awkwardly bears the mark of a kind of mastery, at least a mastery of the history that has made power wear the mask of biopower. For Derrida, however, resistance cannot become a question of styles of subjectivation; resistance exceeds any concept of sovereignty because it fractures such a concept with its, perhaps unconscious, inheritance. This is most clear when Derrida gestures indirectly at Deleuze, as when he writes, "who, besides God, has ever created, literally 'created,' a concept? Freud had no choice, if he wished to make himself understood, but to inherit from tradition" (*Resistances*, 19).

In the title essay of *Resistances of Psychoanalysis* and tracing the figure of "a knot or many knots,"[7] Derrida takes another tack altogether to argue that resistance is not only a matter of being roused by injustice or suffering; resistance is not a unified concept but a set of relations that obstruct, limit, refuse, repeat, and rebel. The intricacy of the reading he offers is beyond summarizing here, though a faithful recapitulation would amount to reading it aloud, so resistant is its movement to the conventions of academic narration. He begins in the preface with two forms of resistance, the first a repeated cultural resistance to psychoanalysis that "returns" to say that psychoanalysis is done for, "expired like an outdated prescription." This return, a cultural disavowal that compulsively revisits the reviled science, is analogous to the patient's own resistance to analysis, which Freud describes as one of the patient's resources in analysis, which he resists by disbelieving or not subscribing to psychoanalytic notions. And so a cultural refusal of psychoanalytic insight carries over to the personal encounter with analysis and supplies the patient in analysis with a resistant tool and a defense that cannot be his own invention. As if in parody of the very self-defeating symptoms that sent the patient seeking help, the resistance to psychoanalysis turns once more against the self in analysis and forces the dramatic history of a cultural refusal of psychoanalytic knowledge into the narrow confines of belief or disbelief, now rehearsed within the intimate and singular theater of the analytic session. A recursive motif in the remaining essays of *Resistances* and again in *Without Alibi*, this concern over the marginal status of the only writing devoted to psychic suffering and the turn against the self overshadows Derrida's reflections on the future of such a denigrated body of knowledge, the only one that addresses the paradoxical problem of cruelty to oneself, "suffering just to suffer" (*Without Alibi*, 239). Repeated throughout these considerations is the suggestion that psychoanalytic knowledge of gratuitous and perhaps inescapable cruelty should enrich our sociopolitical reflections, especially those that aim to change the present. The very intractability or insensibility of cruelty, which resists rationalist explanation, demands that politics, ethics, and law take stock of the knowledge that psychoanalysis has gathered regarding the turn against the self and the other.

The second resistance is a resistance of psychoanalysis to itself, which "comes to its own aid" and, in doing so, provides the interpretive tradition of psychoanalysis with a theory of transformation, including the intellectual transformation of its own precepts.[8] Pursuing the knotted relation of the power of technical knowledge to the resistance of analytic material, Derrida follows the trail of a curious obstacle to analysis that comes to light only through the exhaustion of an analytic enterprise taken to its limit when, in deciphering his own dream, Freud proposes that he can go no further with the analysis. Interpretive exhaustion becomes not only a limit to knowledge but also a subject of psychoanalytic reflection, for Freud accepts the limit, the resistance, as a principle of dream interpretation, one that inscribes the resistance of the unknown and the indecipherable within the very method of reason. Here, a resistance to interpretation constitutes a limit to knowledge, an inappropriable otherness that both exhausts and excites thinking. Against Deleuze's assertion regarding the creation of concepts, which is for him the mode of philosophy's resistance to the present, Derrida states that psychoanalysis does not have a unified concept of resistance or of itself. Psychoanalysis does not create the concept; instead, it analyzes right up to the limit of its powers of interpretation. This limit to interpretation is also doubled. On the one hand, there are mysteries that can be solved if one finds a way around the obstacle or resistance, which, as *Resistances* puts it, "prevents our understanding or analysis without prohibiting it." On the other hand, there are passages that remain in the dark "because a structural limit prevents us from going beyond" (14). Far from founding original concepts, analysis unravels prior constructions, knots of compromise, and fantasy that divide the subject, but it does so without any guarantee of final elucidation or discovery. At the very moment that interpretation runs out of possibilities, another resistance quietly persists to save interpretation from itself, from its own powers of decipherment, and for another day.

Both these understandings of resistance—as an obstacle to analytic knowledge and as the name of a limit that cannot be overcome simply by offering explanations or meanings or even concepts—contribute to the further notion that the analyst must work through resistance by other means. Derrida proposes that resistance, and the suffering of which it is a sign, even a pleasurable and stubborn sign, is not "lifted by the revelation of its meaning(s), it can only be lifted by the intervention of an affective factor" (18). A spectacular but unmasterable effect of analysis, the intervention that lifts or razes the constructions of resistance relies on a tie of affection and a bond of affinity, and this bond of transference must include as well the ties of aggression and hatred between the analysis and the resistance that meets it. Because resistance in and to analysis can be resistant to the revelation of its own meaning—a patient's resistance does not melt away upon analytic disclosure of its origin—and because lifting resistance is the key to successful mediation of suffering, psychoanalysis must keep in view a "resistance not only comprehended and communicated in its intelligibility, but transformed, transposed, transfigured" (18). When resistance transports itself away from itself, another resistance befalls analysis, for such a transfiguration yields no systematic or generalizable map of approach, no determinate form. Analysis may await it expectantly, but each banished resistance follows its own singular path, and, in going across, transfigured, resistance leaves behind another resistance, in a series that, unlike the resources of creative ingenuity whose lack Deleuze laments, can never be exhausted. This secret emerges in analysis, multiplying its resistances, communicating them well beyond reason's intelligibility. Suffering thus infects analysis, contracting it to secrecy.

This analytic secrecy, a secret from itself and for which analysis cannot adequately account, suggests a double bind: "Every resistance supposes a tension, above all, an internal tension. Since a purely internal tension is impossible, it is a matter of an absolute inherence of the other or the outside at the heart of the internal and auto-affective tension" (*Without Alibi*, 26). Freud analyzes such a doubly bound resistance, an outside in the most intimate space of an autoaffection, in "A Child Is Being Beaten," via the language of obligation. There, Freud describes the bondage of a structure that promises the child to resistance for having obliged him twice over: to love and to repression. Confronted with adult patients who present sadomasochistic fantasies, the analyst must imagine a prehistory of love and loss that persists only as remnant or ruin. Neither reconstruction nor rediscovery, the analytic enterprise must produce a fictional discourse to account for the fragmentary evidence, and it must do this in view of the possible "structural limit" that could at any moment foreclose the possibility of interpretive reason. The analyst is charged with imagining a lost fantasy, a desire that could not survive the censorship of repression entire but persists, a resistant element, in a compromised and symptomatic form. For this reason, Freud speaks in place of the departed child whose traces remain as an "archaic inheritance" in the discourse of the adult patient. These remains of the child never emerge as the personal recollections of the speaking subject. Rather, they can only be spoken as analysis or as a "construction of analysis." It is analysis that will voice the archaic obligation, never remembered because unconscious, indeed, the "origin" of the unconscious but so twisted and redirected that it could never claim itself as origin. In short, the child, "obliged to effect an incestuous object choice and obliged to repress it later," retains the passive resistance or inherence of that love, now transmuted into an incestuous wish in the unconscious where it lives out its life in fantasies also unremembered and uncollected (116). This doubled obligation doubly binds the child with love and with the secret that falls into the knot to divide the self continually against itself.

If Freud theorized resistance not only as the patient's defensive effort to avoid the lifting of repression but also as an inherent and inappropriably foreign element within the psyche, viewed through the lens of psychoanalysis, suffering is intimately allied with repetition and the double bind. In fact, Deleuze has said rather more on the topic of psychoanalysis and resistance than either the letter *R* or the question *What Is Philosophy?* reveals. Much earlier, in his reading of Sacher-Masoch, Deleuze notes Freud's analysis of "forms of resistance which in various ways imply a process of disavowal." As a path away from the superego, disavowal "should perhaps be understood as the point of departure of an operation that consists neither in negating nor even destroying, but rather in radically contesting the validity of that which is: it suspends belief in and neutralizes the given in such a way that a new horizon opens up beyond the given and in place of it" ("Coldness," 31). Such opposition to the present, such a resistance, is allied already at the beginning of Deleuze's writings on psychoanalysis, both with a desexualization of the body and the libido and with an act of imagination that founds a new subjectivation or redistribution of the subject. The art of masochism lies essentially in disavowal and the power of disavowal to conjure imagination: "It is nothing less than the foundation of imagination, which suspends reality and establishes the ideal in the suspended world. Disavowal and suspense are thus the very essence of imagination" (128). Neither purely passive nor purely active, the imagination, which derives from its own essence in disavowal, is known to us as fantasy in psychoanalytic reflection.[9]

We might wonder what grounds the proposition of an essence that finds its source in a resistance or unwishing such as disavowal. Where Deleuze asserts the formality of an aesthetic practice endowed with the power to redraw the contours of a subjectivation, Freud speculates: by analyzing perverse fantasy as always in need of translation into its unconscious and phantasmatic origin in a repressed wish, Freud restages the double bind of love and secrecy as something more than an essential disavowal. Deleuze, like Freud, argues for an understanding of fantasy as a form of ideality that is essentially an event, one not captured by the division passive/active. There, Deleuze references Laplanche and Pontalis's reconception of fantasy as a drama of subjectivation within which the subject is disseminated in the very landscape or scenography of the fantasy.[10] This move allows us to understand the formal syntax and grammar of a given text as a field saturated by the very politics of subjectivation that Deleuze believes is the source of a resistance to power. Indeed, Freud's analysis shows that fantasy does intrude upon the subject, destining him to scenes that stage both his desire and its obstruction. Yet the central insight of "A Child Is Being Beaten" disturbs the careful formalism of Deleuze's Masochian scenography: the essential event of fantasy is the one that never happened, even as and in fantasy. As Freud fully admits, unconscious fantasy, the unattested sign of that double bind sharing the subject's origin, is a "construction of analysis."

There is another kind of resistance, one that offers no egoic satisfaction and no legible symptom other than its own repetition in a stubborn return; this Derrida calls a resistance that is a nonresistance, for it persists without meaning and remains impervious to interpretation. Freud calls it the repetition compulsion. We find it at the subject's unremembered origin doing its work to divide that source between love and secrecy, desire and repression; we find it again in the repetitions of fantasy that come unbidden, not yet or ever harnessed to a luxuriating aesthetic, not yet or ever regimented in the formal schema of a perverse poetics. The repetition compulsion resists excessively, to the point of unintelligible repetition; it resists neither passively nor actively, quite without resisting. Melville's Bartleby lends his name to this figure of hyperresistant resistance that spins itself into a nonresistant lingering or repeating that brings the subject and the science of psychoanalysis to the very summit of resistances, which is, paradoxically, a passage to repetition without meaning: "The repetition compulsion, hyperbolic resistance of nonresistance, is in itself analytic; it is that whose resistance psychoanalysis today represents, in the surest form of its ruse: disguised as nonresistance" (*Resistances*, 24). Unraveling analysis, such a suffering in repetition offers, according to Derrida, the chance of transfiguration, intervention, working through, while simultaneously and from the perspective of an analytic knowledge, it threatens to dissolve the very figure of resistance into its disparate and contradictory threads.[11] For Derrida, this analytic threat bound up in the repetition is the closest thing to a "concept" that Derrida will offer to describe deconstruction, for "deconstruction is also the interminable drama of analysis."[12]

Between the interminable deconstruction of resistance and the insistence on the power of resistance to inspire the creative concept and the utterly new, only the former can begin to address the consequences of resistant action. Unending analysis promises to follow a resistant act from the event and into its survival as memory and forgetting. Although Deleuze does not ignore the "abominable suffering" of social protest, he does disarticulate creativity from its inspiring occasion by locating in the concept a kind of vanguardism: "The philosopher is quite incapable of creating a people, [he] can only summon it with all his strength" (*What Is Philosophy?* 110). In this sense, resistance remains a liminal figure for Deleuze, whereas, for Derrida, resistance is the very putting into play of limits and obstacles to meaning; resistance marks the shifting border between meaning and nonmeaning. But where do we situate resistance when unintelligibility is its salient feature? How might we delimit the resistance of social protest, harnessing rebellion, when resistance always proliferates and multiplies its borders?[13]

Turning back to that other quarter of resistance, resistance to power, we might now argue that in the field of political resistance there are interventions analogous to the analyst's successful working-through and -with the other's resistance, but while such interventions may transform and transfigure resistance, communicating it but also allowing it to move out, they cannot prevent resistance from branching out in other ways and as a source of other sufferings. Interminable resistance would be a form of haunting that relegates the subject to ceaseless wandering at the border or threshold of collective norms, even the norms of resistance.

Putting into play the limit of intelligibility, setting it to work, this is the consequence of that "opening of an interval for political subjectivization," and it is no mere figuration of a resistant limit: such intervention is neither a state of exception nor an ethos of styles of life; rather, this opening within the limit generates intervals of intermittent agency and dispossession, sovereignty and loss that never promise the "solid ground," which for Agamben would enable a resistance to "the demands of sovereign power." Earlier I asked what conditions the subject who assumes the capacity to make a scene; now I may answer by resituating the subject of rebellion as something other than the sovereign subject of disavowal who cultivates his conscious fantasy into political subjectivation; Deleuze's subject of disavowal may well be the figure that inspires Agamben's skepticism regarding the body and its potential to oppose power. But insofar as Agamben locates, paraleptically, a claim for the body's capacity ("nothing in it or the economy of its pleasure") for political subjectivization, we must consider this body in all its resistant dimensions; the biopolitical body is also a psychic body, a subjectivity, an array of collective subjectivations, an ethos, a history, and a stylization. By definition, the biopolitical body is always already the knotted intersection of *zoē* and *bios*, private life and political existence. This unsovereign subject draws her capacity to stage a scene from the very dispossession Agamben identifies; when the figure of a limit or law is set to work through catachrestic means, an interval for the appearance of the political subject opens. In this way, dispossession can become the occasion of a political catachresis of bare life itself.[14] But the subject who undergoes this transformation will also survive it to suffer in repetition the intermittence of political subjectivation, which thus becomes a source and resource of resistance. Let us turn now to a singular case of the political catachresis of bare life.

THE SHANTYTOWN: *UKU HAMBA 'ZE! (TO WALK NAKED)*

The year before our couple, Deleuze and Derrida, dwelt "together" so serendipitously on resistance, 1990, the year of Nelson Mandela's release from prison, also the year that a series of apartheid laws are repealed in preparation for the Convention for a Democratic South Africa, the country is gripped by widespread violence. In a migrant workers' shantytown outside a black suburb of Johannesburg, the inhabitants' shacks are threatened with demolition by the South African Police. Facing the bulldozers, the people mount a resistance, responding to the disturbance by acting out the program of demonstration that they know all too well. Some houses fall, and this proves too much for a group of wives and mothers, of women anyway, who intervene for them, in unprecedented fashion: they strip off their clothes and stand again before the bulldozers. It is a resistance that cannot be exhausted by the rhetoric of "spontaneous action," for many reasons, not the least of which is its duration; the women stand naked for quite some time before succeeding.[15]

The event was documented by the South African Broadcasting Corporation television news, shown nationally and thus became part of the national archive. Later, the same television footage resurfaced in a documentary, *Uku Hamba 'Ze! (To Walk Naked)*, which details the event and returns to interview three of the women five years later.[16] These interviews also happen to take place one year after the first nonracial democratic election in the new South Africa and in an atmosphere of preparation for the Truth and Reconciliation Commission's commencement by year's end. But this fact of freedom confronts those interviewed with another struggle. In the early years of the postapartheid state, the talk is of a new nation, a liberated people united in a new freedom. South Africa in 1994 was the very emblem of a people who so believed in the world that they created it anew. This conception of the state and of new beginning is not without consequences for shameful acts committed under apartheid; to have walked naked becomes newly resistant, unincorporable as the economy of freedom-achieved spread through the "earth and the people."

The women justify their actions to the camera: "Even the police could not explain the truth or explain who had sent them to demolish our shacks." Though they could speak the policy, even with feeling or conviction, the police could not speak the truth, a truth that would convince the women that their only homes should be destroyed: "These police dogs knew that they were comfortable in their [own] homes. Whilst they are comfortable in their homes, we are suffering." The women resist the law for which the agents of the law could not convincingly account. But why does this failure send the women off to lose themselves in nakedness? Thandi Mthaphe says of this moment of resistance, "I had lost myself for a while because what was happening had disturbed me." But why does that nakedness become an effective and affective intervention, one that brings the police to a standstill and keeps them there until they go?

A common reading of subversion would hold that, stripped of everything else, these displaced and abject women throw back the figure of resistance and, in triumph over their oppressors, perform the primitivism feared by a racist phantasm. Such a reading holds that, confronted with the *truth* of resistance, the colonial powers lose their bearings and are overcome. But the fact that, for most who walked naked, this was not their first home lost to unjustified police action and that therefore this scene represented a repetition of a state compulsion to destroy rather than an action to which the women could respond "spontaneously" complicates the narrative of instinctive subversion or irruption of revolutionary rebellion. I propose another reading: in the violence of that transitional year, 1990, the police lose their certainty, lose their hegemonic resistance to the analysis of their own sovereign violence; the map of certain power relations comes unmoored, and even the police cannot explain the truth. And no one can tell the story.

We may rebel against a reading that threatens to rob the spectacle of defiant black bodies of its performative force. Certainly, the documentary style and even its distributor's advertisements suggest a preordained genre and prefigured viewing of the women's action: speaking truth to power, such an action might be assumed to be admirable without remainder, a true resistance. Listen again to Thandi Mthaphe: "I was heartbroken when my shack was gone, my shack, my home that I loved very much was gone." What does she voice when she tells us that the destruction of her home, and with it everything she owned and had worked for, reduced her to a nakedness before which her bare body could appear as a retort? "I felt powerful but I was hurt." What does this destruction, this drive to level and destroy, threaten for her? Nothing less than the home, which Derrida also has taught us to understand, in Greek, as an archive.[17] The record of previous dislocations and forced removal conditions the women's failure to abide within the confines of the possible and the script of right resistance. This complexity or divisibility of affiliation and action multiplies the kinds of resistance in the scene and, in this sense, follows Derrida's reading of the proliferating effects of resistance and what counters it. The figure of a limit—for instance, that between the victims and the police—here divides.

To preserve the home, the women act as though they were strangers to the customs governing the body, the home, the neighborhood: "I had forgotten that as a woman I wasn't supposed to walk naked among the people." But this forgetting does not go unchallenged when the community, in the form of the civic association, surrounds them, demanding meanings for the incomprehensible resistance to meaning that the women have become: "They said sit down! Hold on to discipline! Sit down! I didn't want to sit down and be disciplined." It is this strangeness, this becoming stranger to the community around them, that sets their nakedness apart from the disciplines of resistant protest sanctioned by community norms—including community norms of triumph and revolutionary freedom—for this is a struggle that involves them all and within which criminality or shame can attach itself more tenaciously to those within the home than those beyond its bounds, for instance, police dogs. In a community bound by a history of dislocation and abuse, there are still distinctions to be upheld and communal norms to be respected, especially in collective resistance to the violence of "others."[18] The violation of home to conserve the home that their nakedness represents cannot be domesticated once again under the name of spontaneity. The women resist even this misrecognition. In the place of madness or an upsurge of revolutionary fervor, in the place of unfettered release, they offer another bind, another bondage. "Everyone wanted to know what our problem was. You would explain that they didn't have the same spirit that we had, there were no painful memories as we had. People thought we were mad to strip off, being adults." To be compelled by painful memory and forced to justify oneself before the laws of the state and the laws of the home: these conditions suggest a disturbance of the map of power and resistance, self and community, which loses them by knotting them, leaving the naked to find their way home, after the fact and alone.

In the summer of 2002, a group of Nigerian women protesters engaged in a labor dispute with Shell Oil Inc. and, at the end of their rope, threatened to bare themselves in protest. Their successful tactic—negotiations were resumed and demands met—was dutifully explained in the international media, by experts, and even on the organizers' Website, by reference to a traditional practice and a semiotics of shame. When wronged, the injured party may expose himself to show what the other's harm has wrought; according to this conventional and anthropological elucidation, the bare body of the wronged, especially the bare body of an elderly woman or mother, holds a mirror to the shame of the wrongdoer and materializes it in the visual field. By these lights, an affect becomes a sign. The dynamic relation of one to the other, of reflection on the bare body, operates, we are told, by virtue of a mutually transparent and conventional understanding that both precedes the encounter and provides a system of signs for its exercise. The bare body, even the mere threat of it, as in the 2002 Nigerian case, means what it shows.

It is startling, then, to recall that in 1993 a group of Nigerian woman who performed this act of ethical and public reflection, understood and sanctioned by traditional practice, was fired on by agents of the state. More devastating to such a traditionalist understanding of resistance and shame, the women who threatened in 2002 to replay the act well knew the risk they took and were prepared to face the guns with their "bare life." The Nigerian women not only knew the possible cost of their proposed action, they calculated this cost with the knowledge that their resistance might be met with sovereign resistance. Here is a scene in which Deleuze's remark "resistance comes first" finds its sense, for here the relay of power/resistance leaves us only with mounting resistance (*Foucault*, 89). Resistance seems to come from outside the representation or diagram of power, and yet it is utterly local to the scene of struggle and can modulate or calculate that representation of power or code of tradition against the fluctuations of the present. But while this capacity to enter resistance and reason within it, to repeat it, exhibits all the signs of a Deleuzian subjectivation, it does not reflect the dynamic becoming-stranger that enabled the South African women to intervene against sovereign force.

As they clearly attest, the South African women became unintelligible to themselves and to their community. This unintelligibility, which seems to catch the traditionalist explanation somewhat off guard, is equivalent to resistance even if there exists a convention by which the performance might be understood, even if their oppressors could understand them.[19] There remains an excess at the heart of any performative and any citation of convention. This excess or unintelligibility that they became resists but overcomes resistance as well, and not by superior force but by other means. The women's resistance to exclusion, to the loss of community, is lifted by an affective factor, suffering, which enables their flight from home and into nakedness and is itself intimately connected to another collapse, that of the power that subjects them. Bare bodies mirroring shame transfigure the social field so that the police, too, become unintelligible, their defenses disordered and their certainties dispersed, but this suddenly shared unreadability cannot be the product of a game or a well-rehearsed ethical system. Nor is it the child of a convention or a code, despite an authorizing history of at least 150 years that could effectively contextualize the event according to a known tradition of practices in South Africa of ethical reflection and of the so-called impossible.[20]

Did they cite a convention? Doubtless, as such exists even if they were unaware. Did they know themselves to be thus citing an archive of past shames? Doubtful, as they cannot explain or "know" what they did, inhabited as they were by this strange bondage in resistance. They cannot and do not offer the precedent of tradition to cover their tracks or render the illegible suddenly clear. Fanon, approaching a similar disarticulation of the social map, puzzled over the sometimes simultaneous backward and forward movement of resistance when confronted with a colonial domination so oppressive that resistance to it often takes the form of a politically retrograde return to traditional practices, no matter how deeply divided the native culture might be with respect to them. When discussing the rebellious uses of the veil among Algerian and Moroccan subjects of French colonial predation, Fanon notes that some resistant permutations of veiling, though obviously and directly addressing a French audience, went unremarked by the colonizer, unattuned to the possibility that the racial sign of difference might become the medium of resistance, the very language of repudiation of colonial rule.[21] This deafness to the clamor of political resistance begins to collapse when Algerian revolutionaries turn to radio to broadcast in French as a means of rallying the people and forewarning the coming of independence. When Algerians no longer approach the French language as Caliban but seize upon French as the tool of communication across linguistic barriers, suddenly, according to Fanon, the colonizer's image of a country subdued and the colonized's picture of violent subjugation began to merge into a coherent map of social discord. As resistance mounts, it overcomes the gap between divergent realities and fuses the social landscape into a common ground, a threatening and disturbing image of reality that exposes misshapen and deformed social relations formerly rendered invisible by colonial structures of domination. With the advent of a new perception, the defenses of the powerful were disordered, their confidences rendered illegible, their aspirations no longer the norm. This sudden unintelligibility, ironic product of a dramatic, new visibility of risk and threat, disordered a collective resistance to "reality," which emerges in this new light as a monstrously novel and inscrutable possibility of further alteration. Where the defenses of the colonizer come unmoored, the actions of the colonized travel a foreign terrain in improvisational modulations of surrender to the unfamiliar landscape. No doubt, Fanon's theory of crumbling colonial defenses owes much to his analytic practice, where lifting resistance is a major aim, and this sharpens his insight into the social dynamics of revolutionary change. For Fanon, political transfiguration of the social field happens through the intercession of affective factors that challenge and shift the boundaries of intelligibility; more important, this shifting of the norm owes little to convention, reason, or truth. The transfiguration of political relations effected by the now-veiling and now-unveiling Algerian woman does not depend on the dictates of reason or the disclosure of truth. According to Fanon, colonial norms are most at risk precisely when their phantasmatic character is materialized as the social map and precisely when a convention or tradition has been decathected so that it might be deployed strategically. Deterritorialization and reterritorialization are certainly at work in such a strategic intervention on a received norm, but a host of affective factors—for instance, suffering—conditions these calculations and acts of resistance with the result that, rather than merely negating colonial domination, these acts radically contest the given, radically alter the map of power "in such a way that a new horizon opens up beyond the given and in place of it," and, in so doing, this anticolonial contestation moves well beyond the explanatory force of Deleuze's theory of subjectivation ("Coldness," 31).

A singular resistance, which we could follow back into the home, preserves itself, unexplained across the many figures of psychoanalytic resistance, across Deleuze's philosophical gesture that asserts the creativity of resistance, through to the errant action of these mothers, who could not hold on to discipline and let it slip away, leaving them to wander, illegible and untold. Each of these scenes or figurations or events of resistance shares in a vulnerability to an otherness that assumes several names in Derrida's many works but follows along the lines of thinking itself, as when he writes in "Provocation," "What remains to be thought remains to come and thus resists thinking. The word 'thinking' thus takes in, without being able to house or contain it, this inappropriable resistance of the other. To take in without being able to lodge the other *chez soi* is one of the formulas, among others, for the possibility of the impossible that provokes all these provocations" (*Without Alibi*, xxxiii). An abiding resistance, this remaining goes by the names *demeure, restance, désistance* in Derrida's many texts. The inappropriable resistance of the other, while it provokes thought, cannot "become" the collaboration of zones of exchange that situate the concept for Deleuze. This resistance to the sovereignty of thought resists appropriation by any subject. It persists without right or justification, indifferent equally to the heroism of acts and the shame of an unwilled transgression. Under the name "the repetition compulsion," psychoanalysis has much to say about the afterlife of this unsovereign resistance, its lingering shame, and the complexities of its narration. In like manner, psychoanalysis has affinities with the intervention the women brought about; analysis practices such intervention. And like the women, psychoanalysis can attest to the double bind of equally pressing obligations to the laws of the home and to forgetting or repressing that original, archaic bond, even to preserve it. Promised to resistance, "what remains to be thought" challenges any conception of the unity of thinking, including the thinking of suffering, without being able to take it in or to mingle in a "double becoming" (*Foucault*, 109).

Invited to address a gathering of psychoanalysts, Derrida reiterated the creative and resistant promise of this possibility of impossibility, a paradoxical necessity that links responsibility to a radical alterity, by once again beginning with resistance, telling us that cruelty and sovereignty resist. Each resists and so, he asked, "whether, today, here and now, the word and the concept of resistance remain still appropriate. Do they represent the most strategic, most economical lever for thinking what is going wrong, what is not going well in the world on the subject and in the vicinity of psychoanalysis?" (*Without Alibi*, xxxiii). This query does not revoke resistance or seek to replace it with a newer "concept," as earlier Derrida professes his commitment to the university as a place of resistance to power (or, in his terms, sovereignty, even in its state form and even if it only lingers as a phantom of sovereignty) when the university preserves its "force of resistance, this assumed freedom to say everything in the public space" (207).

If we are going to imagine Deleuze and Derrida together around the "R" of resistance, we will have to carry the social or popular dimensions of resistance as the resistance to oppression along with us all, for neither philosopher invites us to forget it, and neither would they welcome its repression. Indeed, we will need these mothers to provoke our thinking, for without an attunement to the constantly renewing forms of cruelty, including cruelty toward oneself in the form of inassimilable remorse, our notions of political resistance become indifferent to the alterations and oscillations of power and revolt. The science of psychoanalysis provides Derrida with a signal example of this risk, and never more than when he admonishes psychoanalysis to take stock of technological transformations in knowledge and social relations, to know what is "happening in the world today," and to exercise a "free responsibility [that] will never be deduced from a simple act of knowledge" (278). This responsibility pledges psychoanalysis to the analysis of injustice and the desire for cruelty from within the limits of its own practice of knowledge, but Derrida notes as well that "psychoanalysis developed not only as analysis of personal resistances, but also as analysis of the cultural, political and social resistances represented by hegemonic discourses" (20). When Freud extended resistance to analysis beyond the borders of the clinic and began to describe the refusal of analysis more generally in the rationalist prejudices of dominant discourses, he also began a deconstruction of sovereignty for which resistance can never be the master term. Analysis unravels and, potentially, intervenes in the resistance to analysis that is sovereignty. This is not a tautology but a repetition that returns the supplement of responsibility as an affective element to our thinking of political resistance to the present; without the possibility of the transfiguration of resistance and without attention to the only discourse that constantly and consistently interrogates gratuitous suffering, the women are, indeed, promised to resistance, for they become the very figures of what cannot be reassimilated to symbolic norms. And as the "mondialization" of cruelty, sovereignty, and resistance mounts to such a degree that, according to Agamben's analysis of biopolitics after Foucault, there is no longer a distinction between the rule and the exception, the norm and the taboo, the state and its dissidents, law and life, our modern habit of resistance, relying as it does on power to offer it determinate form, may no longer resist. [22]

"Psychoanalysis Searches" affirms the alterity of the event—for us, the event of being lost at home, as exemplified in the women's action—beyond sovereignty and "the economy of the possible. It is attached to life, certainly, but to a life other than that of the economy of the possible, an im-possible life no doubt, a sur-vival, not symbolizable, but the only one that is worthy of being lived" (*Without Alibi*, 276). Where Deleuze argued through his reading of Foucault that life is invested with resistance when biopower takes life as its object to be disciplined and regulated, Derrida moves beyond the circumscription of life as regulated and put to death to affirm the presumption, the unconditional affirmation, of a life beyond calculation, economy, and system. This affirmation—what he calls another figure of the impossible that harkens back to his previous explorations of this theme under the name of hospitality, the gift, and forgiveness—is the gratuitous affirmation of the impossible: "Wherever there is law and performative, even if they are heteronomous, there can certainly be event and some other, but they are right away neutralized, in the main, and reappropriated by the performative force or the symbolic order. The unconditional coming of the other, its event without possible anticipation and without horizon, its death and death itself are irruptions that can and must put to rout the two orders of the constative and performative, of knowledge and the symbolic" (278).

What the law or the norm circumscribes as the unintelligible, criminal, deviant, and exceptional joins the impossible without defining or substantializing radical alterity as a concept. The women's unprecedented action exposed them in the performance of an impossibility, for, despite the claims of the traditions of ethical reflection, it was not possible for a woman to walk naked within the symbolic economy of this community, as in many others. Their resistance to domination led to exposure and a scandalous event, yet the moment almost immediately fell prey to its own fragility and was reinscribed within the demands of home. As soon as they became newly answerable to the symbolic norms of home, the women fell back into shame, into suffering, and the resistant refusal of their own rebellion to die down. They remain there as the melancholy survivors of a public shame. Resistance, residue of the event, continues to trouble the women's narratives, for how shall this story of public shame be incorporated in the epic of antiapartheid resistance? These dilemmas cannot be domesticated by a traditionalist explanation, and neither can they be tamed through reference to historical precedent, for neither of these saving graces are sufficient to fold the liminal figure of this resistance back into the social norms of the home and the state, which also survive political upheaval and social revolution. Nor can we say with Deleuze that doubling back upon the self, which might be another figure for becoming stranger to oneself, yields a "style of subjectivation," for the impossible act rebounded upon them, haunting them with shame as they later tried to fold impossible rebellion into the now transformed norm of survival, reterritorialized as the advent, the successful coming of the people.

Home. How to explain, justify, narrate, and respect a performance that preserved the home, the archive, by forgetting it? The predicament is heightened to a suddenly dizzying degree when one registers that, even five years after the fact, the presence of the cameras on the scene had created another misery for these women: their nakedness was recorded, broadcast, mediated in a way that exposed them to the repetition of their nudity in public and as public record. This became a problem for one of the women on the spot as she tried to hide behind others, so that her husband would not see her, she tells us. For another, the mediatized repetition became again, raised again, the question of the home, the future of the home even after it was preserved from destruction: "even my parents, when they see me in these wars, they will understand that it was a struggle," Thandi tries to convince us before she bursts into tears. Or, as Nthabiseng Hlongwane puts it, "I had to strip to fight the police. I always ask myself a sorrowful question. I tried to explain to my kids why I stripped. I was trying to fight for them so that they could find their home." Stubbornly, this experience continues to interrupt their lives even after it saved them; it haunts them as "a thing which has not been understood inevitably reappears; like an unlaid ghost, it cannot rest until the mystery has been solved and the spell broken" (cited in Laplanche and Pontalis, *The Language of Psychoanalysis*, 79). It breaks apart even the tie of kinship because this thing must be tried and explained, to the children at the moment of origin in the event and again, once home is restored, to the grandchildren: "But now I have one problem when it comes to my grandkids because God has helped me find a place, now I become even more sad when I think of those things. I don't know who to blame, the government, the town clerk, the people I used to live with, or blame god. *I don't know who I was because I was naked as anything. My body that is respectable at all time. Even now, when I respect my body, I ask myself, 'Why should I respect it?' Because I'd shown it to the nations*" (emphasis added).

This shame, to use Deleuze's word without analyzing it, follows the rebellion to haunt the women with another misery, another homelessness, which amounts to the question of how to write the history of this resistance for their parents, children, and grandchildren: "I was naked as I was born. . . . I had forgotten that as a woman I was not supposed to walk naked among the people." Returned to the nakedness of birth, this woman fears that her sorrowful question—"why should I respect it?"—will haunt those to come. How to archive this impossible nakedness?

NOTES

1. See Deuber-Mankowski, "'A Zone of Indistinction'" and "Cutting off Meditation."
2. See Žižek, *The Ticklish Subject*, especially 262. As an example of the purist insistence on a unified and singular conception of "resistance,"

one might cite Žižek's assertion of an easily apprehendable distinction between what he calls a "socio-critical" and a "clinical" use of the term. Such a theory of the clean separation of these domains cannot broach the subjects under consideration here: namely, women's symbolic inscription in the state, in the state's narrative of its own birth, and in the popular tale of anticolonial or antiapartheid resistance; neither can such an insistent assertion of difference between the social and the clinical forms of resistance address the place of shame in historical memory. The rhetorical gambit of this distinction is to discredit in advance any argument that what Žižek calls "resistance to social power" and resistance to "unconscious truth" expressed in symptoms may not be distinguishable, that they may condition each other such that resistance to power takes on symptomatic formations, not only for individuals but for groups as well. Finally, for Freud, the clinical form of resistance, evident when a patient defends against self-consciousness of the motor or source of his symptoms, reveals a set of investments and symptomatic defenses that also characterize the hegemonic refusal of psychoanalysis as a form of knowledge evident in the history of the reception of psychoanalysis. There is no single or final form of resistance in clinical analysis; rather, there are multiple forms, as Derrida's "Resistances" shows. That Freud could identify in the notion of resistance a continuum of modulating refusal, from a patient's private deflection of new knowledge and affects to a diverse array of social repudiations of psychoanalytic insight, attests both to the difficulty encountered in attempts to hold the two domains, the critical and the clinical, apart and to the continued usefulness of "resistance" as a term when approaching the disavowal of psychoanalysis still performed by hegemonic forms of knowledge and authority. Beyond the forms of resistance experienced in the clinical account, Freud's writings reveal limits to interpretation that are also resistances. Finally, Derrida points out that the repetition compulsion constitutes yet another form of resistance, one that utterly blurs the distinction between clinic and sociocritical domains.

3. The French offers "des résistances" for what the English translates as "a plurality of resistances." One could add to this the following passage from *Power/Knowledge*: "Resistance to power does not have to come from elsewhere to be real, nor is it inexorably frustrated through being the compatriot of power. It exists all the more by being in the same place as power; hence, like power resistance is multiple and can be integrated in global strategies" (142). In her *States of Injury*, Wendy Brown critiques a popular notion of resistance and empowerment when under-

stood as substitutes for a practice of freedom. It is clear that, for Foucault, resistance and power generate a mutuality that makes their distinction utterly relative in the abstract, hence the necessity of identifying in the particular historical or textual instance what moves what. This is why a politics that takes empowerment as its only ally and thereby forgoes the responsibility to articulate and inhabit a "practice of freedom" must run aground of its own resistance. Yet the notion of practice, what Foucault explored under the rubric of ethos in the second volume of his *History of Sexuality*, is also conditioned by and productive of—indeed, "practices"—the modes of symptomatic haunting and exclusion that psychoanalysis exposes analytically.

4. In Rancière's essay, the exemplary case of political subjectivization is that of women's demands for human rights during the French Revolution. From within the limit of human rights, they claim human rights, thus setting the limit to work in what Judith Butler calls the labor of "political catachresis" (*Antigone's Claim*, 82).

5. Even this common feature divides, for Derrida deliberately begins his essay on resistances by speaking of his love of the word; for his part, Deleuze has more than one philosophical affect in his repertoire and even in *What Is Philosophy?* he treats a host of feelings.

6. Deleuze analyzes Sacher-Masoch's invention of a style in "Coldness and Cruelty," 133. See also his *Foucault*, 92.

7. This phrase, repeated throughout Derrida's *Resistances*, echoes a chapter title in Deleuze and Guattari's *A Thousand Plateaus*, "1914: One or Several Wolves," which in turn refers to a dream analyzed in Freud's "History of Infantile Neurosis," or "Wolf Man." This echo was again repeated in Derrida's address to the "Derrida/Deleuze: Psychoanalysis, Politics, Territoriality" conference, where he deconstructed *Plateaus*' accusation that Freud ignores the importance of multiplicity and the social unconscious in the Wolf Man's symptoms and fantasies (Derrida's address is reproduced here as the opening essay of this volume). For the authors of *Plateaus*, the psychoanalyst is guilty of using the oedipal narrative to "make patients believe they would produce individual, personal statements, and would finally speak in their own name" (38). The aim of "Resistances" is to show that Freud's theory of "persuasion" is one of affective transfiguration of the analytic method, the analyst's presumptions, and the patient's relation to his defenses and to the social as mediated by and projected onto the analyst. The analytic cure cannot simply confer meaning on the patient's suffering, symptoms, and fantasies, for such an exercise of institutional reason would be incapable of transfiguring resistance.

For example, Freud tells us that the Wolf Man's analysis reached an impasse almost immediately, leaving him "entrenched" in a "submissive indifference. He listened, understood and did not permit anything to touch him." Freud gave him a deadline of one year to complete his analysis or break it off. The "threat made the Wolf Man give up his resistances and produce new material" ("From the History of Infantile Neurosis," 401). Yielding resistant silence for productive sharing of the "material," the Wolf Man does not capitulate to a normative enforcement; rather, he enters into the new affective relation with the analyst via the alibi of a new social compact or contract. The normative and ideological pressure to produce individual, personal statements invoked by a discourse of empowerment (e.g., when projects of social redress assume the function of inciting, gathering, and hearing victim's testimonies) would be analogous to the role of oedipal coercion proposed by Deleuze and Guattari in their critique of the normative presumptions of Freud's methods. However, this reading will have to negotiate the other pole of interpretation here emblematized by Derrida: are there not social interventions that can and do lift resistance such that "new material" makes its way into the discourses of the subject? And can psychoanalysis, as a practice of analysis that must think through exactly what resists and rejects analysis, extend its reflections to a consideration of the pressing sociopolitical dilemmas of a global world? Derrida pursues the question of this responsibility in "Psychoanalysis Searches the States of its Soul: The Impossible Beyond of a Sovereign Cruelty," in *Without Alibi*.

8. The enumeration of resistances becomes comic as the essay progresses, for while we seem to have six forms of resistance—(1) cultural resistance to psychoanalysis; (2) resistance of psychoanalysis to itself in the form of a limit to interpretation; (3) egoic; (4) idic; (5) superegoic resistances, of which each possesses three subvariants; and (6) finally, the repetition compulsion—several of these forms of resistance are shown not to be resistance at all or shown to be divisible into still other forms. The repetition compulsion, a resistance of nonresistance, in part because it has no meaning and cannot be interpreted or decoded, becomes on closer inspection the principle that destroys the very concept of resistance, while simultaneously it is the most analytic principle in play. Indeed, as Derrida reminds us, he disentangles "5 + or − 1" different resistances lurking in Freud's single word in *Without Alibi*, 246. See also *Resistances*, 22.

9. See Deleuze, *The Logic of Sense*, 210–238, especially 210–216, for a discussion of the phantasm.

10. Laplanche and Pontalis, "Fantasy and the Origins of Sexuality," 26.

11. Repetition and iterability condition the constitution of identities while also destining them to dissolution. The repetition compulsion that drives Freudian analysis to divide and question itself also organizes the greatest resistance of psychoanalytic reflection to deconstructive analysis. Derrida reiterates a scene from the encounter between a hegemonic version of psychoanalysis and the analytic exigency of deconstruction by referencing, quickly, his exchange with Lacan between *The Post Card* and the "Seminar on 'The Purloined Letter.'" The crux of the matter hinges on the question of dissociation, divisibility, indeed the formal techniques of analysis, and leads Derrida to the uncharacteristic definition of deconstruction: "If, in an absurd hypothesis, there were one and only one deconstruction, a sole *thesis* of 'Deconstruction,' it would pose divisibility: difference as divisibility" (*Without Alibi*, 33).

12. Derrida urges the States General of Psychoanalysis to cease inhibiting their practice and become responsible for a reading of political, social, and technological mutations (*Resistances*, 29).

13. The problems raised by the perpetual figure of woman as threshold of intelligibility are posed in Judith Butler's *Antigone's Claim*, where she argues, for instance, that "Antigone figures the limits of intelligibility exposed at the limits of kinship" (23). I pursue this line of thought in my "Archiving Resistance" in connection with Zoë Wicomb's novel *David's Story* and several accounts of the South African Truth and Reconciliation Commission to explore the problem of gendered resistance and the state.

14. This term is borrowed from Judith Butler's *Antigone's Claim*, where the "inhuman" can speak as human and thus lay claim to the human because the very language that demarcates the difference can become the occasion of a political claim.

15. For the canonical demystification of spontaneous action as a resource of anticolonial resistance see Fanon, "Spontaneity: Its Strength and Weakness."

16. Many thanks to Janet Neary, who has written compellingly on the politics of sight in this scene, for introducing me to *Uku Hamba 'Ze! (To Walk Naked)*. The most detailed and considered study of the Dobsonville protest of 1990 is Sheila Meintjes's "Women's Local Troubles and National Demands."

17. In *Archive Fever*, Derrida draws our attention to the etymology of the word "archive," which bears the trace of its Greek setting—quite literally, as archives are housed—and suggests the selection and authority of *archons*, keepers of the archives. In the context of the shantytown, the

dwellings function as archives, though the story they tell of forced removal and traumatic displacement disrupts the conceit of untroubled location characteristic of the archive. Significantly, the women who engaged in the action later suffered from a problem of the archive; several women directly addressed this to their interviewers and perhaps to the nation (via the camera's mediation) when they asked how to tell this story to their relations.

18. Zakes Mda's novel *Ways of Dying* portrays the social structure and affective bonds of a community of shantytown dwellers who organize their own community needs through their civic association. Consistent with his commitment to exploring the lives of the socially abject, Mda builds the novel around the figure of a professional mourner, male, who lives out of a shopping cart and is brought back into the human community by a woman, a key organizer and caretaker of her fellow shantytown dwellers. Like the women of *Uku Hamba 'Ze!* the characters of *Ways of Dying* live the consequences of having practiced an inassimilable mode of survival.

19. Derrida argues that every code of intelligibility, including Lacan's symbolic, is organized through a performative power of authority, convention, and institution (*Without Alibi*, 258). But every system or code, even the symbolic order of authorized social intelligibility, is haunted by its own limit, and this limit is embodied in the unintelligibility legislated at its border. For two investigations of this performative excess and two distinct figurations of limit as border and as internal fold, see Judith Butler, *Antigone's Claim* and "Arguing with the Real."

20. The women did not openly cite a convention to authorize their action (citing instead their personal histories). However, they do perform against a historical and regional context where baring one's body has been practiced as a mode of signifying dispossession. The action of 1990 takes place against the background of the 1856–1857 Xhosa cattle killings, which are vividly referenced in Zakes Mda's recent novel *The Heart of Redness*, a novel that recasts contemporary political struggles in South Africa in terms of legacy, madness, and prophecy.

21. When Moroccan women began to wear black veils to mourn the exile of their king in 1953 and did this despite the fact that black has never been the color of mourning in the region, they directly addressed a colonial audience that could or would not hear them. See Fanon, "Algeria Unveiled" and "This Is the Voice of Algeria."

22. For instance, "The Foucauldian thesis will then have to be corrected or, at least, completed. . . . Instead the decisive factor is that, together with

the process by which the exception everywhere becomes the rule, the realm of bare life—which is originally situated at the margins of the political order—gradually begins to coincide with the political realm, and exclusion and inclusion, outside and inside, *bios* and *zoē*, right and fact, enter into a zone of irreducible indistinction. At once excluding bare life and capturing it within the political order, the state of exception actually constituted, in its very separateness, the hidden foundation on which the entire political system rested" (Agamben, *Homo Sacer*, 9).

BIBLIOGRAPHY

Agamben, Giorgio. *Homo Sacer: Sovereign Power and Bare Life*. Trans. Daniel Heller-Roazen. Stanford, Calif.: Stanford University Press, 1998.
Al-Kassim, Dina. "Archiving Resistance." Unpublished manuscript.
Brown, Wendy. *States of Injury: Power and Freedom in Late Modernity*. Princeton: Princeton University Press, 1995.
Butler, Judith. *Antigone's Claim: Kinship Between Life and Death*. New York: Columbia University Press, 2000.
———. "Arguing with the Real." In *Bodies That Matter: On the Discursive Limits of Sex*, 187–222. New York: Routledge, 1993.
Deleuze, Gilles. "Coldness and Cruelty." In *Masochism*, trans. Jean McNeil, 15–138. London: Faber and Faber, 1971. Reprint, New York: Zone, 1989. Originally published as "Le froid et le cruel," in *Présentation de Sacher-Masoch* (Paris: Minuit, 1967).
———. *Foucault*. Trans. Sean Hand. Minneapolis: University of Minnesota Press, 1988.
———. *Negotiations 1972–1990*. Trans. Martin Joughin. New York: Columbia University Press, 1995.
———. *The Logic of Sense*. Trans. Mark Lester with Charles Stivale. Ed. Constantin V. Boundas. New York: Columbia University Press, 1990. Originally published as *Logique du sens* (Paris: Minuit, 1982).
———. *What Is Philosophy?* Trans. Hugh Tomlinson and Graham Burchell. New York: Columbia University Press, 1994.
Deleuze, Gilles and Félix Guattari. *A Thousand Plateaus: Capitalism and Schizophrenia*. Trans. Brian Massumi. Minneapolis: Minnesota University Press, 1987.
Deleuze, Gilles and Claire Parnet. *L'abécédaire de Gilles Deleuze*. DVD. Dir. Pierre André Boutang. Paris: Montparnasse, 2004.

Derrida, Jacques. *Archive Fever*. Trans. Eric Prenowitz. Chicago: University of Chicago Press, 1996.
——. *The Post Card*. Trans. Alan Bass. Chicago: University of Chicago Press, 1987.
——. *Resistances of Psychoanalysis*. Trans. Peggy Kamuf, Pascale-Anne Brault, and Michael Naas. Stanford, Calif.: Stanford University Press, 1998. Originally published as *Résistances de la psychanalyse* (Paris: Galilée, 1996).
——. *Without Alibi*. Trans. Peggy Kamuf. Stanford, Calif.: Stanford University Press, 2002.
Deuber-Mankowski, Astrid. " 'A Zone of Indistinction': A Critique of Giorgio Agamben's Concept of Biopolitics." www.thomaslemkeweb.de/engl.%20texte/A%20Zone3.pdf. Originally published as "Homo sacer, das bloβe Leben und das Lager. Anmerkungen zu einem erneuten Versuch einer Kritik der Gewalt," *Die Philosophin* 25, no. 2: 95–114.
——. "Cutting Off Mediation: Agamben as Master Thinker." Paper presented at the Critical Theory Institute, University of California, Irvine, March 2005.
Fanon, Frantz. "Algeria Unveiled" and "This Is the Voice of Algeria." In *A Dying Colonialism*, trans. Haakon Chevalier, 35–63 and 69–98. New York: Grove, 1963.
——. "Spontaneity: Its Strength and Weakness." In *The Wretched of the Earth*, trans. Constance Farrington, 107–147. New York: Grove, 1963.
Foucault, Michel. *The History of Sexuality*. Vol. 1, *An Introduction*. Trans. Robert Hurley. New York: Vintage, 1990.
——. *Power/Knowledge: Selected Interviews and Other Writings, 1972–1977*. Trans. Coin Gordon, Leo Marshall, John Mepham, and Kate Soper. Ed. Colin Gordon. New York: Pantheon, 1980.
Freud, Sigmund. "A Child Is Being Beaten." In *Sexuality and the Psychology of Love*, ed. Philip Rieff, 107–132. Collected Papers of Sigmund Freud 8. New York: Collier, 1963.
——. "From the History of Infantile Neurosis ('Wolf Man')." In *The Freud Reader*, ed. Peter Gay, 400–428. New York: Norton, 1989.
Hardt, Michael and Antonio Negri. *Empire*. Cambridge: Harvard University Press, 2001.
Lacan, Jacques. "Seminar on 'The Purloined Letter.' " Trans. Jeffrey Mehlman. *Yale French Studies* 48 (1972): 39–72.
Laplanche, Jean and J.-B. Pontalis. "Analysis of a Phobia in a Five-

year-old Boy." In *Formations of Fantasy*, ed. Victor Burgin, James Donald, and Cora Kaplan. London: Methuen, 1986.

———. "Fantasy and the Origins of Sexuality." In *Formations of Fantasy*, ed. Victor Burgin, James Donald, and Cora Kaplan, 5–34. London: Methuen, 1986.

Mda, Zakes. *The Heart of Redness*. New York: Picador, 2000.

———. *Ways of Dying*. New York: Picador, 2002.

Meintjes, Sheila. "Women's Local Troubles and National Demands: The Construction of Women's Citizenship in South Africa in the 1990s." http://66.102.7.104/search?q=cache:TfyUFhnwnmoJ:www.unibas-zasb.ch/redakteure/peclard/Paper_Meintjes.pdf+%22Dobsonville+protest%22+Meintjes&hl=en&gl=us&ct=clnk&cd=1&client=firefox-a.

Rancière, Jacques. "Who Is the Subject of the Rights of Man?" *South Atlantic Quarterly* 103, no. 2/3 (Spring/Summer 2004): 297–310.

Uku Hamba 'Ze! (To Walk Naked). VHS. Directed by Jacqueline Maingard with Sheila Meintjes and Heather Thompson. Third World Newsreel, 1995.

Wicomb, Zoë. *David's Story*. New Edition. New York: The Feminist Press at CUNY, 2002.

Žižek, Slavoj. *The Ticklish Subject: The Absent Centre of Political Ontology*. New York: Verso, 1999.

6

THE RHYTHM OF PAIN

Freud, Deleuze, Derrida

Branka Arsić

Deleuze's and Derrida's relation to Freud was always complicated.[1] On the one hand, psychoanalysis seriously influenced them, whereas, on the other, it became for Deleuze the object of the gay science of *Anti-Oedipus* and for Derrida the object of a secret desistance described in "Passions."[2] In this complex network of influences, it is the question of pain and suffering that not only "from the beginning" put psychoanalysis at a certain distance from both of them but also established an "affinity of the thesis" divided by "very obvious distances" in the strategy and manner of "writing, speaking and reading," as Derrida puts it when he mourns Deleuze's death in *The Work of Mourning* (192).

THE ONTOLOGY OF PAIN—FREUD

Masochism—a certain noneconomical attitude toward pain—threatens psychoanalysis. Such a thesis can be considered extreme if one remembers that psychoanalysis is used to instability and that various threats to the "stability" of thinking are its exclusive interest. To say therefore that masochism threatens psychoanalysis is to say that that masochism threatens the psychoanalytic openness to threats. The openness of psychoanalysis to ambivalences and uncertainties relies on the presumption that something like masochism is impossible or at least that Freud had problems coming to terms with its possibility. For the whole operative system of psychoanalytic terms (identity, id, ego, superego, guilt, unconscious/conscious) can function only on condition that it obey a certain economy. Masochism, however, does not fit this picture. No matter how Freud tried to analyze it, it always appeared as a psychic phenomenon without economy, hence unanalyzable. If, however, there is a psychic phenomenon that cannot be read because it contradicts the very idea of psychic life, then it is possible—as a disturbing consequence that Freud had to face—that everything we know about the economy of psychic life is affected by what we cannot know.

Already in *Three Essays on the Theory of Sexuality*, the explanation of the economy of perversion cannot account for masochism. In contrast to sadism, which was presented as explicable,[3] masochism is defined as a "passive attitude towards sexual life." It appears to be a life lacking in an attitude toward itself and thus a life without economy, for it is neither an exaggeration of sexual instinct (as is the case with other perversions) nor its active reduction but a sheer passive exposure, a type of waiting for the gift of pain. At least, that is how it appears in what Freud calls the "extreme case of masochistic perversion." In such a case, even masochistic enjoyment is "conditional upon suffering physical or mental pain at the hands of the sexual object" (24). In contrast to other perverts, the "extreme" masochist does not do anything to gain his own enjoyment. He appears to constitute a passive attitude even toward his own perversity (thus undoing its status of perversion).

Masochism disturbs the difference not only between inversion and perversion but also between perversion and neurosis. In contrast to the neurotic translator, who transcribes emotionally invested mental processes into a different type of text (symptoms),[4] the pervert transgresses the text into an act, which is why Freud can say that the symptoms (of neurotics) "are formed in part at the cost of abnormal sexuality; *neuroses are, so to say, the negative of perversions*" (31). But, by reading neurotic textuality, psychoanalysis discovers that the sexual instinct of psychoneurotics is, in fact, driven by "perversion": "An especially prominent part is played as factors in the formation of symptoms in psychoneuroses by the component instincts, which emerge for the most part as pairs of opposites and which we have met with as introducing new sexual aims . . . the active and passive forms of the instinct for cruelty. The contribution made by the last of these is essential to the understanding of the fact that symptoms involve *suffering*, and it almost invariably dominates a part of the patient's social behavior" (32). Masochism—now determined as the passive instinct for suffering cruelty—"almost invariably dominates" the social behavior of neurotics. Neurotics not only suffer their symptoms but enjoy their suffering. Their superego punishes their ego, which has been reduced to an object enjoying the cruelty inflicted on it (the structure Freud will call "moral masochism," which he always thought of as the climax or "peak" of masochistic perversion).

Psychoanalytic classifications are further threatened when hypnosis shows that the technique of analysis capitalizes on this masochism of neurotics: "In this connection I cannot help recalling the credulous submissiveness shown by a hypnotized subject towards his hypnotist. This leads me to suspect that the essence of hypnosis lies in an unconscious fixation of the subject's libido on the figure of the hypnotist, through the medium of the masochistic components of the sexual instinct" (16). The hypnotized person (here playing the role of the masochist in love with the analyst) will reappear later in *Group Psychology and the Analysis of the Ego* as an ordinary person in love. For, in *Group Psychology*, Freud will determine that "from being in love to hypnosis is evidently only a short step. The respects in which the two agree are obvious. There is the same humble subjection, the same compliance, the same absence of criticism towards the hypnotist as towards the loved object. There is the same sapping of the subject's own initiative; no one can doubt that the hypnotist has stepped into the place of the ego ideal" (58). Love is the experience of humble subjection and the enjoyment of that subjection. If one falls in love because one loves love itself, then it follows that what one actually loves about it is submission, pain, and suffering. One is in love with passivity ("the sapping of one's own initiative"), or, rather, one is in love with masochism. It is at this point that psychoanalysis faces the absolute disaster of its classifications. For not only are neurotics perverts, but everybody is a pervert, at least to the extent that everybody can fall in love.

Beyond the Pleasure Principle could be seen as Freud's effort to articulate a logic of being that would account for noneconomical suffering.[5] By explaining what is inexplicable for psychoanalysis, the ontology of pain that Freud develops there would thus serve to back up psychoanalysis itself. This ontological grounding of psychoanalysis (its metapsychology) is dualistic: "Our views have from the very first been *dualistic*, and today they are even more definitely dualistic than before—now that we describe the opposition as being not between ego-instincts and sexual instincts but between life instincts and death instincts" (326). Everything is hereafter dual. It is a matter of supporting the thesis that there is a separate existence for death drives, a properly "autonomous" labor of death working against life.

Freud launches his analysis of the masochistic side of this ontological divide by remarking on an essay that treated the phenomenon carefully. Freud was convinced that masochism confirms the existence of the death drive by reading an essay by Sabina Spielrein, a very "instructive and interesting paper, which however, is unfortunately not entirely clear to me" (328). He was thus enlightened by a paper that remained obscure to him. On the basis of this nonunderstanding, he can say that masochism is a far more destructive instinct than sadism. For whereas the sadist directs his aggression toward the external object and so preserves his own ego (sadism is thus a form of the life instinct), the masochist's instinct acts against his own ego. Masochistic life turns on itself in order to destroy itself. Such a turning of life on itself is the action of the death drive: "Masochism, the turning round of the instinct upon the subject's own ego, would in that case be a return to an earlier phase of the instinct's history, a regression. The account that was formerly given of masochism requires emendation as being too sweeping in one respect: there *might* be such a thing as primary masochism—a possibility which I had contested at that time" (328). Somewhat later, in "The Economic Problem of Masochism,"[6] what was suggested as a mere possibility in *Beyond the Pleasure Principle* becomes a claim: "Another portion (of the destructive instinct) does not share in this transposition outwards; it remains inside the organism and, with the help of the accompanying sexual excitation described above, becomes libidinally bound there. It is in this portion that we have to recognize the original, erotogenic masochism" (418). We have therefore to recognize the original love for pain that is "structurally" inscribed in every organism.

Guided thus by its own desire to affirm the death drive (we could even say "guided by its own masochism"), psychoanalysis establishes an originary enjoyment in pain and again encounters a problem. For if masochism is originary and primary, then it exists in the "thing itself," as it were, or, more precisely, the "thing itself" is masochistic (masochism thus becomes the noumenon of psychoanalysis). Masochism is in the origin of the substance; the being itself is masochistic. And it is such a masochistic being that now subverts psychoanalysis. For if the being is masochistic, if masochism and the forces of life are something like two Cartesian principle attributes, then one has to conclude that masochism is an ontological category that negates the psychoanalytic idea of a necessary economy (turnovers with capital gains) of our psychic life. But to negate that idea is to negate psychoanalysis. Evidently, something in masochism threatens psychoanalysis.

IMPERSONAL PAIN—DELEUZE

To say that Deleuze's philosophy is saturated by an effort to affirm masochism is not to say that it seeks to affirm death, for in his philosophy masochism is an affirmation of a thinking and identity radically different from Freud's. In other words, Deleuze creates a concept of masochism that presumes a critique of the Freudian understanding of the economy of subjectivity. His redefinition of masochism is based on an idea of the "literality" of pain that is opposed to what in Freud functions as its interiorization (its becoming metaphor).

By claiming that masochism is an interiorization of the destructive instinct that, instead of being transposed outside (as in the case of sadism), remains inside the organism and takes the ego as the object of its destruction, Freud introduces what he calls "secondary" or "moral" masochism. Here, the superego becomes the destructive force, torturing an ego that enjoys that torture: "We shall not be surprised to hear that in certain circumstances the sadism, or instinct of destruction, which has been directed outwards, projected, can be once more introjected, turned inward, and in this way regress to its earlier situation. If this happens, a secondary masochism is produced, which is added to the original masochism" (*Masochism*, 419). The enjoyment of pain, which at first was the characteristic of "original, erotogenic masochism," thus becomes enjoyment of the pain inflicted by bad conscience. That is to say, the pain itself becomes the feeling of guilt of the bad conscience (which is why in the final analysis masochism finds its climax in the desire to be punished). Freud's insistence on this gesture of interiorization pacifies pain by inventing, in the form of bad conscience, a "sensualised, spirtualised" version of it. It is through this "spiritualization," says Deleuze echoing Nietzsche, that *"a new sense is invented for pain, an internal sense, an inward sense*: pain is made the consequence of a sin, a fault. You have produced your pain because you have sinned, you will save yourself by manufacturing your pain. Pain conceived as the consequence of an inward fault and the interior mechanism of salvation, pain being interiorised as fast as it is produced, 'pain transformed into feelings of guilt, fear and punishment.'"[7] The translation of pain into the feeling of guilt ("secondary masochism") is its becoming metaphor. Thus, Deleuze suggests, if guilt can be a metaphor for pain, it is because spiritualized pain becomes the reactive force that distances us from the body (hence life) that is always in pain: guilt becomes a metaphor for that pain. By making pain a metaphor and then dramatizing masochism as enjoyment of it (enjoyment of painful punishment) so as to produce pleasure, psychoanalysis effects a dialectical gesture par excellence. For, and this is the point of Deleuze's objection to the psychoanalytic treatment of masochistic pain, when pain is interiorized and spiritualized, punishment is desired only in order to arrive finally at pleasure. Masochism therefore always confirms the pleasure principle. This speculative-dialectical gesture should be seen precisely in the fact that the whole maneuver of interiorization of pain has been performed only in order to conclude with what was there from the very beginning: the pleasure principle. The (a priori) pleasure principle structures the interpretation of pain to such an extent that that interpretation puts at risk the fundamental dissymmetry between pleasure and pain. According to the pleasure principle, pleasure is always pleasing, but pain is not always painful: some pain is pleasurable. In the final analysis, masochistic perversion would be nothing but a detour that the masochist takes in order to accommodate pleasure (which, turned into an a priori principle, also becomes a metaphor).

If the psychoanalytic idea of pleasure and pain is only a metaphor, what then is a nonmetaphorical pleasure? What would be an affirmative understanding of pain? "Biopsychical life," says Deleuze, "implies a field of individuation in which differences in intensity are distributed here and there in the form of excitations. The quantitative and qualitative process of the resolution of such differences is what we call pleasure. A totality of this kind—a mobile distribution of differences and local resolutions within an intensive field—corresponds to what Freud called the Id. . . . The word 'Id' (*Ça*) in this sense is not only a pronoun, referring to some formidable unknown, but also an adverb referring to a mobile place, a 'here and there' (*Ça et là*) of excitations and resolutions."[8] The id is both a mobile place—which moves from place to place—and a place that is "within" itself movable from itself, hence open and multiple. Thus conceived it cannot be a (pro)noun referring to a substance or a being; rather, it has to be an adverb without either a subject or a predicate.

According to Deleuze's critique, it is precisely the fact that pleasure is a process rather than a being or state that presents Freud with a serious difficulty: "It is here that Freud's problem begins: it is a question of knowing how pleasure ceases to be a process in order to become a principle.... Obviously, pleasure is pleasing, but this is not a reason for its assuming a systematic value according to which it is what we seek 'in principle'" (96). The question is to know according to what principle "excitations," "free differences," or "contractions" (what Deleuze calls the first layer of the unconscious) become bound. Freud's answer to that question is that differences are already invested with pleasure; pleasure is the principle of binding. Hence the speculative circle reappears: pleasure, which is supposed to be produced by binding, is bound by pleasure. Deleuze, on the other hand, advances the reverse thesis: pleasure is only the effect of binding. If pleasure is the result of binding, then what makes the binding possible? What is there, beyond the pleasure and pain?

"This binding is a genuine reproductive synthesis, a Habitus" (96). That, in short, is Deleuze's answer to the question. Reproductive synthesis or habit means at least two things: (1) it is an activity "that takes as its object the difference to be bound"; (2) more important, it is a *passion* of repetition from which a new difference emerges. Each excitation (which is in itself already a contraction, what Deleuze calls "a primary passive synthesis") participates in repetition and so is raised to a reproductive synthesis, or habit, which is, like contraction, passive: "Investments, bindings or integrations are passive syntheses or contemplations-contractions in the second degree" (97). They are called "second-degree" syntheses not because they are "secondary" or interiorized but because they are repetitions. Each investment and binding, each pleasure, is thus an effect of habit. Several consequences follow:

1. If habit is what binds and ties excitements, it is also what precedes the drives and instincts (integrations). Drives are thus effects of habit and not vice versa, for drives are "nothing more than bound excitations" (97).
2. To say that habit synthesizes drives and thus precedes them is also to say that habit occurs before any ego is constituted.

Habits are "here and there" (id) before any I. Id is made of habits. Preceding the ego, habits are always impersonal, something which the ego will come to inhabit. And because they synthesize before the ego appears, they are called passive syntheses. They are passive not because they don't move or function but because they do not "belong" to an "I."

3. Each time a repetition or a habit binds excitations (contractions), an ego is formed. That ego is not an ego of apprehension or recognition. It is a passive larval ego. There are as many egos as there are habits for *each habit is a little passive ego* (the existence of so many passive egos all over the body explains, then, the stubbornness of our habits and addictions for they act independently of the ego and its preferences). The id is populated with egos: "At the level of each binding, an ego is formed in the Id: a passive, partial, larval, contemplative and contracting ego. The Id is populated by local ego" (97).

4. The contraction-habit "structure," excitements and their habitual reproduction, is what produces pain or pleasure. This is not to say that the contraction-habit structure is the pleasure principle. On the contrary, this activity of reproduction and passion for repetition constitutes the beyond of pleasure, which is to say "beyond" the principle, a *beyond without a principle*.

Needless to say, this "beyond" constitutes a different transcendental aesthetic (and a different understanding of subjectivity), for it introduces a different understanding of pleasure and pain. For Kant (and we are not far away from Freud here at all) defined the passive self of the transcendental aesthetic as the merely receptive self that assumes "sensations already formed." According to Deleuze, by claiming that sensations come from elsewhere and get translated into sensations within us, Kant "cuts the Aesthetic into two parts: the objective element of sensation guaranteed by space and the subjective element which is incarnate in pleasure and pain" (98). Pain (as well as pleasure) becomes in Kant the temporal translation of a spatial, objective sensation, which is why pain is always the pain of the subject and always an effect of the process of interiorization.⁹

The "beyond" the principle posited by Deleuze, however, opens up the possibility of something altogether different. Since habit—the synthesis of reproduction of differences—is already a network of contractions, this union of contraction and habit announces the collapse of the difference between objective sensation and subjective (translated, metaphorical) pain. "Objective" sensation is "subjective" pain without there being any translation of objective into subjective. This means that local selves possess at the same time the capacity to produce pain and to receive it. Passive synthesis does precisely that: it synthesizes contractions (produces pain and pleasure) and by so doing receives and experiences what it has synthesized. Production and reception fall into one and happen at the same time. It is a question of a receptivity that produces both the reception and what is received as one and the same thing. Pain is thus not translated but becomes a literal, nonrepresentable pain. Because there is no apprehension of an "I," "passive syntheses are obviously sub-representative" (84), which is to say pain is purely and simply presented. The question of whether "sensation or perception [is] thus merely hallucinatory (because it does not have its object) or merely objective (because it does not have its subject)" loses its meaning. For pure presentation is nothing other than the negation of that difference. Pain thus takes place as a literal pain that cannot be metaphorized into enjoyment of pain (enjoyment of pain presupposes precisely the transcendental doubling whereby a transcendental subject appropriates pain as its own pleasure).

But this idea of pain (of its literality and exteriority) is possible only because of a difference in the very idea of passivity. Far from being conceived of as a "passive attitude towards life" (and thus as the force of death, as Freud has it), passive syntheses in Deleuze are nothing less than the constructive force of life itself, of which everything is made (including death). Passive syntheses are the originary affirmative power of life: "However, in order of constituent passivity, perceptual syntheses refer back to organic syntheses which are like the stability of the senses; they refer back to a primary sensibility that we *are*. We are made of contracted water, earth, light and air—not merely prior to the recognition or representation of these, but prior to their being sensed. Every organism, in its receptive and perceptual elements, but also in its viscera, is a sum of contractions, of retentions and expectations . . . this primary, vital sensibility" (73). Everything is made of primary sensibility or passivity that is contracted before being sensed (even before the senses and their forms appear). The primary sensibility of passive contractions constitutes impersonal life (a sensibility that does not sense itself, the sensibility of earth, of water, or of light).

Deleuze called that life of originary passivity "the plane of immanence," which is neither the interiority that absorbs all difference into itself nor a plane of "individuation" that constitutes subjectivity in its various forms. Rather, it is a network of "contractions" and their relations, each of which (relation) comes about to form a singular event: "It is a haecceity no longer of individuation but of singularization: a life of pure immanence, neutral, beyond good and evil, for it was only the subject that incarnated it in the midst of things that made it good or bad. . . . A singular essence, a life" (*Pure Immanence*, 28–29). The plane of immanence is this impersonal proliferation of passive syntheses or larval selves.

It is the plane of immanence that constitutes desire. This says several important things about desire: (1) it is the endless dissemination of passive syntheses; (2) being a motion of passive synthesis, it is the desire of larval selves and therefore always impersonal; (3) being impersonal, it implies no lack (for only the ego knows of lack); (4) being a changeable network of larval selves, of contraction and habits, it is an assemblage of various heterogeneous elements; (5) being an assemblage, it is not a "natural given"; (6) being a changeable assemblage, it does not have a structure (it is opposed to structure or genesis, says Deleuze); (7) being a process without a structure, it is a singularity as opposed to a person or subject (it constitutes, as Deleuze would say, the individuality of a moment, of a day or season). Thus the best way to establish a difference between the plane of immanence and desire is to say that the plane of immanence refers to the network of habits and their always external relations, whereas desire refers to the way the plane of immanence works. It refers to processes, affects, and impersonal contemplations. Desire implies a plane of immanence, whereas the plane of immanence bears witness to desire.

Those two ideas—pain-pleasure as impersonal contraction of habit on the plane of immanence and passivity conceived of as vital force or desire—bring us closer to Deleuze's radically different interpretation of masochism. But in order to arrive there, we must make a detour and address the question of active syntheses, for masochism appears as a reaction to them.

Active synthesis operates reactively with respect to the little larval selves: It "is defined by the test of reality in an 'objectal' relation and it is precisely according to the reality principle that the Ego tends to 'be activated,' to be actively unified, to unite all its small composing and contemplative passive egos, and to be topologically distinguished from the Id. The passive egos were already integrations but only local integrations, as mathematicians say; whereas the active self is an attempt at global integration" (*D&R*, 98). The ego as global integration of identity is thus the power of negation of differences—the power of their totalization—insofar as it negates its disconnectedness and establishes an organic *dispositif* of power ("organic" here means an attempt at connecting what is free and unstable). As Deleuze puts it: "Whereas active synthesis points beyond passive synthesis towards global integrations and the supposition of identical totalisable objects, passive synthesis, as it develops, points beyond itself towards the contemplation of partial objects which remain non-totalisable" (101).

The integrative power of active synthesis first of all synthesizes the body. Instead of being a surface of relations constituted by contractions of pure pain and populated by passive egos, the body becomes an "organized" or organic body, a body with forms and determinate organs. This reactive becoming-into-"being" happens through the process of specularization and interiorization. Active syntheses therefore introduce a different idea of the body and by the same token change the concept of pleasure and pain.

Another way to put this would be to say that the active synthesis of the ego gathers little selves into "shapes" and thus changes the body of indeterminate sexuality (relations of contractions) into a stabilized, sexed body. The point of agreement between Deleuze and Foucault, according to Deleuze, was precisely Foucault's thesis in *The History of Sexuality* that the speculative power of active synthesis forms organs and reduces sexuality to sexes and their molar differences: "I take one of the most beautiful theses of *History of Sexuality*: the dispositif of sexuality [*"dispositif"* is here understood as the power of active synthesis] reduces sexuality to sex (to difference between sexes . . . etc, and psychoanalysis is full of this reductionism)" ("Desire and Pleasure," 186–187). Deleuze has in mind Foucault's notorious statement from *The History of Sexuality*: "We must not make the mistake of thinking that sex is an autonomous agency which secondarily produces manifold effects over the entire length of its surface of contact with power. On the contrary, sex is the most speculative, most ideal, and most internal element in a deployment of sexuality organized by power in its grip on *bodies and their materiality, their forces, energies, sensations and pleasures*" (155). As in Deleuze, bodies are here conceived of as the pure materiality or literality of forces, relations, energies, and sensations (contractions). By referring to sex as the most internal or ideal element of sexuality, Foucault is obviously insisting on the Hegelian speculative-dialectical terminology. The question becomes: how are we to understand the thesis that sex is the most speculative point of sexuality? Keeping in mind the Hegelian understanding of those terms (speculative, ideal, internal), one could say that sex, as the "most speculative" moment, is the point of actualization of sexuality. Even though neither Deleuze nor Foucault spelled it out in these terms, sex, I am suggesting, is the moment when sexuality turns into reality, which in Hegel is the reality of the idea. Sex is thus the idea or reason of sexuality. In order for this realization of sexuality as reasonable sex to occur, however, there must exist a nonreasonable, merely "natural" force of negation of ideality that will be sublated by the realization of that very ideality into sex, by the collapsing of sexuality into sex. And it is only when reality and self-consciousness fall into one, that is, when sexuality or the body without organs collapses into the "idea," that the body becomes the sexed body. Sex (as the speculative moment) is an effect of the belief that the "ideal" moment will become real (sexual difference is thus nothing but a speculative difference).

It thus seems that the production of sex takes the same form as the production of (metaphorical) pain. In order to appear, sex has to idealize sexuality in the same way that metaphorical pain spiritualizes pure pain. The constitution of sex is thus nothing other than the production of (transcendental) pain. Sex could thus be determined as the transcendental principle of pain (or vice versa). And it is only against the backdrop of this structure that pleasure comes into play as quasi-transcendental concept, as it were, as the translation and appropriation of the subject's own pain and/or sex. For pleasure now appears not as a "contraction" or passion but as a process of reconciliation (mediation) of the subject with its own pain, or sex, or body. That is why, I am proposing, Deleuze's main question becomes not how to achieve pleasure but how to get rid of it, how to liberate desire from the oppressive (identifying) force of pleasure.

"I cannot give any positive value to pleasure," says Deleuze, "because pleasure seems to me to interrupt the immanent process of desire; pleasure seems to be on the side of strata and organization.... Pleasure seems to me to be the only means for a person or a subject to 'find itself again' in a process that surpasses it. It is a reterritorialization" ("Desire," 190). Appropriated by active synthesis, pleasure becomes one of its forces, precisely, the force of individualization. And it is because pleasure is always personal that it is fundamentally opposed to desire and that it interrupts it. In contrast to pleasure, desire is a motion or process that surpasses the person. Desire negates the person who lets himself go into desire so that there is only desire, impersonal life, passive contractions. The question of whose desire it is or who takes pleasure in this desire is therefore particularly inane, for the whole point is precisely to travel on the waves of desire without pleasure.

But how are we to succeed in this effort to reach desire as the nonprinciple that resists pleasure? This is where masochism comes into play in a decisive way. For masochism is a complex strategy that works against pleasure, against the ego and therefore against the politics of globalization; it is a strategy that reestablishes free, little, local differences, which is why its main characteristic is its resistance to the law. Masochism achieves that through several maneuvers, the most important of which is the contractual relation.

Deleuze never tired of repeating that masochism depends on a contract that has nothing to do with understanding it as the regulation of the system of punishment, nothing to do with reinforcing the Freudian idea that it culminates in moral masochism, in the desire to be subjected to the law and its force of sanction. For the masochistic contract is, in fact, the very resistance to the law. It is the freeing of desire as process that negates the law: "desire is in no sense connected to the Law."[10] But how is that achieved? The way the contract is rooted in masochism "seems to have something to do with breaking the link between desire and pleasure: pleasure interrupts desire, so that the constitution of desire as a process must ward off pleasure, repress it to infinity."[11] The contract negotiates the possibility of a process that would repress pleasure to infinity and thus make it inaccessible. The contract contracts the infinite postponement of pleasure. By so doing, it breaks the link between desire and pleasure, freeing one from the other. As a result, the process of self-constitution of the subject is blocked (postponed to infinity). For once pleasure (which constitutes the subject) is obviated, the process of impersonal desire comes into play: "Desire cannot be attained except at the point where someone is deprived of the power of saying 'I'. Far from directing itself towards an object, desire can only be reached at the point where someone no longer searches for or grasps an object any more than he grasps himself as subject" (89). The contract therefore "contracts" the impersonal and wards off the law (for the impersonal is precisely what cannot be identified by the law).

Warding off the law is the negation of pleasure because it opens up a space for the formation of a plane, for the formation of desire as an endless wave of contractions. Masochistic desire is all about waves or events. A wave-event is an extension or else an "element stretched over the following ones such that it is a whole and the following elements are its parts" (Deleuze, *The Fold*, 77). As an extension, it "contains neither a final term nor limit." In contrast to how one might commonly understand it (a dramatic turnabout, a theatrical reversal of everything, a momentous blow that interrupts certain processes), the event is here conceived of as a delicate, very fragile, and elegant thing, an almost imperceptible vibration, "an audible wave, a luminous wave."

Deleuze makes it clear that there is also a second component to the event: "Extensive series have their intrinsic properties (for example, height, intensity, timbre of a sound, a tint, a value, a saturation of color)" (77). And it is this combination of extensions and their intrinsic properties that constitutes an event-wave, properly speaking. The wave comes as what will come: it is both arrival and its postponement. And masochism would be precisely about receiving and delaying pain waves that suspend the "I" (hence warding off active syntheses). As Deleuze puts it: "The woman-torturer sends a delayed wave of pain over the masochist, who makes use of it obviously not as a source of pleasure but as a flow to be followed in the uninterrupted process of desire" (*Clinical*, 53). The masochist does not use the waves of pain as a source of pleasure precisely because pleasure gathers together. For the same reason, Deleuze insists, it is wrong to say that the masochist wants the pain for pain's sake: "It is false to say that the masochist is looking for pain but just as false to say that he is looking for pleasure in a particularly suspensive or roundabout way" (*Plateaus*, 152). Masochism is about neither pain nor pleasure but the extension and intension of desire.

Masochism is thus organized around this suspension or waiting that is a vibration without a timbre and therefore a wave: "What becomes essential is waiting or suspense" (*Clinical*, 53). But, inasmuch as it is composed of the motion of desire, that waiting is already impersonal; it is a vibration of desire, its flow. Waiting never happens as its own self-reflection, in the form of "I am waiting." Such an attitude is, strictly speaking, impossible, for its occurrence mobilizes the subject, forcing him to interrupt the process. Masochistic waiting occurs as the suspense that precisely suspends the "I." This impersonal waiting therefore has the form of "it is coming, it is not coming," "it is and it is not," the form, that is, that connects "is" with "is not" and so suspends both being and nonbeing.

The literality of pain, the absence of self-reflection that arrives as pain waves, suggests that pain always happens as the transformation of extension into pure intensity (we thus arrive at the process of passive syntheses). This transformation is of crucial importance for Deleuze, for it introduces the possibility of constructing a new body. When extension becomes pure intensity, there appears what Deleuze already called in *The Logic of Sense* the "body without organs" (188). It is called the "BWO" precisely because all extension becomes intense. There is now only the timbre (of pain). The body without organs is such an impersonal timbre. It is neither a metaphor nor a phantasm but a quite literal and unthinkable spreading of pain waves: a proliferation of pure intensities, pure pain, an entity event. The best one can say about it is a rather "empty" circular thesis: it cannot be interpreted because it is literal, because it is a meaning that has collapsed into its referent: "Only intensities pass and circulate. Still, a BWO is not a scene, a place, or even a support upon which something comes to pass. It has nothing to do with phantasy, there is nothing to interpret. The BWO causes intensities to pass; it produces and distributes them in a spatium that is itself intensive, lacking extension" (*Plateaus*, 153). It is from this intensive "spatium" that a space is produced step by step and each time in a different way, with no a priori categories. Intensities spread around, connecting themselves in various ways, thus forming yet new extensions as arrivals of so many new intensities. The process is endless as long as it is not interrupted by pleasure (by the reappearance of the "I"). It is a spreading of the ocean of impersonal, neutral waves of pain.

RHYTHM OF SUFFERING — DERRIDA

Speculating on Derrida, who cultivated a habit of speculating on Freud, one might venture to say that Deleuze's creation of the concept of masochism, as a theory of "identity" based on pain that would escape any psychoanalytic apprehension of it, could be seen—from the vantage point of "Resistances"—as nothing but a frontal attack on psychoanalysis. Being a blunt attack, it would have to fail, or so Derrida would think, for like all such full frontals it would amount only to a calculable effect of obedience to the modern injunction to resist psychoanalysis: "Must one resist? And, first of all, psychoanalysis?" If one must resist, then Deleuze's resistance, far from being a creation of a concept that undermines the psychoanalytic understanding of personal identity, would be a symptom of a more general—epochal—resistance to psychoanalysis that itself would have to be analyzed: "If it were necessary to resist analysis, one would still have to know whence comes this 'one must' and what it means. One would still have to analyze it" (Derrida, *Resistances of Psychoanalysis*, 1). Such an analysis could then conclude that resistance to psychoanalysis is the resistance of an analysis that is susceptible to analysis, as though it wanted to keep its distance from the analyst in order to keep its secret for itself and thus capitalize on it. But, in offering such a reading, an analysis of the resistance to psychoanalysis would risk turning itself into a psychoanalytic reading, which would again be a very calculable outcome, destined to fail in advance. Resistance to psychoanalysis and analysis of it would have to be read as an affirmation of what is being resisted. It is for that reason that, in contrast to Deleuze, Derrida—to speculate a little further—resists such a resistance. Another reason is related to the ethics of deconstruction: a frontal attack as total refusal never does justice to the refused. There must be something in the refused worth praising and accepting. Derrida's resistance to resistances would be related to his effort "to do justice to Freud."

"To Do Justice to Freud" is, however, the quotation from Foucault that Derrida makes the title of his essay on Foucault's resistances to Freud, there where he tries to attune us to the fact that, in his book on madness, Foucault didn't quite manage to do what he said he would do: "justice to Freud." As Derrida puts it: " 'To do justice to Freud' will more and more come to mean putting on trial a psycho-analysis that will have participated . . . in the order of the immemorial figures of the Father and the Judge" (90). According to Derrida's reading of Foucault, the "mystical foundation of the authority" of the analyst (the Judge) and hence of psychoanalysis (being the verdict of the judge) would be based on a certain "unjust" exchange between analyst and analysand. The latter would secretly (imperceptibly to himself) let go of something that he wanted to keep for itself or would betray a fear of doing so, or else the analyst would act as if he were appropriating secret knowledge about the analyzed. In any case, elaborating on Foucault's suggestions, Derrida suggests that in the end psychoanalysis would come down to something like a "technique of the secret" (at this point, in a section entitled "The Other Secret of Psychoanalysis," Derrida reads Foucault in such a way that his and Foucault's voices are somewhat mixed, and it is not quite clear if this is Foucault talking or Derrida ventriloquizing). As such a technique, psychoanalysis would operate according to an economy of the secret that makes its turnover on the black market of blackmail. As if the analyst were making a secret approach to the analysand's "secret" and then profiting on that capital, speculating with it. Hence "it would be necessary to follow throughout these pages all the ins and outs of the value of a secret, of a certain secrecy value," says Derrida concerning pages from *Madness and Civilization*: "This value would come down in the end, to a technique of the secret, and of the secret without knowledge. Whenever knowledge can only be supposed, whenever, as a result, one knows that supposition cannot give rise to knowledge . . . there is the invisible production (for no one ever witnesses it) of a secrecy effect, of what we might call a speculation on the capital secret or on the capital of the secret" (92). It is this capital of the secret—even if in the form of the simulacrum of "real" knowledge—that enables the analyst to assume the position of a "devilish" power "entrusted" with a role like that of the evil demon in Descartes's *Meditations*. The very "uncertainty" of the analyst's knowledge (does he know or doesn't he; he looks as if he saw through me) and secrecy puts the analysand in the role of a hunted "victim," deluded by the analyst himself, who thus comes to play the role of "unreason." And so the analyst becomes for Foucault, according to Derrida, the embodiment of the Evil Demon. Derrida writes: "Fictive omnipotence and a divine, or rather 'quasi-divine,' power, divine by simulacrum, at once divine and satanic—these are the very traits of an Evil Genius, which are now being attributed to the figure of the doctor. The doctor suddenly begins to resemble in a troubling way the figure of unreason that continued to haunt what is called the classical age after the *act of force* [*coup de force*] of the *cogito*" (95).

Presuming, however, that the title of Derrida's essay is ironic—if, by (ironically) quoting Foucault, it undoes the claim that it does justice to Freud—then Derrida's resistance to Foucault's reading of the position of the analyst is driven by the same argument that organized his response to Foucault's understanding of the Evil Demon. The problem with Descartes's *Meditations* or with Freud's understanding of psychoanalytic technique is not, for Derrida, that they exclude unreason (from meditations, from analysis) only in order to introduce it secretly in the figure of the evil god or malicious analyst. Rather—and this was Derrida's main point in his dispute with Foucault regarding the status of unreason in *Meditations*—the "scandal" of modern, classical thought is that it generalizes madness by turning reason into one of its variations. In other words, if the economy of the secret and mystical inauguration of authority is based precisely on a technique of the secret, it is because the exchange that Foucault considers to be exclusive for psychoanalysis is a "general economy" of modern subjectivity: the subject of modern thinking is constituted through a process of re-turning to itself through a self-mirroring in which it gets a glimpse of itself. Armed with this "knowledge" (the momentary, secret appropriation) of his image, the subject would assume mastery over himself. He would become autonomous, his own author or authority. And if, for Derrida, resistance to psychoanalysis is nothing other than a symptomatic obedience to a certain injunction that needs to be analyzed, if such a resistance consequently always fails, it is because it never goes in the "right" direction. For it takes the answer to the question of how radically to resist psychoanalysis to be found in the accusation that analysis oppresses thought, whereas radical resistance to psychoanalysis (one that cannot be analyzed) is achieved by "inventing" a thinking that would not be caught in the economy of secret.

One should notice that elsewhere, as if still siding with the thesis that the analyst capitalizes on a secret through a secretive technique, Derrida develops a theory of subjectivity on whose secret no one could capitalize. His "Passions" thus could be read as a secret resistance not only to the mystical authority of the analyst but also, by extension, to any authority, to the authority of subjectivity as well (for any form the *autos* or *auctoritas* assumes is based on cashing in a secret value with interest). And, to the extent that his text is an effort at formulating such a nonanalyzable secret, it is, by the same token, a secret (nonanalyzable) resistance to psychoanalysis, one that neither accepts nor negates it but desists (from) it.

The secret Derrida speaks of as a place of passion would not be a question of "a representation dissimulated by a conscious subject, nor, moreover, of the content of an unconscious representation, some secret or mysterious motive that the moralist or the psychoanalyst might have the skill to detect, or, as they say, to demystify" ("Passions," 24). As if echoing Foucault in reverse, Derrida is saying that the secret in question could not be the source of the mystical foundation of the analyst's power for he could not demystify it. The secret he has in mind would thus entail a dethroning of the analyst's authority for the latter would be prevented from capitalizing on it. But if such a secret is unanalyzable, it is not because the analysand has learned how to resist analysis by hiding his secret better but because the secret is of a kind that neither resists nor accepts anything (for example, analysis). In something that resembles a long list of the characteristics of such a secret, Derrida consistently defines it by means of double negation, something that is "neither" this "nor" that: it is like the abyss of separation whose meaning neither speaks nor hides anything; it is neither reflective nor anamorphic; rather, it is simply in the mode of nonbelonging, a passive "there is something secret"; its truth is related neither to remembering nor forgetting; it cannot be stabilized by an idea of *adequatio* or of *mimesis*; it is nonphenomenal and "its nonphenomenality is without relation, even negative relation, to phenomenality" (26). The nonphenomenal "nature" of the secret refers then to a different understanding of truth and, as Derrida puts it in "Desistance," another experience of truth is always conditioned by a new "question of the subject" (25). In short, the secret would thus lack any identifiable being.

The "there is (some[thing] secret)" that incapacitates the power of the analyst also incapacitates the power of subjectivity. Its possibility negates transcendental subjectivity in all its modern forms but—and Derrida is very clear here—most explicitly in the form given to it by psychoanalysis. For the secret in question is neither the content of an "unconscious representation" nor the "dissimulation of the conscious subject." "Neither conscious nor unconscious" refers to a subjectivity different from that imagined by psychoanalysis. Therefore, if the secret can escape the analyst, it is because it does not derive from the specular order at all: it escapes the representational economy of subjectivity. Secrecy is constitutive of a self that does not see itself.

In other words, through a motion "proper" to it, the secret constitutes a self for which nothing is proper. In the "depths" of identity (of the proper and of the proper name), it is something that constantly disappears in its own name: "What returns to your name, to the secret of your name, is the ability to disappear in your name" ("Passions," 13). The re-turn (something like a "trope of reflection") that constitutes subjectivity by giving it the ground on which to represent itself (and hence itself for another—the analyst, for example), here returns, but as the ability to disappear: more than is required for reflection, therefore, and more than the analyst would like. Its re-turn turns against itself by going through itself; through such an invagination, it disappears precisely in the moment of return. In its return, it surpasses itself, as if going beyond itself and opening a "new" way for its motion, but one that no one can see and testify to. It makes a "hole" in the self at the "place" where representation can occur. For that reason, I am suggesting, Derrida calls the return of re-flection that tears the subject apart a wound: "Yes, the wound is there, over there. Is there some other thing ever that may be legible? Some other thing than the trace of a wound? . . . Do you know another definition of event?" ("Sauf le nom," 60). Reflection, as a "proper disproportion" of the self that disappears through itself, becomes a "living" trace that is not even a scar but a persistently painful injury that does not speak (is secret) precisely because it exists at the place where representation (including the possibility of talking about itself) would occur.

The wound cuts the subject in a way that is radically different from the psychoanalytic divide. The subject constituted by the secret would not exist separated within itself by an unstable and porous borderline that divides conscious and unconscious but would be this very divide as the self absent from itself. The disappearance of the self through itself would mean precisely this "ability to disappear in your name . . . and thus not to return to itself, which is the condition of the gift (for example, of the name) but also of all expansion of self, of all augmentation of self, of all *auctoritas*. In the two cases of this same divided passion, it is impossible to dissociate the greatest profit and the greatest privation" ("Passions," 13). The self that "remains" in this return is not an *autos*, not autochthonous, but neither is it authoritarian. By extension, then, it is barely a self, or, rather, it is a self only as a "divided passion," the passive suffering of its own cut. And insofar as the self gets surpassed in this return, the greatest profit from it (the "constitution" of the nonappropriative self) is the effect of its greatest privation (for the exposed and passive self is precisely bereft of itself). With this idea of the self as privation of selfhood (as impersonal wound), Derrida comes close to Deleuze's passive syntheses of impersonal life.

The "event" that Derrida describes—reflection becoming an arrow that passes through and surpasses the self—would have to have a paradoxical effect. For in traversing the self, it turns it into a self that is fundamentally open (the wound is always open). But since this openness appears at the "site" of re-flection (making it blind to itself), no one can bear witness to it. The openness of the wound thus has the form of a seal. In Derrida's words, "an event, if I understand right, that would have the form of a seal, as if, witness without witness, it were committed to keeping a secret" ("Sauf le nom," 60). Such a commitment is structurally necessary. For it is not that somebody decides to keep the secret; it is rather that the secret cannot be "memorized," transferred, revealed, communicated, or translated; indeed, we might have to call it "literal." It does not belong to something that has happened but is something that is its own happening: "We testify to the secret that is without content, without a content separable from its performative experience, from its performative tracing" ("Passions," 24). Not that the secret is without content, a passive blankness; rather, its content is (or is inseparable from) its performative inscription, hence inseparable from the affliction of a wound. It is thus the moment (endless, because endlessly repeatable) of injuring and dividing that prevents the subject from healing itself by sublating the wound (for that would mean, precisely, to separate the content from its performative inscription and to testify to it). The event is "offered," but it can be understood only as an immediate experience of direct suffering, which, analytically speaking, has to be invisible. To say "we testify to the secret" is thus to say "we experience the wound," we are exposed to the injury, but such an utterance is to be differentiated from the performance of an endurance to which no one testifies. We are thus not only the endurance of such an event but its very trace. The self exists as this passive, incommunicable exposure to the wound.

In *The Gift of Death*, the content of the secret inseparable from its performative inscription will be referred to as an "experience of trembling." "A secret always *makes* you tremble" because it does not announce its arrival as a quiver or a shiver (53). And if "makes" is here italicized, it is because the secret is what makes the self by turning it into a sheer trembling. It is like a "solicitation," an earthquake of a being in the sense in which, as Derrida put it already in "Différance," "*solicitare* in old Latin means to shake as a whole, to make tremble in entirety" (21). The "secret" self is made of intensities like the shocks or waves of an earthquake. The selfless self that Derrida talks about is a passive tympanum of waves of suffering.

Thus, it seems, in deciding to talk about waves of passion and suffering (passion means "to suffer," from Latin "*passus*," past participle of "*pati*," "to endure, to suffer"), Derrida is strategically close to Deleuze's enterprise even though his "reading" of pain is radically different. For if he opts for the term "suffering" rather than pain, it is for the same reason Deleuze prefers "pain"; namely, it is suffering that, for Derrida, is impersonal, whereas it is pain that personalizes. In "opting" for this terminological distribution, Derrida is also "secretly" performing his desistance with respect not only to psychoanalysis but also to Heidegger. First, in carefully avoiding the term "pain" and almost "systematically" choosing "suffering," Derrida resists Freud's negation of the difference between the two terms. According to Freud's thesis advanced in *Civilization and Its Discontents*, "in the last analysis all suffering is nothing else than sensation" (27), hence always reducible to physical pain and thus always "personalized" (always the pain of my body). But he perhaps also had in mind Heidegger's remark from *The Question of Being*, which Lacoue-Labarthe analyzes in *Typography*, in turn the subject of Derrida's "Desistance." For Heidegger: "If anyone indeed dared to think through the relationship between 'work' as the fundamental trait of being and 'pain,' moving back past Hegel's *Logic*, then the Greek word for pain, namely *algos* would first come into speech, for us. Presumably, *algos* is related to *alego* which, as an intensive of *lego* signifies intimate gathering. Then pain would be what gathers in the most intimate" (quoted in Lacoue-Labarthe, 57). In referring "elliptically" to the most intimate gathering of the labor of pain, Heidegger is "extremely prudent," says Lacoue-Labarthe. For he precisely avoids explicitly addressing "what could well be the essential, namely, the 'intimate implication' between *work*, *pain*, and *Gestalt*" (56). What is essential, in other words, "is the relation between *work* and *pain*, on the one hand, and *(re)presentation by figure, gestalthafte Darstellung*, on the other" (56). It could be, then, that the representation or self-representation by figure (and, by the same token, the firm standing of the subject as specular "figural" subject) is possible only through the activity of pain.

In contrast to a pain that subjectivizes, suffering, as Derrida points out, would be outside the economy of representation and thus of "work, pain and figure." It would be a dissemination of intensities of passions without the intimate gathering and erection of the subject within itself. Instead of an (analyzable) "I am," there would be a "there is" or, indeed, "something secret." And the "there is," as impersonal (not intimately gathered) rhythms and waves of intensities, would not only correspond to what Deleuze called literal impersonal pain but come closer to "another" psychoanalysis. It would reveal its secret collusion with Reik's rhythmic-melodic individual or its perhaps less secret alliance with Lacoue-Labarthe's analysis in "The Echo of the Subject" (a chapter in *Typography* also analyzed by Derrida in "Desistance"). Such a "suffering" self, made of waves (or, more faithful to Lacoue-Labarthe's terminology, a "melodic" self that writes its "allobiography," a life written by sound waves), would touch on a "phenomenon that, despite the catharsis, begins to exceed and broach the subject's economy, and ruin it from within. Laughter and tears, sarcasm and cheers . . . , and all those emotions . . . in which consciousness disappears and the body is in spasms, where there is produced a suspension or a fundamental and rending 'caesura,' all of them are perhaps of the order of *l'emoi*. Meaning *powerlessness*" (*Typography*, 189). And Derrida's "secret" dividing of the self would be precisely that caesura: a nonrepresentable and nonanalyzable wound torn out of the "wholeness" of an identity. The sheer existence of such a tear.

The nearly "total" affinity in thesis between Deleuze and Derrida that Derrida spoke of in mourning Deleuze should now be somewhat clearer. For whether the "new self" is thought of in terms of impersonal waves of pain or passion (which is not to reduce the irreducible difference between the two), what is unsettled in both cases is the firm standing of psychoanalysis and its "figural" or specular subject. In both cases, something like the groundlessness of psychoanalysis is not only exposed but endured.

NOTES

1. The argument I am pursuing here will appear in a more elaborate version in a book on the micropolitics of pain that I am writing in collaboration with Gregg Lambert.
2. See also Derrida's "Desistance."
3. See Freud, *Three Essays on the Theory of Sexuality*, hereafter *Sexuality*: "As regards . . . sadism, the roots . . . are easy to detect in the normal. The sexuality of most male human beings contains an element of

aggressiveness—a desire to subjugate" (23). And, "Thus sadism would correspond to an aggressive component of the sexual instinct which has become independent and exaggerated" (24).

4. Symptoms of neurotics are "substitutes—transcriptions as it were—for a number of emotionally cathected mental processes, wishes and desires, which, by the operation of a special psychical procedure (repression), have been prevented from obtaining discharge in psychical activity" (Freud, *Sexuality*, 30).

5. Freud, "Beyond the Pleasure Principle," hereafter "Pleasure."

6. Freud, "The Economic Problem of Masochism," hereafter "Masochism."

7. Deleuze, *Nietzsche and Philosophy*, 129.

8. Deleuze, *Difference and Repetition*, 96, hereafter *D&R*.

9. This logic then enables the construction of a Kantian ethics (the interiorization of a duty imposed from outside) that is very similar to Freud's explanation of masochism and the interiorization of pain. One should keep in mind that Freud recognizes this masochistic element in Kantian ethics when, in "Masochism," he relates moral masochism (the sadistic superego torturing the masochistic ego) to the Kantian categorical imperative: "The super ego—the conscience at work in the ego—may then become harsh, cruel and inexorable against the ego which is in its charge. Kant's Categorical Imperative is thus the direct heir of the Oedipus complex" (422).

10. Deleuze and Guattari, *A Thousand Plateaus*, 89, hereafter *Plateaus*.

11. Deleuze, *Essays Critical and Clinical*, 53, hereafter "*Clinical*."

BIBLIOGRAPHY

Deleuze, Gilles. "Desire and Pleasure." Trans. Daniel W. Smith. In *Foucault and His Interlocutors*, ed. Arnold I. Davidson, 183–192. Chicago: University of Chicago Press, 1997.

———. *Difference and Repetition*. Trans. Paul Patton. New York: Columbia University Press, 1994. Originally published as *Différence et répétition* (Paris: Presses Universitaires de France, 1968).

———. *Essays Critical and Clinical*. Trans. Daniel W. Smith and Michael A. Greco. Minneapolis: University of Minnesota Press, 1997.

———. *The Fold: Leibniz and the Baroque*. Trans. Tom Conley. Minneapolis: University of Minnesota Press, 1993.

———. *The Logic of Sense.* Trans. Mark Lester with Charles Stivale. Ed. Constantin V. Boundas. New York: Columbia University Press, 1990. Originally published as *Logique du sens* (Paris: Minuit, 1982).

———. *Nietzsche and Philosophy.* Trans. Hugh Tomlinson. New York: Columbia University Press, 1983.

———. *Pure Immanence: Essays on A Life.* Trans. Anne Boyman. New York: Zone, 2001.

Deleuze, Gilles and Félix Guattari. *Anti–Oedipus: Capitalism and Schizophrenia.* Trans. Robert Hurley, Mark Seem, and Helen R. Lane. Minneapolis: University of Minnesota Press, 1983.

———. *A Thousand Plateaus: Capitalism and Schizophrenia.* Trans. Brian Massumi. London: Athlone, 1987.

Deleuze, Gilles and Claire Parnet. *Dialogues.* Trans. Hugh Tomlinson and Barbara Habberjam. New York: Columbia University Press, 1987.

Derrida, Jacques. "Desistance." In Philippe Lacoue-Labarthe, *Typography*, trans. Christopher Fynsk, 1–42. Stanford, Calif.: Stanford University Press, 1998.

———. "Différance." In *Margins of Philosophy*, trans. Alan Bass, 1–28. Chicago: University of Chicago Press, 1982.

———. *The Gift of Death.* Trans. David Wills. Chicago: University of Chicago Press, 1995.

———. "Passions: 'An Oblique Offering.'" In *On The Name*, trans. David Wood, John P. Leavey, Jr., and Ian McLeod, ed. Thomas Dutoit, 3–34. Stanford, Calif.: Stanford University Press, 1995.

———. *Resistances of Psychoanalysis.* Trans. Peggy Kamuf, Pascale-Anne Brault, and Michael Naas. Stanford: Stanford University Press, 1998. Originally published as *Résistances de la psychanalyse* (Paris: Galilée, 1996).

———. "Sauf le nom (Post-Scriptum)." In *On The Name*, trans. David Wood, John P. Leavey, Jr., and Ian McLeod, ed. Thomas Dutoit, 35–88. Stanford, Calif.: Stanford University Press, 1995.

———. *The Work of Mourning.* Trans. Pascale-Anne Brault. Ed. Pascale-Anne Brault and Michael Naas. Chicago: University of Chicago Press, 2003.

Foucault, Michel. *The History of Sexuality.* Vol. 1, *An Introduction.* Trans. Robert Hurley. New York: Vintage, 1990.

———. *Madness and Civilization: A History of Insanity in the Age of Reason.* Trans. Richard Howard. New York: Vintage, 1988.

Freud, Sigmund. "Beyond the Pleasure Principle." Trans. James Strachey. In *On Metapsychology: The Theory of Psychoanalysis*, ed. Angela Richards and Albert Dickson, 11:269–338. The Penguin Freud Library. London: Penguin, 1991.
———. *Civilization and Its Discontents*. Trans. James Strachey. New York: Norton, 1989.
———. "The Economic Problem of Masochism." Trans. James Strachey. In *On Metapsychology: The Theory of Psychoanalysis*, ed. Angela Richards and Albert Dickson, 11:409–426. The Penguin Freud Library. London: Penguin, 1991.
———. *Group Psychology and the Analysis of the Ego*. Trans. James Strachey. New York: Norton, 1989.
———. *Three Essays on the Theory of Sexuality*. Trans. and ed. James Strachey. New York: Basic Books, 1962.
Heidegger, Martin. *The Question of Being*. Trans. Jean T. Wilde and William Kluback. New York: Twayne, 1958.
Lacoue-Labarthe, Philippe. *Typography*. Trans. Christopher Fynsk. Stanford, Calif.: Stanford University Press, 1998.

THE ONLY OTHER APPARATUS OF FILM

(A Few Fantasies About *Différance, Démontage,* and Revision in Experimental Film and Video)

Akira Mizuta Lippit

"THIS IS ONLY A DREAM"

"This is only a dream." An unknown voice interrupts the dream. It enters the mise-en-scène from elsewhere, from a place both within and without the dream, a slight excess infused into the world of the dream. "Das ist ja nur ein Traum." There and not there, the voice is *folded* into the dream as a trace of exteriority, inside and out, inside-out. The nondiegetic utterance suggests, for Sigmund Freud, evidence of a secondary revision, habitual, he argues, in all dreams. Another apparatus has interrupted the flow of the dream, leaving a trace of its intervention in the form of a *différance*: another subject (of enunciation) from another temporal order has entered, like Chris Marker's time traveler, the dreamwork.[1] The topography of the dreamwork has been, to use Gilles Deleuze and Félix Guattari's idiom, "deterritorialized." Without a time and territory proper to it, the dream—the mechanism of this particular dream—has been dismantled; its machinic structure, the components of its apparatus, reduced to parts. The anonymous voice divides the subject, multiplies and displaces it from the dream: it adds a second voice, which now also speaks, "This is only a dream." Freud's emblematic phrase disrupts the illusion of temporal coherence and exposes the presence of another subject and temporality already at work within the dream. "We must be several in order to write," says Jacques Derrida, "and even to 'perceive'" ("Freud," 226).

Freud devotes the sixth chapter of *The Interpretation of Dreams* (1900) to the dreamwork, identifying four factors that contribute to the construction of dreams. The "displacement of psychical intensities," "considerations of representability" (as visual and acoustic memory traces), "condensation," and "secondary revision" serve as mechanisms by which dream thoughts evade censorship and congeal as dream texts. Each factor is designed, according to Freud, to relieve the pressures of the unconscious without damaging the psychic economy of the subject. The fourth element of Freud's scheme, secondary revision, contributes less to the content of the dream than to its agency. Only in instances of extreme affect, when the continuation of the dream is threatened, does the second agent appear, make itself seen or heard, and attempt to reassure the dreamer: "I am here but not entirely present; you are not where you think you are, so you can return there, where you were, safely." The representation of chaos as coherence. Freud says: "In my view the contemptuous critical judgment, 'it's only a dream,' appears in a dream when the censorship, which is never quite asleep, feels that it has been taken unawares by a dream which has already been allowed through. It is too late to suppress it, and accordingly the censorship uses these words to meet the anxiety of the distressing feeling aroused by it" (489). When the censor also falls asleep; when both subjects are asleep. Something has evaded the censor; an idea, suffused with affect, has entered into thought, and the contemptuous utterance "it *is* only a dream" seeks to control the damage of a thought unleashed from the unconscious, by dismissing it and the entire work into which it has entered. The phrase serves as the index of a lapse, a failure of the censorship to prevent the entry of surplus affect—usually, but not always, associated with anxiety or displeasure—into the sleeping subject. It also exposes, on the occasion of the utterance, the presence of a censoring agent, a second apparatus at work in the construction of dreams. ("The apparent exteriority of political censorship," says Derrida of Freud's dreamwork, "refers to an essential censorship which binds the writer to his own writing" ["Freud," 26].) Two machines construct the dream, or, put another way, the dream emerges from a divided machine disguised as one. Dream and dream machine consist in Freud's thought as assemblages of parts, authors, and agencies that are designed to appear organic. As with most Freudian structures, the exception or anomaly provides the rule, in this case, a law of the dreamwork. All dreams, Freud insists, are reworked in the first instance, have already been revised at the moment of their appearance as dreams. Those dreams that appear the most coherent have been the most revised during sleep. "Dreams occur," says Freud, "which at a superficial view, may seem faultlessly logical and reasonable; . . . they appear to have a meaning, but that meaning is as far removed as possible from their true significance. . . . It is in these dreams that the secondary revision has played around with the materials most freely. . . . They are dreams which might be said to have been already interpreted once, before being submitted to waking interpretation" (490).

Insisting on the habitual nature of secondary revision, Freud sees the working-over of dreams as a necessary process by which unadulterated dream thoughts are reassembled and realized as dreams. Secondary revision "fills up the gaps in the dream-structure with shreds and patches" (490). It imposes an order where there is none, an impression of narrative and structural unity against the chaotic force of the unconscious. At stake in Freud's claim is a defense against the void that threatens to open within each psyche, the unrepresentable form of the unconscious, which relies on the activity of imagination—the production of visual and acoustical images—to disguise the presence, always, of nothing. Of *only* nothing. In this sense, secondary revision functions as a form of editing, as a practice of arranging dream materials into semblances of order and causality. Rarely, says Freud, does secondary revision "create new contributions to dreams. . . . It exerts its influence principally by its preferences and selections from psychical material in the dream-thoughts that has already been formed" (491). Psychical materials *already there* are revised and rearranged, producing new sequences, narratives, and effects. Constructed like Vertov's cinema, dreams are assemblages forged in a psychic "factory of facts."[2] In Freud's view of the dreamwork, one finds a theory of writing: Editing as authorship; revision as inscription. An other as author; another who writes with me, beneath and alongside me, in place of me. Only an author; one author and another, one other author.

Although they seek to disguise the fact, dreams are essentially heterogeneous, authored by multiple subjects at different stages in the dream cycle and after. In this sense, the "only" of Freud's phrase also can be understood to insist on the singularity of the dream, "this is the only dream," "only this dream is." Only one, one dream. Just (*nur*) a dream, a just dream, just one dream. Beside the practical necessity of dismissing the dream as "only a dream" (in order to reassure the dreamer), another purpose of the statement may be to maintain, paradoxically, the singularity of the dream, its unity. "This is only one dream." An untenable unity, for Freud, given his view of dreams as originary translations. Dreams are, already in the first instance, translations drawn from a vast semiotics, conscious and unconscious. The dream emerges always from an irreducibly other site, an other world—the unconscious—that the dreamwork seeks to naturalize and integrate into consciousness. Only on the occasion of a failed dream, in which the surveillance has broken down, does the structure and radically foreign nature of the dream thought—the ideas and affects that constitute it—become apparent. "This is only a dream" signals a disturbance in the dramatic and temporal order of the dream, it functions like a stutter, a tear in the matrix of the dream, that reveals its internal modes of production. That is, secondary revision generates the semblance of meaning and coherence in dreams, largely in order to continue the dream but also to mask the absence of meaning as such in the unconscious. "This is only a dream" produces a rupture, a small hole through which the profound absence that sustains each psychic subject is made visible. The fundamental question of psychoanalysis asks, says Slavoj Žižek, "Why is there something instead of nothing?" (48).

The intervention of the second voice, "This is only a dream," exposes the industrial structure of the dream and implements a mode of reparative reflexivity: "You are there in that dream only. And you are here, safe, there was only a dream." The slight distance introduced by the reflexive *différance* of the statement renders the dream closer to a phantasy,[3] which Freud likens to a dream and calls a daydream (*Tagtraum*): "Closer investigation of the characteristics of these daytime phantasies shows us how right it is that these formations should bear the same name as we give to the products of our thought during the night—the name that is of 'dreams.' They share a large number of their properties with night-dreams, and their investigation might, in fact, have served as the shortest and best approach to an understanding of night-dreams" (492).

"THIS IS ONLY A PHANTASY"

In contrast to the intensity of dreams, phantasies are marked by a degree of reflexivity, by the ironic distance between the subject and its work. "(I know) this is only a dream." At the moment when the censoring mechanism, at work in all dreams, fails and the schizoid apparatus is revealed, the dream becomes a phantasy. Like dreams, phantasies are traversed by secondary revisions that inscribe a series of agents or moments of agency on a single scenario. Unlike dreams, the secondary revisions are part of the manifest structure of phantasies. Phantasies are dreams in which the process of secondary revision, rewriting, has been made transparent. "This is only a phantasy" no longer signals the termination of a reverie but rather its beginning. It doesn't end the state but prolongs it, acting as its opening. A phantasy is like and unlike a dream; it begins where the dream ends but also acts, like dreams, as a revision of the world.

Jean Laplanche and J.-B. Pontalis define a phantasy as an "imaginary scene in which the subject is a protagonist, representing the fulfilment of a wish (in the last analysis, an unconscious wish) in a manner that is distorted to a greater or lesser extent by defensive [perceptual] processes" (314). Although the mechanisms are more conscious than in dreams, the wishes remain unconscious ones. In phantasies, the subject inscribes itself always as protagonist, often against the evidence of the senses. (The author is bound neither by perceptions nor physical laws. I can be you, only you, or you and me.) Like dreams, phantasies serve as opportunities to fulfill wishes, to revise one's experience of the empirical world. They are productions, and Laplanche and Pontalis infuse the language of phantasy with the idiom of theater and film: "What Freud means in the first place by '*Phantasien*' are day-dreams, scenes, episodes, romances or fictions which the subject creates and recounts to himself in the waking state" (316). Phantasies, say Laplanche and Pontalis, are episodic, characterized by movement and narrative identification: "Even where they can be summed up in a single sentence," write Laplanche and Pontalis, "phantasies are still scripts (*scénarios*) of organised scenes which are capable of dramatisation—usually in a visual form" (318). The subject of a phantasy is inscribed as protagonist in a *sequence* "in which permutations of roles and attributions are possible" (318). Staged and performed, phantasies can be seen as psychic film projections, animated and dynamic, susceptible to habitual revision.

Apart from their classification in psychology, phantasies also carry the popular connotation of an activity outside the boundaries of reality; they suggest the work of imagination and fiction. In English, the distinction between psychoanalytic and popular uses of the word is often marked by a homonymic shift in spelling from "f" to "ph." A *différance*: the "graphic difference itself vanishes," says Derrida, "into the night, can never be sensed as a full term, but rather extends an invisible relationship, the mark of an inapparent relationship between two spectacles" ("Différance," 5). "Into the night," an "inapparent relationship between two spectacles." At work in a thinking of ph/fantasy is a dialectic between the structure of the dream, Freud's figure for and point of entry into the psychical apparatus and the unconscious, and a mode of rumination, "daydreaming," that leads to nothing, is itself of no consequence, represents the antithesis of action and meaningful thought. A thinking of two spectacles, two forms of spectacular thinking (or wishing, or representing) that "eludes both vision and hearing" (5). In psychoanalysis, everything is at stake; in the popular idiom, nothing. In psychoanalysis, phantasy represents the very possibility of a politics of the unconscious. Outside of psychoanalysis, there is no politics proper to fantasy. To fantasize, even if it signals a more dangerous line of thought and action yet to come (exposure to graphic violence, for example), does not in itself constitute a political act. In the end, "it *is* only a phantasy."

A popular view of cinema regards dramatic narratives as fantasies, forms of escape. Christian Metz likens the fiction film to a daydream or phantasy and notes the periodic convergence of film and phantasy in a spectator. This "little miracle," he says, temporarily suspends the dialectic between perception (of external images) and imagination (internal reverie) by bringing together the disparate experiences of exteriority and interiority. Of this effect peculiar to film, Metz writes: "This is the specific joy of receiving from the external world images that are usually internal, images that are familiar or not very far from familiar, of seeing them inscribed in a physical location (the screen), of discovering in this way something almost realisable in them, which was not expected, of feeling for a moment that they are not inseparable from the tonality which most often attends them, from that common and accepted yet slightly despairing impression of the impossible" (136). An impression of the impossible opens onto but also follows from a world that is at once inside and out, a world in which the distinction between interiority and exteriority has been momentarily halted and replaced with the impossible and miraculous impression of synchronicity. Inside and outside converge; psyche and world collapse. An "artificial psychosis," says Jean-Louis Baudry.[4]

Another dialectic of phantasy opens between two minor genres of film, experimental film and documentary. Minor because they exist at the limits of the cultural, political, industrial, financial, and aesthetic film economy, along with Third, minoritarian, and other forms of alternative global media. Collectively, one can refer to this world as a "minor cinema," in the sense that Deleuze and Guattari ascribe to Kafka's oeuvre: languages are deterritorialized, the individual is connected to a political immediacy, and each enunciation is always part of a collective assemblage (16–18). The minor cinema can be seen as an inversion, even a perversion, of the feature-length fiction film. Both interior and exterior worlds are made unfamiliar, distant, irreducibly foreign. Before this media, I no longer recognize the world around me or, for that matter, myself. I am only a spectator, but never the only one. Experimental film and video, which often foreground the enunciation of an individual or subject, complicate the machinery of phantasy and expand it. By contrast, the documentary, a term coined by John Grierson, which follows the earlier designation "actualities," emphasizes objectivity, history, and, ultimately, an indexical relation to reality as such.[5] (This is only a provisional distinction, already unpleasant and in need of revision.) Phantasies, or historical revisions, are superfluous in documentaries: their presence is understood to detract from the success of a work. One could posit a dialectic between documentary film or video, which is generally understood to adhere to conventions of truth, and experimental cinemas, which are permitted, even expected, to develop the presence of a discernible subjectivity, which actively interferes with objectivity. Fact and fiction, reality and fantasy, objective representation and subjective interpretation, history and memory, documentary and experimental media operate according to contradictory imperatives and could be seen, in some instances, as antinomies. To the list of oppositions, one might add another ultimately fantastic opposition: politics and psychoanalysis.

Laplanche and Pontalis, who have produced a map of psychoanalysis, a chart of its world, inscribe the operations of phantasy at the intersection of "imagination and reality." They write: "The use of the term 'phantasy' cannot fail to evoke a distinction between imagination and reality (perception). If this distinction is made into a major psycho-analytic axis of reference, we are brought to define phantasy as a purely illusory production which cannot be sustained when it is confronted with a correct apprehension of reality" (314–315). The contradiction (between imagination and reality) embodied by a phantasy is transformed into an antinomy in its encounter with "a correct apprehension of reality." But as Fredric Jameson notes in *The Seeds of Time*, a false dialectic haunts the distinction between contradictions—which share a common framework and retain the possibility of resolution—and antinomies—which, like Lyotard's *differends*, can never be resolved because of a foundational incommensurability. Contradiction and antinomy, says Jameson, are not themselves oppositional but, rather, symptomatic. They form, he writes, invoking the idiom of psychoanalysis, a symptomatology. He continues: "I will organize my symptomatology accordingly, and operate as though an antinomy were a *symptom* of a contradiction" (4). In a language infused with its own symptoms, with a massive deterritorialization of the unconscious, philosophy, visuality, politics, technology, athletics, infection, earthquakes, and inscription, Jameson suggests this line of escape: "So it is that depth forms (if any exist, like prehistoric monsters) tend to be projected up upon the surface in the anamorphic flatness of a scarcely recognizable afterimage, lighting up the board in the form of a logical paradox or a textual paralogism. We have to swim in both these worlds at once; learn to work the remote-control glove within the contamination chamber; posit a noumenal shadow world of seismographic movements and shoulderings that inscribes itself with grotesque delicacy as minute and pencil-thin lines on the graph" (4–5). At work in Jameson's assertion is a fantastic rhetoric, impossible in any one register, possible only in the polyphony of multiple subjectivity and authorship. A symptomatology, a wildness that escapes in and into the disruption of order. A phantasy.

The complex frame that surrounds documentary and experimental media, which can share political sympathies but display deep ideological, aesthetic, and practical divides, can be seen as such a symptom of contradiction, appearing as an antinomy. Even when they actively subvert the terms, documentaries return inevitably to the registers of truth and the real, which are embedded in the discursive foundations of the genre. Experimental films and videos, by contrast, are grounded in the forces of the subject. Personal, subjective, my voice or your voice, only. History and enunciation, the adherence to facts and their revision, seem to establish an irreducible distance between documentary and experimental work.

The provisional opposition between documentary and experimental form is called into question by a minor genre, form, style, or practice known as "found footage" or "recycled" cinema. Working with film and video documents that have already been established in one context, found footage works rewrite and reconfigure the material to produce a revised text that retains the material traces of the original, beneath its revision. They are assemblages and collages of other work. They are, in a sense, revised documentaries, even when the original material was not a documentary. That is, the documentary is created in the revision, an effect of the revision. Bruce Conner's reworking of atomic test footage in *Crossroads* (1976), Harun Farocki's dissection of state media representations of the final days of the Ceauşescu regime in Romania in *Videograms of a Revolution* (1992), Peter Forgács's reinscription of archival home movies of Dutch Jews condemned to death in *The Maelstrom* (1997), Naomi Uman's erasure of women from porn films in *Removed* (1998), and many other recycled cinemas from around the world have implemented a political practice of revision, a resistance to the orders inscribed on commercial and national media. Found footage works defuse the conflict between fact and figure, archive and invention, by insisting on an aesthetics and politics of revision. They undermine the originality of the original, as well as its immutability, drawing into question the singularity of any text. Revised and recycled, found footage films engender a *différance* between the original and its revision, the past and the present, and the imaginary (fantastic) divide that separates documentaries from experimental films and videos. Derrida offers this description of the chronogeographic economies of *différance*: "It is because of *différance* that the movement of signification is possible only if each so-called 'present' element, each element appearing on the scene of presence, is related to something other than itself, thereby keeping within itself the mark of the past element, and already letting itself be vitiated by the mark of its relation to the future element, this trace being related no less to what is called the future than what is called the past, and constituting what is called the present by means of this very relation to what it is not: what it absolutely is not, not even a past of a future as a modified present" ("Différance," 13).

The present is possible only as a relation to something other than itself, to something prior and outside; it is possible only if it carries a trace of the past (and future): the mark of what it is not. Only this if it is also (only) that. A distance between elements and times, from one to the other, but also a distance within the work, like a dream, that divides it from within. "An interval must separate the present from what it is not in order for the present to be itself," continues Derrida, "but this interval that constitutes it as present must, by the same token, divide the present in and of itself, thereby also dividing, along with the present, everything that is thought on the basis of the present" (13). The architectures of *différance*, dream, and recycled cinema require an internal division, spatial and temporal, that carries the trace of an other, a spectral mark of the past and the outside, in its material organization. Phantasy is the inscription—either conscious or unconscious—of this distance. As revisions, found footage works resemble dreams; the dimension of reflexivity brings them closer to phantasies.

"THIS IS ONLY A FILM," "IT'S ONLY A MOVIE"

Jay Rosenblatt's found footage film *Human Remains* (1998) exemplifies the stakes of phantastic revision. Superimposed over archival footage of a number of infamous twentieth-century figures, Rosenblatt appends what appear to be their voices, always in two languages, one native, the other English. The acoustical form, borrowed from the conventions of TV documentaries, renders the translation as a form of revision, a second voice in the film. The first-person narrations consist of anecdotal, personal, and otherwise intimate details. The effect is a synchronicity between image and sound, the illusion of a unified subject. One hears, in *Human Remains*, Hitler, Mussolini, Stalin, Franco, and Mao speak from beyond the grave. Or, rather, one hears acoustic representations of their thought. The disembodied voice-over suggests the convergence of the image with a profound interiority. It speaks, the image. This illusion of unity is assailed by the sheer intimacy of detail and the synthetic quality of the simulated voices. Rosenblatt scrambles the synchronicity with the use of selective single-track audio: some gestures produce sounds, most others silence. A pen scratching on paper, footsteps, a kiss, pierce the silence of the world (of the dead) from which these figures call.

The monstrosity of Rosenblatt's historical figures has been revised by the indices of corporeality reinscribed on their remains, on their film shadows. Another voice speaks, a human voice, always two; defensive, anxious, and depressed. On the defensive tone of phantasies, Laplanche and Pontalis write: "Such defences are themselves inseparably bound up with the primary function of phantasy, namely, the *mise-en-scène* of desire—a *mise-en-scène* in which what is prohibited (*l'interdit*) is always present in the actual formation of the wish" (318). To be perceived, in this case, as human. Rosenblatt's revision introduces the structure of phantasy into historical objects, a desire inherent in the "impossible impression," to return to Metz's term, of history.

In addition to the polyphony that *Human Remains* engenders, the questionable veracity of some material—Hitler's digestive apparatus, Mao's personal hygiene, for example—creates a rupture between the apparently reliable historical footage and the ambiguous text, indicating the marks of a revision. Rosenblatt, a former psychotherapist, produces an impure documentary, part fact, part speculation, that reveals a series of agencies inscribed on the surfaces of a finite history. A paradoxical document, outside the conventional space of documentary practice and doxa, a type of paradocumentary, a *paradoc*.

The acts of revision that emerge from the surplus intimacy of Rosenblatt's text expose the archive as dynamic, accessible, and vulnerable. By evoking the specters of doubt, Rosenblatt transforms the nightmare of history into a violent daydream. A waking nightmare. Freud identifies daydreams as "immediate fore-runners of hysterical symptoms," which "are not attached to actual memories, but to phantasies erected on the basis of memories" (529–530). *Human Remains* hystericizes the interred bodies of history, forcing them to return like repressed thoughts and effect new symptoms. At the intersection of history and expression, figure and voice, *Human Remains* exposes the vulnerability of historical representation to phantastic revision. Neither history nor memory, it problematizes the notion of the "only" of "only a film." "It is only a film"; history is only a film; only film can speak (in) the voice of history. Rosenblatt's sabotage of the documentary "I," the formal device that promises the authenticity of history, opens the field of history as such to the vicissitudes of revision. If, as Laplanche and Pontalis claim, phantasies are acts of imagination that posit the subject always as protagonist, then *Human Remains* has rewritten the screenplays of history, exposing them to a habitual and indefinite rewriting. Rosenblatt turns history into a vast repository of phantasies, where the singularity of the subject no longer remains. I am no longer only me. The first persons that appear to speak in *Human Remains* are no longer embodied; they represent the forces of an indeterminate and hysterical subjectivity at work in the representation and apparatus of history.[6]

Another historical phantasy explores the limits of thinking and writing history. In *The Dead Weight of a Quarrel Hangs* (1998), Lebanese videographer Walid Ra'ad searches for distinct moments of subjectivity, for the possibility of a single instant of total subjectivity that would render the Lebanese Civil War (1975–1991) intact. While not a found footage work in the strictest sense, Ra'ad's video appropriates the logic of recycled cinema by simulating the discovery and reworking of documents, artifacts, and traces from a history yet to be constituted.[7] Traversing the media of photography, film, and video, the brief arrests that constitute *Dead Weight*—photo finishes, anniversaries, the ends of war, cryptic blue photographs, sunsets—seek to capture moments of finitude, departure, and disappearance. A phantasy that sustains Ra'ad's work concerns the desire to pause the flow of a symptomatic history, an event (or series of events) that has ceased to be legible. Ra'ad questions the very capacity to experience even a single moment of a hysteric history. The only moment of a history made meaningful as finite. Again, for Laplanche and Pontalis, phantasies are never constituted by single moments but rather by movements: "It is not an *object* that the subject imagines and aims at, so to speak, but rather a *sequence* in which the subject has his own part to play and in which permutations of roles and attributions are possible" (318). Like Rosenblatt's strategy in *Human Remains*, Ra'ad introduces a set of historical figures that appear, in the end, permeable. They hover like phantoms between fact and fiction, displaced and hybrid, unable to stop in one place.

One of Ra'ad's key sources of information is Zainab Fakhouri, the wife of Dr. Fadl Fakhouri, "the foremost historian of the civil war in Lebanon." The presence of both Fakhouris, always as traces, remains a crucial feature of Ra'ad's work, but, like the episodes that constitute *Dead Weight*, the question of authenticity is ultimately exceeded and put in the service of a larger framework: the phantasies that accrue to a historical trauma. Facts assume significance once they have been revised in the economy of phantasy. Dr. Fakhouri first appears in Ra'ad's tape as a chronicler of Lebanon's leading historians, who, Ra'ad asserts, were avid gamblers and bet regularly at the races, not on the actual outcomes but on the images of winning horses that were published in the next day's newspapers. Regarding Dr. Fakhouri's racehorse photos and annotated notebooks, Ziad Abdallah and Farah Awada urge one to approach them as " 'hysterical symptoms' based not on any one person's actual memories but on cultural fantasies erected from the material of collective memories" (ii). A Borgesean revision, a paraphrase and citation of Freud's thesis on phantasy. In an echo of *Human Remains*, Dr. Fakhouri's notebook describes the day's winning historian: "He undeniably drank to excess, and as far as women goes, he is essentially very shy. One feels that he is sexually terribly inhibited. He is obsessively clean and tidy" (v). At stake is not the accuracy of the detail but its supplementary quality. It is in the supplementarity of revisions and phantasies that the other subject appears. Always beside the point, Fakhouri's secondary revisions push the practice of history into the space of a daydream.

The desire that propels Ra'ad's video—that of a unified subject of the Lebanese Civil War, secure in a distinct moment of time— gives way to the phantasies that determine any historiography. To write history is to daydream, to allow for the fluidity of its subjects, and to relinquish the possibility of its finitude. The secondary revision of a history is what makes that history possible in the first instance, always too late.

From history to memory, Austrian filmmaker Martin Arnold's

Alone: Life Wastes Andy Hardy (1998) provides another version of phantastic revision. Cutting scenes from the filmwork of Mickey Rooney and Judy Garland, Arnold's found footage work rewrites the compulsively repetitive narratives that constitute Rooney and Garland's *Andy Hardy* and other films. In *Alone*, Hollywood films assume the status of historical documents. Arnold's rewriting of the Hollywood artifacts comes to expose the phantasies that inform the desires repressed in the original films. Or, rather, the revisions ascribe symptoms to the original *as if* they had been repressed.[8] Arnold superimposes Freud's primal phantasy of the oedipal crisis over Hollywood narratives of romance, allowing the two layers of myth to generate a new set of hysterical symptoms. Oedipus and its exaggeration. Arnold's revisions of the oedipal scene—the erotic caresses between mother and son, the father's violent eruptions and assault of the son, the mother's despair at the arrival of a new erotic object—are all exaggerated by the stutters and repetitions that Arnold introduces into scenes that might have already sustained an oedipal form. This is a strategy, according to Deleuze and Guattari, a line of escape from the grand narrative of the psychosexual subjectivity after psychoanalysis. From their analysis of oedipal structures in Kafka: "To expand and augment Oedipus by adding to it and making a paranoid and perverse use of it is already to escape from submission. . . . Opening the impasse, unblocking it. Deterritorializing Oedipus into the world instead of reterritorializing everything in Oedipus and the family" (10). An exaggerated Oedipus releases the subject from the grip of its tyranny and back into the world, deterritorialized. Exaggeration represents a way out. "But to do this, Oedipus had to be enlarged to the point of absurdity, comedy" (10). The absurd enlargements in *Alone* take the form of repetition. Rather than adding to the text, Arnold repeats pieces of it, enlarging and expanding the family structure to the point of absurdity. Arnold dismantles Hollywood cinema in a manner similar to the dismantlings that Deleuze and Guattari discover in Kafka. In the French original, "*démontage*," anti-Oedipus, anticinema. Of Kafka, they write: "The dismantling of the assemblages makes the social representation take flight in a much more effective way than a critique would have done and brings about a deterritorialization of the world that is itself political and has nothing to do with an activity of intimacy" (47).

Arnold's *démontage* thrusts Andy Hardy's desires outward, outside familial territories and into the world as a comic phantasy.[9] Each inscription, each act of *démontage*, scratches the surface of a desire, its mise-en-scène, accumulating, in the process, a set of marks along its exterior. This construction of exteriority determines, according to Žižek, the place where all phantasies are destined, the outside. "The Unconscious is outside," Žižek writes, "not hidden in any unfathomable depths" (3). On the outside, *Alone* generates a series of symptoms that implicate the viewer in a transgression of the law that determines the original myths. The revisions and perversions of order, of the law, implement the very conditions of desire. Žižek says, a "fantasy does not simply realize a desire in a hallucinatory way," rather, it "constitutes our desire, provides its co-ordinates; that is, it literally 'teaches us how to desire'" (7).

Phantasies are, in Žižek's reading, pedagogical and, one might add, as he does elsewhere, fundamentally political in nature. As supplements to established orders—myth, narrative, truth, law—they subvert a politics of the unique subject or single author. They disorder the world, and, in the case of found footage cinema, they dismantle even the revision. The secondary revisions that constitute found footage cinema revise and *devise*, assemble and dissemble, the originary documents, materials, and forms, as well as their orders.

"To create is to understand," says Trinh T. Minh-ha, "and to understand is to re-create" (194). For Trinh, the fluid lines of inscription between author and viewer provide an exemplary relation between media producer and consumer. Operating according to a practice of interminable revision, she offers this scenario, which can be read as a manifesto of media reinscription:

> The maker constantly reads and re-reads, and is the first as well as the nth . . . viewer of her own text, while the viewer is co- and re-creator of the media text in the diverse readings it is able to engender. Thus, the media text which challenges its commodity status by letting itself be experienced only in an activity of

production ... radically acknowledges the plural texture of life—of intervals among words, images, sound, silence. It invites the perceiver/reader to follow what the creative gesture has traced, therefore rendering visible *how it can be unmade, restored to the void, and creatively re-made*. It reflects on itself as social/textual activity by apprehending the same language with a foreigner's sight; hearing, looking, and listening with intensity in unexpected places; making mistakes repeatedly where it is not supposed to; displacing thereby the stability of correct syntaxes and fixed nominations.

(194–195; emphasis added)

Like the intervals and gaps that determine Freud's dreamwork, Trinh's media text resembles a dream that has been exposed by the productive logic and politics of revision. It resembles, *reassembles*, a phantasy that has punctured the continuity of a work and destabilized its "correct syntaxes." Like phantasies, Trinh's media renders visible how every idea, every object, and every instance of the real "can be unmade, restored to the void, and creatively re-made." It teaches one to perceive reality with a "foreigner's sight," to discover at the center of one's thought and experience of the world the irreducible distance of another world. Found footage films and videos, which are also, by definition, heterogeneous, inscribe those traces of revision and offer the possibility of a practice based on the operations of phantasy, *différance*, *démontage*, and deterritorialization. The convergence of fact and figure, the document and its revision in found footage work, illuminates the possibility of conceiving a documentary aesthetics of the phantastic. Jay Rosenblatt's *Human Remains*, Walid Ra'ad's *The Dead Weight of a Quarrel Hangs*, and Martin Arnold's *Alone: Life Wastes Andy Hardy*, among many other works, provide an opportunity to begin to think about the rhetoric of phantasy in the realm of the documentary—a category that has perhaps already been conceived phantasmatically. To recycle, revise, and reinscribe media opens a line of escape to another topography of representation. In the deterritorialization of commercial media, another world of cinema becomes possible outside, only.

NOTES

1. "*Différance*," Jacques Derrida says of his neologism, refers "to an order which no longer belongs to sensibility." Neither sensible nor intelligible, *différance* "belongs neither to the voice nor to writing in the usual sense" but to "the strange space . . . *between* speech and writing" ("Différance," 5; original emphasis). A "strange space" shared also by the dream.

2. Sections of Vertov's numerous Kino-Eye manifestoes bear a resemblance to Freud's dreamwork, especially to secondary revision and the censoring agency. "Instead of surrogates for life (theatrical performance, film-drama, etc.)," wrote Vertov in 1925, "we bring to the workers' consciousness facts (large and small), carefully selected, recorded, and organized from both the life of the workers themselves and from that of their class enemies" ("The Essence of Kino-Eye," 50).

3. I discuss my reasons for using this spelling below, on page 176.

4. "Cinema offers," says Jean-Louis Baudry, "an artificial psychosis" (315). For Baudry, the comparison of cinema to the unconscious, especially the dream, is premised on the ability of both to simulate reality, to generate the experience of a "real perceived from the outside" (310). The result is a "fusion," he says, "of the interior with the exterior," which effects a simulation and representation of the subject to itself (311). In dreams and films, Baudry concludes, "The subject is induced to produce machines which would not only complement or supplement the workings of the secondary process but which could represent his own overall functioning to him: he is led to produce mechanisms mimicking, simulating the apparatus which is none other than himself" (317).

5. See, in this connection, Philip Rosen, "Document and Documentary," 58–89. Rosen writes of Grierson's "phraseology": "An arena of meaning centering on the authority of the real founded in the indexical trace, various forms of which were rapidly disseminated at all levels of industrial and now postindustrial culture" (66).

6. Many of Rosenblatt's found footage works forge relations between the individual and the historical, the singular and the universal, the personal and the mythical, and the particular and the general. *The Smell of Burning Ants* (1994), about a boy's relation to his own violence and masculinity, and *King of the Jews* (2000), about a boy's relation to Jesus Christ's Judaic heritage and the representation of Christ and Judaism, in addition to *Human Remains*, search for the point of contact between

singular voices and the archive, small tensions in the historical spaces and times of the filmed image.

7. In a subsequent work, *Hostage: The Bachar Tapes* (2000), Ra'ad invents the author and autobiography of Lebanese hostage Souheil Bachar, who was kidnapped in Beirut in 1983 and held in solitary confinement for ten years, except for twenty-seven weeks in 1985, when he was held with famous American hostages Terry Anderson et al. Of the fifty-three tapes that Bachar made, only the seventeenth and the thirty-first, says Ra'ad, are available in North America and Western Europe. The tape opens with a white screen. In a voice-over narration, Souheil Bachar introduces himself and then gives instructions for voice-over and subtitle translations: his narration is to be translated into the "official" language of the country where it is shown (i.e., "English in the US and UK"); the voice-over should be that of "a neutral-toned female"; and subtitles should be set against a gray or blue background. The background turns blue ("like the Mediterranean"), a small magnetic storm, and then Bachar appears.

8. Elizabeth Cowie suggested this structure of retroactively applied symptoms.

9. In his digital video installation *Deanimated: The Invisible Ghost* (2002), Martin Arnold continues the *démontage* of his previous found footage films in another direction. He erases characters from a minor horror film—*The Invisible Ghost* (1941), directed by Joseph H. Lewis and starring Bela Lugosi—removing them entirely in some instances from the film. Arnold digitizes the film image and then removes just the human figures, replacing the background to create a seamless erasure. At other times, Arnold removes only the spoken dialogue from the film's soundtrack and then, using a morphing technique, seals the characters' mouths shut. Arnold induces a kind of oedipal *différance*, in which characters have been displaced from themselves in space and time and from the meaningful relations that would define them. The results are comical and, in places, dreamlike, but only as an effect of the horror from which they originate.

BIBLIOGRAPHY

Abdallah, Ziad, and Farah Awada. Foreword to "The Plates." *Public Culture* 11, no. 2 (Spring 1999): i–xiv.

Arnold, Martin. *Deanimated: The Invisible Ghost*. Digital Video Installation. N.p., 2002.

Baudry, Jean-Louis. "The Apparatus: Metapsychological Approaches to the Impression of Reality in Cinema." In *Narrative, Apparatus, Ideology: A Film Theory Reader*, trans. Jean Andrews and Bertrand Augst, ed. Philip Rosen, 299–318. New York: Columbia University Press, 1986.

Conner, Bruce. *Crossroads*. Video/Film. Directed by Bruce Conner. N.p.: Bruce Conner, 1976.

Deleuze, Gilles and Félix Guattari. *Kafka: Toward a Minor Literature*. Trans. Dana Polan. Minneapolis: University of Minnesota Press, 1986.

Derrida, Jacques. "Différance." In *Margins of Philosophy*, trans. Alan Bass, 1–28. Chicago: University of Chicago Press, 1982.

———. "Freud and the Scene of Writing." In *Writing and Difference*, trans. Alan Bass, 196–231. Chicago: University of Chicago Press, 1978.

Farocki, Harun. *Videograms of a Revolution*. Video/Film. Directed by Harun Farocki. N.p.: Drift Distribution, 1992.

Forgács, Peter. *The Maelstrom*. Video/Film. Directed by Peter Forgács. N.p.: Lumen Film, 1997.

Freud, Sigmund. *The Interpretation of Dreams*. In *The Standard Edition of the Complete Psychological Works of Sigmund Freud*, trans. James Strachey, Anna Freud, Alix Strachey, and Alan Tyson, vols. 4 and 5. London: Hogarth and the Institute of Psycho-Analysis, 1953–1974.

Jameson, Fredric. *The Seeds of Time*. New York: Columbia University Press, 1994.

Laplanche, Jean and J.-B Pontalis. "Phantasy (or Fantasy)." In *The Language of Psychoanalysis*, trans. Donald Nicholson-Smith. New York: Norton, 1973.

Lewis, Joseph H. *The Invisible Ghost*. Film. Directed by Joseph H. Lewis. California: Banner Productions/Monogram, 1941.

Metz, Christian. "Film and Phantasy." In *The Imaginary Signifier: Psychoanalysis and the Cinema*, trans. Celia Britton, Annwyl Williams, Ben Brewster, and Alfred Guzzetti, 129–137. Bloomington: Indiana University Press, 1976.

Ra'ad, Walid. *Hostage: The Bachar Tapes*. Video/Film. Directed by Souheil Bachar. Beirut and New York: The Atlas Group in collaboration with Walid Ra'ad, 2001.

———. *The Dead Weight of a Quarrel Hangs*. Video/Film. Directed by Walid Ra'ad. Beirut and New York: Atlas Group in collaboration with Walid Ra'ad, 1999.

Rosen, Philip. "Document and Documentary: On the Persistence of Historical Concepts." In *Theorizing Documentary*, ed. Michael Renov, 58–89. New York: Routledge, 1993.

Rosenblatt, Jay. *Human Remains*. Video/Film. Directed by Jay Rosenblatt. New York: Jay Rosenblatt Film Library/Transit Media, 1998.

———. *The Smell of Burning Ants*. Video/Film. Directed by Jay Rosenblatt. New York: Jay Rosenblatt Film Library/Transit Media, 1994.

———. *King of the Jews*. Video/Film. Directed by Jay Rosenblatt. New York: Jay Rosenblatt Film Library/Transit Media, 2000.

Trinh T. Minh-ha. "The World as Foreign Land." In *When the Moon Waxes Red: Representation, Gender, and Cultural Politics*, 185–200. New York: Routledge, 1991.

Uman, Naomi. *Removed*. Video/Film. Directed by Naomi Uman. N.p., 1998.

Vertov, Dziga. "The Essence of Kino-Eye." In *Kino-Eye: The Writings of Dziga Vertov*, trans. Kevin O'Brien, ed. Annette Michelson, 49. Berkeley: University of California Press, 1984.

Žižek, Slavoj. *The Plague of Fantasies*. London: Verso, 1997.

8

DE/TERRITORIALIZING PSYCHO-ANALYSIS

Gregg Lambert

I would like to begin by rephrasing the title to this chapter as a question: "De/Territorializing Psychoanalysis?" I believe this phrase is advantageous in that it provides us with two senses we can begin to explore; at least, it is sufficiently ambiguous to require further clarification. Are we talking about (a) "deterritorializing psychoanalysis" in the imperative sense of causing psychoanalysis itself to become deterritorialized from the historical legacy and dominant institutions that belong to the psychoanalytic movement after Freud? (To be more precise, since I am limiting my questions to the subject of psychoanalysis in the American university, I am not talking about the entire history of the psychoanalytic institution, including the historical migration of various traditions and schools to non-European countries and to "the rest of the world," a phrase that Derrida uses to chart its partial globalization, but rather about a certain Freudian-Lacanian tradition of psychoanalytic theory belonging to a geographic zone that is, to employ Derrida's chart again, somewhere "North of the Mexican border" and has come down to us from . . . well, Baltimore!) Or are we talking about (b) a "deterritorializing psychoanalysis" in the sense that we could conceive of a psychoanalysis that would itself be deterritorializing, a psychoanalysis that would be without walls or institutions, out in the open, so to speak? Both senses of the phrase are equally valid for a discussion of Deleuze and Guattari's historical assault on the Lacanian institution in France, and, as I will argue, for Derrida's conception of "Geo-psychoanalysis"; therefore, in an act of homage to Derrida's own manner of resolving such double binds, I have chosen to leave the question undecided and will address both senses of "deterritorializing psychoanalysis" in two propositions, which correspond to each sense of the phrase.

PROPOSITION 1

"DETERRITORIALIZING PSYCHOANALYSIS"
(AS IN, "TO DETERRITORIALIZE" OR IN THE IMPERATIVE FORM: "DETERRITORIALIZE PSYCHOANALYSIS!")

In addressing the first sense of the phrase "deterritorializing psychoanalysis," a further question I would raise, hypothetically, is whether we can imagine a rigorous concept of the unconscious *outside* the discourse of psychoanalysis itself, that is, removed from its institutional history, its apparatus, its associations and protocols, its so-called technique, or its metapsychological theory. This is a question that can be understood to resonate with Derrida's own interrogations, which appear in *Résistances de la psychanalyse* (1996), as well as in many of his earlier writings on the psychoanalytic institution, and concern the historical limits that have shaped the field of psychoanalytic knowledge. On first glance, one might think this impossible, given that the concept is so thoroughly inscribed in the history of the psychoanalytic movement and was invented by Freud, who still holds a certain patent on its application to social, cultural, and individual phenomena. But then, is the invention of the concept the same as the production of the signified?

A fundamental thesis that one can find throughout the writings of Deleuze and Guattari is that the unconscious does not exist, or, more accurately, the unconscious does not exist prior to the moment of its production. To say it did would be to accord it an ontological determination, something that Freud subtracted from the concept in his article "The Unconscious" (1915), in which he submitted the notion to a purely topological definition of the psychic apparatus, which looks a bit like Hjelmslev's screen projected over an indeterminate signifying matter. Thus, as Deleuze writes, "it is not a question, by one method or another, of reducing the unconscious; it is much more a question for us of producing it—there is no unconscious that could be said to be already there, since the unconscious must be produced and it must be produced politically, socially, and historically" (*L'île déserte*, 381).

The imperative of "deterritorializing psychoanalysis" therefore immediately poses a problem for us to resolve: Deterritorialize it from what? What is the specific form of territory that appears so problematic for Deleuze and Guattari and motivates their imperative to deterritorialize? They give many responses to this question, of course: Oedipus, the family, castration (that is, the "splinter in the flesh"), and, most of all, *Desire*. (I will take up some of these later on.) But are these territories, properly speaking? Are they not rather the "forms of *signifiance*" that are constantly reproduced by psychoanalytic interpretation? One can certainly claim that the family is a territory that has been colonized by Oedipus, which produces the relays that are necessary for individual and social desire to become interchangeable, that is, part of a larger social assemblage (for example, that of capitalism). This doesn't explain much, however, and it certainly doesn't explain Oedipus but merely assumes that Oedipus is already there as an operator of this entire network of relays of desire. Consequently, in their critique of the psychoanalytic interpretation of the family, for example, their emphasis is always on the role played in the enunciation of statements and proper names. They do not deny that oedipal statements already exist—in other words, they are not accusing psychoanalysis of making them up—and neither do they blame psychoanalysis for selecting them exclusively as forms of *signifiance*, "for such statements are to a certain extent already part of a machinic assemblage." Rather, as they write, "We are criticizing psychoanalysis for having used Oedipal enunciation to make patients believe that they would produce individual, personal statements, and would finally speak in their own name" (*A Thousand Plateaus*, 38).

To deterritorialize psychoanalysis, consequently, can mean nothing less—although perhaps it will mean something more—than to remove it from the one constant that defines its formal operation and the reproduction of its authority, and by this I mean the analytic space itself (that is, to deterritorialize the very space in which the unconscious is produced and reproduced). According to Deleuze and Guattari, psychoanalysis produces the unconscious by means of a machinic assemblage that remains consistent across its various institutions. The components of this machine are as follows: (1) a closed space strictly defined by time—the infamous five-minute session employed by Lacan is only an exaggeration of this principle but, at the same time, confirms the restriction of time as a fundamental component—and by an indefinite number of articles (the chair or couch, the desk, the notepad, the pen, a few books on the table next to a table against a wall, a painting or paintings that must exhibit some relation to culture, and, of course, professional journals); (2) a subject defined as the patient, which could also be a group (it does not matter how many, since the rule "only one person can speak at a time" is strictly observed, and so the quantitative difference is thereby effectively negated); and finally (3) the analyst, the one who stands in for what Deleuze and Guattari define as the "subject of enunciation" in such a way that even the silence of the analyst is accorded a dimension of speech (*la parole*). The assemblage of these components defines the form of analysis itself, a form that arranges the contents and counts for much more than the contents. It is, according to Deleuze and Guattari, a "machine" that produces the unconscious by a regular rhythm inserted into the interstice of speech and silence: symptoms, transference, interpretation, the incessant rumblings of unconscious desire. It is this machinic dimension of psychoanalysis that Deleuze and Guattari have made into such an object of contestation. I say this in order to clarify a long misunderstanding: they are not opposed to psychoanalysis per se but rather to a certain Freudo-Lacanian analytic machine of interpretation that remains a constant throughout its incarnations.

As an aside, it is somewhat odd that the machinic assemblage that belongs to psychoanalysis bears more than a passing resemblance to any number of plays by Beckett, particularly the later plays. I don't think this is purely accidental since a number of the components involved (the voice, the imago, the dyadic ensemble of characters) bear a striking similarity, although I don't have the time to go into a long digression on this resemblance. I note it in passing only to underline the fact that there is a certain similarity between the goals of Beckett's work and psychoanalysis: in the end, the exhaustion of the subject's speech, an emptying-out of his or her complaint ("*Oh my suffering! Oh my life! What has become of my happiness?*"), and the reduction of the subject's mot juste (which, in the end, is revealed as just another cliché that already belongs to the reparatory of sadness). If, in the beginning, there was the word and the word was made flesh, then the end of the psychoanalytic session is the word made shit, into the excrement of the drive. It is precisely the word that reveals its true performative dimension as an acting-out of silence; by reducing the word to its signifying dimension, that is, by inserting into a chain of signifiers that have captivated the subject, the famous silence that the subject has so long sought in order to fill it with the drive is reduced to nothingness. It is here that silence could be said to belong to two different registers: the full silence (in all its phallic glory!) becomes the silence that marks a pause between two different constructions of desire, the anticipated silence that marked the aim of the subject's demand returns in the form of non-sense, a residue, or leftover. Here, a major distinction could be said to emerge in the comparison: for Beckett, this silence assumes a properly comic significance accompanied by an impossible imperative to "get over it" or to "give it up"; psychoanalysis, however, retains a tragic attitude with regard to the possibility of ever finishing—that is, the possibility of ever not saying "I"—so that even while it empties out the signifier, it leaves the unconscious structure intact and awaiting a freshly determined object. One could say that it is not by chance that Freud, late in his life, despaired over the idea of an "interminable analysis," much in the same way that one of Beckett's characters also can be heard to complain, "I thought I had done with preliminaries. No, no, we have all been here forever, we shall all be here forever. I know it" (333).

Returning to our discussion of the analytic machine, now that we have taken a survey of its components, how does it function? According to Deleuze and Guattari, the psychoanalytic machine of interpretation operates by one simple procedure: *to negate the subject of the statement in favor of the subject of enunciation.* "You say one thing, but what you are really saying is something else." This is the lever by which the subject's own statement is razed in favor an unconscious enunciation. "You say you want strawberries, but you really desire x." As Deleuze writes, "What I say is returned to me as the subject of the statement; what I wanted to say returns to me (in my relation with the analyst) as subject of enunciation" (*L'île déserte*, 383). Thus the analytic machine "produces" the unconscious by splitting the subject of the statement from the subject of enunciation, and it is by means of this simple procedure of division (or cleavage in the heart of the speaking subject) that the unconscious suddenly appears—somewhat like Heidegger's lightning bolt that causes the night to appear against its abyssal ground—on the side of the subject's *vouloir dire*. The analyst only materializes the division by occupying the position of the subject's true enunciation (a place that is first of all handed over by the subject) and by refusing any immediate or direct object of the statement as the subject's true intention.

Given the above observations, perhaps the question I evoked earlier concerning whether there could be an unconscious outside psychoanalytic discourse could be rephrased in the following manner: is there an unconscious, properly speaking, *outside* the analytic session? For example, this question emerges when the psychoanalytic apparatus of interpretation is plugged into all sorts of things: culture, film, literature, myth, history, and current events (September 11th being an event most easily recalled to mind, along with the nausea of psychoanalytic interpretation that occurred in its wake). It is in these circumstances that the machinic dimension of psychoanalytic knowledge has emerged so dramatically in the contemporary period, in the sense that any "text" can become, willy-nilly, an occasion for the production of the unconscious. As Deleuze later remarks in *Dialogues* (1996), "the psychoanalytic critic is now more like a journalist: he creates the event, then in various fashions, offers his services afterwards" (Deleuze and Parnet, 105).

In the psychoanalytic interpretation of culture, however, where the position of analyst is lacking to operate the division between an overt signification and a latent or hidden enunciation of truth, it has often been observed, this distinctive procedure operates allegorically. At this moment, the "text" assumes the position of the subject of the statement, while the interpretation provided by the psychoanalytic theorist or critic simulates the subject of enunciation, providing the unconscious signification of the text's overt or literal meaning. Thus, when the analytic machine is removed from one of its most critical components, the relation to the analyst, it begins to go wild, producing interpretation after interpretation, most of which are thinly veiled allegories of the same basic interpretation. This is especially true, according to a very interesting observation made by Deleuze, after psychoanalytic interpretation acquired *a statutory claim over all enunciation*, that is to say, when it adopted a notion of structure after Lacan (*L'île déserte*, 383). Here, we could say that the analytic machine works—and perhaps it works all too well! And yet we could also argue that the true status of all these interpretations is not that different from the discourse of the patient who overinterprets everything. The critic does not occupy the same position as the analyst vis-à-vis the position of subject of enunciation in the act of interpretation; this must be accorded to a certain enunciation of *savoir* that is referred to the place of a psychoanalytic body of knowledge, that is, to a prior enunciation, which the critic cites or performs in his or her interpretation of the statement or text (as when a critic cites Lacan or Freud). The given text (of literature or film) occupies the position of the subject of the statement, whereas psychoanalytic *savoir* now occupies the position of the subject of enunciation, which is referred to by the critic as the former's true enunciation. In the end, it appears as though the text itself were motivated by the subject of enunciation that the psychoanalytic interpretation provides as its basis and only serves to illustrate its concepts, something that Derrida has critiqued already in his famous commentary on Lacan's reading of Poe's "Purloined Letter" ("Le Facteur de la Vérité," in *The Post Card*). Hence the famous "*Wo es war, Soll Ich werden*," which can be translated as "where it (the text, the discourse, the statement) was, so the subject of psychoanalysis shall come to be."

I would argue, however, that what is missing in this act of interpretation is, surprisingly enough, the unconscious itself. There is no unconscious! In other words, what is "produced" or "reproduced" is the enunciation of the *truth*, which is the purely performative dimension that belongs to the act of interpretation. In psychoanalytic interpretation, by means of this performative dimension, the truth of the text is referred to the body of psychoanalytic knowledge (which above I designated by the technical sense of *savoir*), although often this knowledge is reduced to a discrete number of formulae or maxims: "the real always returns to the same place," "the letter always arrives at its destination," "man's desire is the desire of the other," "The woman does not exist," and so on. As an example of this, I could point to the body of work by psychoanalytic theorist Slavoj Žižek. One can immediately see something eminently machinic, automatic, in his interpretation of anything cultural or literary. His work has the feeling of a cyclotron that has been left in high gear and that lets nothing go to waste by reusing everything, including old jokes and entire passages from earlier works. In place of the above procedure, however, Žižek's automaton of interpretation operates by means of simple negation (it is a dialectical machine): "You say one thing, but what you really mean is the exact opposite." Here, something is different, which more closely resembles the function of negation that was first outlined by Freud: the subject's own statement is returned to him or her in its opposite form. Thus the letter returns to its destination through an operation of inversion. In this, we can see Žižek is more of a Hegelian than a Freudian, strictly speaking, which is why his chosen subject is "the prose of the world."

It is true that the literary text can be instigated in "a transferential relationship," as the theoretical body of work by Gabriele

Schwab has amply demonstrated. The reception histories of the *Sorrows of Young Werther* or *The Catcher in the Rye* can attest to this as well; however, excluding the well-known instances of psychotic identification, in most cases, the text itself cannot fully occupy the position of the subject of enunciation, which is to say that it is not inaugural. For example, I can give my lover a volume of Proust, and in that moment the saga of Marcel and Albertine is given an enunciating dimension that is, strictly speaking, not found in Proust. The subject of enunciation cannot be said to derive from Proust's narrative but rather from the *parole* of the gift itself, which turns Proust's work into a cryptic cipher of my message and subsumes the work under a symbolic identification assigned to it by another register of significance. This does not mean, however, that the enunciation accorded to my gift of Proust will say exactly what I wanted it to, since my own enunciation, inasmuch as the message still must be deciphered by the intended receiver, is inscribed in what Lacan (1998) aptly called "the defiles of the signifier." Therefore, the unconscious is not in the text, properly speaking, but rather occurs between the text and the enunciating dimension that makes of the text something that is sent, meant to be listened to, even obeyed. This immediately raises the possibility that it could be delayed, deferred, if not missed altogether, and the true intention never to be heard from again—possibilities that Derrida has remarked already by the term *"destin-errance."* I would say that this principle forms the imperative condition of the act of interpretation itself, which is to say *that the very condition of interpretation is misinterpretation*. Consequently, to summarize a very old and well-known debate, the fact that a letter that always arrives at its destination is precisely due to the possibility of its getting lost, to which every act of interpretation responds with a categorical imperative that it always must be found precisely where it was meant to be.

This raises a final question under the first proposition: that is, is the proper dimension of psychoanalytic practice ever achieved by means of interpretation alone? In other words, *is interpretation the proper route for achieving a critical or transformational relation to desire?* I have underlined this question because I think the answer is not at all clear. Ironically, it is here that the responses by Deleuze and Guattari and by Lacan meet on common ground. Psychoanalysis is not a matter of interpretation. As Lacan said quite clearly, "psychoanalysis it is not a hermeneutics." In fact, from the perspective of technique, this is because it has been discovered that interpretation leads more often to the failure of analysis than to the revelation of the unconscious process, something that Freud himself readily demonstrates in his case study of Dora, where a prejudiced and precipitous interpretation of Dora's problems immediately implicated Freud in a secret pact with Dora's father and Herr K. Of course, Dora saw through this and rejected Freud with her famous dismissal: "Well, is that all you have to offer me? Really? I mean, why do I need you to tell me what is already too obvious and sordid about the whole affair?" As for Lacan, whom we know paid scrupulous attention to Freud's mistakes, interpretation was always a last resort and moreover will never take the form of some information that the analyst offers to the patient, even at the end, which, in fact, achieves its desired effect only by the silencing of every interpretation. Nevertheless, even when it is withheld, interpretation could be said to constitute the very ethical substance of psychoanalytic practice (which is to say that it is an ethical demand that binds the analyst to an even greater degree than the patient, who, it is true, cannot be held responsible for the act of interpretation). At the same time, it is here that a major distinction could be drawn between the two positions on the act of interpretation. Thus, if from the perspective of psychoanalytic technique, interpretation is an ethical act, in the strongest sense of the term "act," the analyst here could be said to occupy the position of Antigone before the figure of Creon and to be able to perform this act only with the full knowledge that it already constitutes a death sentence that will land on the head of the analyst himself or herself. To put this enigmatically, the analyst can only speak as a dead man, that is, dead to the question of desire, which is an issue that should only concern the living.

For Deleuze and Guattari, on the other hand, it has never been a matter of interpreting but rather of experimentation. Thus, "it is precisely that we oppose a field of experimentation, personal as well as collective, to the activities of psychoanalytic interpretation" (*L'île déserte*, 384). But what is this? Above, I stated that interpretation is among the most rare and highly scrutinized activities and perhaps the most ethical moment of psychoanalytic technique, whereas Deleuze and Guattari seem to have reduced psychoanalysis completely to the activity of interpretation. This constitutes the underlying point of the intense disagreement over their arguments against psychoanalysis in the collected volumes of the *Capitalism and Schizophrenia* project (*Anti-Oedipus*, *A Thousand Plateaus*, and *Kafka*). This disagreement could be paraphrased as follows: if, according to one of the most forceful theses put forward from *Anti-Oedipus* onward, psychoanalysis knowingly and quite deliberately reduces the unconscious by territorializing it and making it into a universal (that of Oedipus), it could just as well be said that Deleuze and Guattari knowingly and deliberately bastardize the psychoanalytic concept of the unconscious by turning the oedipal construction of desire into a boogeyman that can too easily and precipitously be dismissed. It's as if psychoanalysis suddenly were being accused of wanting to retain a repressive organization of desire rather than providing an analysis of the dominant organization of desire that exists in modern societies. Of course, this is in a certain sense Foucault's argument as well. It seems, for now, we have reached an impasse or at least what de Man would have identified as the rhetorical traits of a strong misreading on their part. (I will return to this problem in the discussion of the second proposition.)

Freud himself addressed the proliferation of so-called psychoanalytic interpretations—in his time, but this admonition also can apply to our own—by saying that knowledge of the unconscious cannot be procured by listening to lectures and reading books, which he described as having the same effect that handing out menus in a time of famine would have on hunger. As Freud writes, "This analogy goes even further than its immediate application; for informing the patient of his unconscious regularly results in an intensification of the conflict within him and an exacerbation of his troubles" ("'Wild' Psycho-analysis," 225). Perhaps this word of warning also should be heeded today by the proliferation of so-called psychoanalytic interpretations of culture and society, including the unconscious formations of gender and racial identity. We might ask what effect these interpretations have on the unconscious cause of these formations? In fact, one could even go further and say that *the inflation of psychoanalytic interpretation today can be read as one of the most pressing and visible signs of the resistance to psychoanalysis that marks our era*—on the part not only of the individual interpreters but also of the association of readers, of a public, a society, and even a culture. I would even venture to say that if our knowledge of the unconscious has increased, and has been discovered to dominate almost every aspect of the subject's anxious attention to the world and to others, this knowledge has brought us no closer, collectively or individually, to the possibility of entering into an effective analysis of this state of affairs. Here, we would do well to remember the first principle of a psychoanalytic technique that could strictly be called Freudian: knowledge of the unconscious is only the beginning of treatment, not its end.

PROPOSITION 2

"DETERRITORIALIZING PSYCHOANALYSIS"
(AS IN THE POSSIBILITY OF A PSYCHOANALYSIS THAT WOULD
ITSELF BE DETERRITORIALIZING)

So far I have been citing from an early interview that occurred immediately after the publication of *Anti-Oedipus* in 1972, "Cinq propositions sur la psychanalyse," in which Deleuze offers the following proposition: "Today, psychoanalysis presents a certain political danger which is proper to it, and which can be distinguished from the dangers that were implicit in the old clinical psychiatry. While the former constituted a place of enclosure that was localized, psychoanalysis, on the contrary, functions *in the open air*" (*L'île déserte*, 233; emphasis added). We might further define this latter phrase as in a place that is nonlocalized and in a space that is without walls. Concerning this new danger that Deleuze talks about, I have already outlined two aspects: the first supposed danger is that the analytic machine gives psychoanalysis a method of ambulation (allows it to get out and move around, since it is not limited to a particular location or social institution); the second aspect is what Deleuze identifies as a certain statutory right over enunciation that psychoanalytic interpretation lays claim to in an absolute manner, which, according to Deleuze, has replaced the earlier temporary contract between the patient and the analyst. According to this observation, this has led to a generalized psychoanalysis that asserts a statutory right over each and every act of speech without regard to its specific location in culture or society and without the specific consent of a subject who submits his or her speech to the rule of analysis in the form of entering into a temporary contractual relationship with an analyst. One might even say that, after the assumption of the structural concept of the sign, today, psychoanalytic interpretation lays claim to every appearance of the signifier as directly an issue pertaining to its own subject (that is, the unconscious). Both these observations can be combined to describe a psychoanalysis that functions without enclosure, which is out "in the open air," although, they could just as easily describe a situation in which psychoanalysis has gone "wild."

It is at this point, surprisingly enough, that we might hear a resonance with Freud's early concerns over a kind of psychoanalysis that is wild, meaning out of control and perhaps too much out in the open. The problem of territory itself, however, can be located in the Freudian reply to this danger, for while Deleuze and Guattari respond by imagining a form of psychoanalysis that would be deterritorializing (which they earlier had baptized with the name of "schizo-analysis," only to abandon this title later as a little too problematic, perhaps), the Freudian institution responds to this danger by territorializing psychoanalysis itself, a decision that continues to have profound repercussions on the current form of the institution and on the transmission of its knowledge. In short, an apparatus (a school, an association) was constructed to house the analytical machine in order to administer it properly. Here unfolds the long saga of the psychoanalytic institution, which

Lacan once compared to the War of the Roses. But, we might ask, was it necessary that the institution of psychoanalysis should evolve in this form—through schism, combat, betrayal, intrigue, and, finally, marriage? Except for the last means of politics, its history could only be compared to the history of the Communist Party.

Again, I would like to recall a certain resonance of this question with Derrida's reflections on the historical institution of psychoanalysis in *Résistances de la psychanalyse*, particularly the pages concerning the possibility of a psychoanalysis to come, one that might emerge *outside* this history, one that would not be *your* psychoanalysis, or *my* psychoanalysis, or even its *own*, for that matter, a possibility that could only arrive through a deconstruction of the analytic situation itself and therefore would appear as something of an "auto-deconstruction" of the institution of analysis (88). Thus, to quote Derrida, the question of the future of psychoanalysis "must sooner or later result in the dissolution of the IPA that Freud founded"—"and its replacement with something else, something quite other, something with a fundamentally different structure, a different aspect, a different topography—in short, a different *chart*" (83).

Returning to Deleuze's critique of this institutional form, I will draw on several points from *L'île déserte*, the early text mentioned above. The first point to be made, according to Deleuze, is that psychoanalysis has assumed (along with Marxism) a form of what Deleuze calls a "culture of memory," which is to say, a knowledge that always advances by means of a veritable "Return to the Source." (The institutional form this tradition most often takes, of course, is the form of "the discourse of the Master.") The second point to be made concerns what I defined above as the analytic machine. Inasmuch as this is a machine, the specific knowledge (or *savoir*) it calls for is technical and thus creates the demand for an institutional policing mechanism that validates and authorizes those in whom this machine is invested to function properly.

It is at this point that we might recall Freud's little article "'Wild' Psycho-Analysis," where we can bear witness to the first hint of this demand for a psychoanalytic police, a self-policing, even the issuing of papers (and moreover, given that no police force then existed to uphold the law of psychoanalysis when he called for its invention, the invention of a psychoanalytic tribunal vested with the office of upholding the responsibility to the name). As Freud announces: "Neither I myself nor my friends and co-workers find it agreeable to claim a monopoly in this way in the use of a medical technique. But in the face of the danger to patients and to the cause of psycho-analysis that are inherent in the practice that is to be foreseen of a 'wild' psychoanalysis, we have had no other choice. In the spring of 1910 we founded an International Psycho-Analytical Association, to which its members declare their adherence by the publication of their names, in order to be able to repudiate responsibility for what is done by those who do not belong to us and yet call their medical procedure 'psycho-analysis'" (227).

In this passage, we are bearing witness to a certain arbitrary decision, which is to say, thoroughly historical or even "historicizing" in its event: the founding of the Freudian monopoly, which can only borrow its apparatus from a number of other historical institutions (the association, the school, the "cause" or political organization, etc.). Moreover, if we follow Freud's argument closely, of the two causes for instituting this form of protectionism—harm to the patients, harm to the cause of psychoanalysis itself—Freud underlines the latter as the principal concern (since "wild" psychoanalysis more often than not produces the effect of recovery in the patient, even if the means for achieving this recovery are purely accidental and are most often caused by the patient's own resistances). In fact, Freud says quite clearly that recovery can be produced by a "resistance to psychoanalysis," but only at the price of harming the name of "psycho-analysis" itself. "And this," Freud says, "can be avoided" (227). This gesture, it is true, did nothing to prevent the spreading of psychoanalytic knowledge, only providing a mechanism for distinguishing, in a patently juridical manner, between legitimate and illegitimate appropriations. It is a mechanism that merely restricts liability to the name of "psychoanalysis" by creating a proper territory (an association of signatories) that will henceforth demarcate a lawful and proper space of a psychoanalytic *civitas*, or *polis*, from a wild and lawless frontier of "wild" psychoanalysis. Perhaps now we can understand why Deleuze constantly refers to Freudian psychoanalysis as a "Ciceronian science" and to Freud as "Roman."

In a very interesting passage that occurs in *Dialogues*, Deleuze asserts that at the same time psychoanalysis passed from its early Freudian phase to its post-Freudian phase—when it abandoned significance in favor of interpretation, the research of signifieds (or symbols) in favor of the structural agency of the signifier, the temporary contract between analyst and patient for the permanent statutory right that psychoanalytic theory now exercises over all enunciation (without regard to its specific location or context)— the site of the unconscious was displaced from its early hereditary model (in Freud) onto relations of political and social alliance. The manner in which the unconscious reproduces itself from one subject to the next is no longer to be located in the institution of the family; rather, the unconscious is produced across relations of alliance and affiliation that have supplanted the family, alliances that reproduce themselves in the manner of a plague and in such a way that the family itself only functions as a secondary feedback loop for these later formations of unconscious desire (Deleuze and Parnet, 101). In this very suggestive remark, Deleuze perhaps opens a line of inquiry (pursued today by Etienne Balibar, among others) for understanding the different schemas of alliance that have emerged in late-democratic societies: racial alliances, ethnic nationalisms, or fundamentalisms. It does not matter if each of these forms of alliance has taken on the image of a hereditary model in the sense of an archaic justification, particularly in the case of racial and ethnic schemas of alliance, since it could be shown that in each case the manner in which these alliances reproduce themselves socially exceeds any model of kinship or heredity. In fact, it is precisely in retaliation for the humiliation suffered from a father—real or imaginary!—that the most horrifying of these new alliances have spread. For example, how many suicide bombers have detonated their bodies in Iraq today, and is the true cause of their act one of political sovereignty or obedience to the ferocious injunction of the superego? Moreover, what did the images of Saddam Hussein unshaven, desolate, haggard, like a horse about to be put down or sent off to the glue factory, his decaying orifices yawning and exposed and in a certain sense invaginated by the probing instruments of U.S. officials, produce in the Iraqi identity if not such a strange funereal desire?

This development corresponds to one of the most forceful theses found in *Anti-Oedipus*. To continue to speak of an unconscious that produces through the institution of the family, according to old hereditary schemas and familial personages (Oedipus), is to continue to speak of a nostalgic or mythical unconscious. In order to discover the true position of the unconscious in social formations today, one must deterritorialize the unconscious and, at the same time, defamiliarize the concepts of psychoanalytic knowledge that are derived from this earlier model. It is this procedure that one finds clearly articulated in *Anti-Oedipus*, which has more than a chance resemblance to the strategy of "defamiliarization" (*Entfremdung*) that defines the practice of a Brechtian political theater. Therefore, if psychoanalysis is truly to regain the empirical validity of a science again, it will be necessary for it to pass through an antipsychoanalytic phase. As Deleuze writes: "The desire or delirium (which are profoundly the same thing), the desire-delirium is by its very nature a libidinal investment of the entire historical field, immediately social. Delirium properly concerns classes, peoples, races, and masses. . . . We say that schizophrenia has to do not with the family but with a global affair, not with the parents but with whole peoples, populations, and tribes" (*L'île déserte*, 382). Here we find, succinctly phrased, the fundamental thesis of antipsychoanalysis: speak no more about the family but rather of whole peoples; not about the cloistered room and its dirty little secrets but rather of the full body of the earth with its yet undefined zones.

All the same, I wonder whether Deleuze and Guattari are a little too categorical on this point in particular, that is, a bit too philosophical and not psychoanalytic enough. How does the constituted individual in a given society accede directly to this political plane of desire, except in bypassing—a bit too precipitously—the entire question of this formation altogether, which is to say, by foreclosing the dimension of the imaginary entirely? Perhaps it is for this reason that Deleuze and Guattari chose Kafka as the subject of the third volume of *Capitalism and Schizophrenia* since Kafka constitutes the true test case of their antipsychoanalytic theory. Kafka is an author who has been oedipalized to a nauseating degree, which echoes the title of the chapter "A Bloated Oedipus." Hence he is the perfect subject for an experiment that seeks to liberate the author and his work through the production of an unconscious that takes place outside its psychoanalytic concept. This is not that farfetched since one can read *The Castle* as an alternative construction or mapping of unconscious processes within a discourse of knowledge that is specifically literary (narrative, descriptive) and not scientific (analytic, inductive). The solution to this problem, which is not a problem of interpretation but is equal to the problem of desiring-production itself, is to find a means of bypassing the family altogether in order plug Kafka's works directly into the various social, political, and bureaucratic machines. Here, the family (meaning the subjective significations of the phantasm that is internalized in the constituted individual) is presented as the obstacle that must be discarded. That is, it is not approached, as in psychoanalytic method, by reducing the significations of the phantasm to their true symbolic designations (for example, the name of the father, the phallus); rather, it is by a more radical means of jettisoning—"forgetting" might be another way of putting this— the problem of the individual phantasm entirely, of producing an image of desire that is immanent to the social production of *"desire-delirium."*

In addition to their treatment of Kafka, the case of the Wolf Man offers another vivid illustration of this thesis, and Deleuze and Guattari return to it several times to pose the following question. "How is it," they ask, "that Freud could have failed to see what is so painfully obvious in the dream of this little Russian aristocrat who could neither get out of bed, nor even dress or feed himself? Of course he was depressed. He was scared of wolves. Not of one wolf, but several, a whole pack gnashing their teeth just outside his apartment window. *How is it, Comrade Freud, you fail see their true representatives?*" (*A Thousand Plateaus*, 37–38). It is here that we bear witness to an amazing piece of political intrigue, and Deleuze and Guattari are right to call our attention to it. Perhaps the overt political interpretation was too obvious for Freud. But perhaps this was lucky for us; otherwise, we would have missed such an amazing feat of interpretation (the reduction of the seven wolves), one that is worthy of a dialogue one would expect to find in a play by Beckett:

> I saw wolves.
> What did you say, you saw goats?
> No, I saw wolves.
> How many goats *did* you see?
> Six or seven, but they were *wolves*.
> Ah, I see, you saw dogs.
> No, six goats . . . I mean, wolves, in a tree outside my window.
> Yes, yes, it is all very clear: one of the dogs was standing up on its hind legs, mounting the other from behind (hence six legs, there we have it!) Was the door to your bedroom left open?
> No, no, damn it! I never saw any dogs at all. You're making things up. They were wolves, I tell you. Although, come to think of it, I do remember a picture of a wolf in a children's book standing upright with its paws on a boy's shoulders, and its huge red tongue about to lick his face.
> Ah! So you saw your father's penis? It was erect, and consequently it was red and very big?
> This is becoming ridiculous!
> Maybe so, but at the same time it is becoming all too clear.

Does this mean that Freud obstinately refused the patently obvious political interpretation of the scene, choosing instead to track the signification of the dream to its true unconscious source in childhood fantasy? And yet what if Freud punctuated the analysis at that point and interpreted the Wolf Man's dream? "So, you are depressed from the revolution. It marks the beginning of your depression." Or even, "So, you desire to become a wolf and run in the pack." I'm not sure that either interpretation would have resolved anything. It's easier, after all, for a man to become a wolf than it is for an aristocrat to become a Bolshevik or (ultimately) for analysis to really become "wild." Finally, it is around this point of the political question of desire that we might understand the motive for Deleuze's argument that psychoanalysis wants to reduce the unconscious, whereas he and Guattari want to multiply it. Nevertheless, a crucial distinction to be made is that by this process of multiplying the unconscious, they are not talking about creating a "wild psychoanalysis," about multiplying interpretations. Can we imagine, one day, a psychoanalysis that would be deterritorializing, that would directly accede to the political enunciation of unconscious desires? Moreover, would such a deterritorializing psychoanalysis only come after deterritorializing psychoanalysis? And how would it come about—by stripping psychoanalysis of its apparatus and its machine of interpretation? But then, wouldn't a psychoanalysis that would accede directly to the political *agencement* of unconscious desire be a form of politics, properly speaking? I will conclude therefore by posing a final question: Can we yet imagine a time when there would be no more psychoanalysis, when the unconscious would be a subject of politics and not of interpretation? That is, can we begin even to imagine such a state of health, *the end of analysis*?

BIBLIOGRAPHY

Beckett, Samuel. *The Three Novels of Samuel Beckett*. New York: Grove, 1995.
Deleuze, Gilles. *L'île déserte et autres textes*. Paris: Minuit, 2002.
Deleuze, Gilles and Claire Parnet. *Dialogues*. Paris: Flammarion, 1996.
Deleuze, Gilles and Félix Guattari. *Anti-Oedipus: Capitalism and Schizophrenia*. Trans. Robert Hurley, Mark Seem, and Helen R. Lane. Minneapolis: University of Minnesota Press, 1983.
———. *Kafka: Toward a Minor Literature*. Trans. Dana Polan. Minneapolis: University of Minnesota Press, 1986.
———. *A Thousand Plateaus: Capitalism and Schizophrenia*. Trans. Brian Massumi. Minneapolis: University of Minnesota Press, 1987.

Derrida, Jacques. *The Post Card*. Trans. Alan Bass. Chicago: University of Chicago Press, 1987.
——. *Resistances of Psychoanalysis*. Trans. Peggy Kamuf, Pascale-Anne Brault, and Michael Naas. Stanford, Calif.: Stanford University Press, 1998. Originally published as *Résistances de la psychanalyse* (Paris: Galilée, 1996).
Freud, Sigmund. "The Unconscious." In *The Standard Edition of the Complete Psychological Works of Sigmund Freud*, trans. James Strachey, Anna Freud, Alix Strachey, and Alan Tyson, 14:161–215. London: Hogarth and the Institute of Psycho-Analysis, 1953–1974.
——. "'Wild' Psycho-Analysis." In *The Standard Edition of the Complete Psychological Works of Sigmund Freud*, trans. James Strachey, Anna Freud, Alix Strachey, and Alan Tyson, 11:221–227. London: Hogarth and the Institute of Psycho-Analysis, 1953–1974.
Lacan, Jacques. "Sexuality and the Defiles of the Signifier." In *Four Fundamental Concepts of Psychoanalysis*, trans. Alan Sheridan, ed. Jacques-Alain Miller, 149–160. New York: Norton, 1998.